AIRCRAFT
RECOGNITION GUIDE

David Rendall

HarperCollins*Publishers*

HarperCollins*Publishers*
77–85 Fulham Palace Road
Hammersmith
London W6 8JB

First Published by HarperCollins*Published* 1999

3 5 7 9 10 8 6 4 2

© Jane's Information Group 1999
ISBN 0 00 472212 4

Design: Rod Teasdale

All rights reserved. No part of this publication may be reproduced, stored in a retrieval system,
or transmitted in any form or by any means, electronic, mechanical, photocopying, recording
or otherwise, without prior permission of the publishers and copyright holders.

Printed in Italy

Acknowledgements
All photographs and artworks via Jane's Information Group except:

Aviation Photographs International: 162, 281 Jeremy Flack (photographs)
Richard Burgess: 60, 118, 191 (artworks)

Contents

Contents

Contents

Contents

Contents

Introduction

This edition of Jane's Aircraft Recognition Guide contains more new aircraft designs than any previous edition. A total of 27 aircraft have achieved their first flight or firm orders since 1995. Manufacturers are hunting markets to replace many of the 30-40 year old designs nearing the end of their lives.

In the 95th year of powered flight the majority of airline fleets and air forces are made up of designs dating back to the 60s and 70s. The world's two most popular airliners the 737 and 747 date from 1967 and 1969 respectively, the West's premier fighters the F-15 and F-16 from 1972 and 1974. The most popular light aircraft the Cessna 172 and Piper Cherokee are older still.

By far the oldest aircraft still in regular service remains the venerable Douglas DC-3 which is now in its 65th year. Yet replacements for this rugged transport aircraft make up the lions share of new aircraft in this edition. Aircraft like the AeroProgress T101, Reims Caravan II and Colombia's first indigenous design the Galivan 358, have been designed as cargo and passenger carriers for the third world.

New designs take so long to develop, that many manufacturers are forced to modernize existing designs rather than start from scratch. At the high-cost end of the market – airliners and combat aircraft – new aircraft include a modified 737, C-130, a Japanese built F-16 (Mitsubishi F-2) and a vastly improved F/A-18E/F. The only new-design combat aircraft since 1981. The EF 2000, F-22, Gripen, Rafale and Su-37, will have taken 20 years to reach their squadrons when they enter service after 2000.

Smaller aircraft however, are prospering. A surge of civil designs from Russia have entered the markets as the swords to ploughshares programme takes bite. Rugged utility designs appear to be their greatest strength, and include innovative designs such as the AeroRIC Dingo with its air cushion landing gear. Only those aircraft with solid funding or launch customers have been included in this edition, as for every one flying prototype, Russian designers produce ten conceptual models.

The expanding use of composite materials continues to affect private aircraft design. To increase efficiency and reduce costs the latest light aircraft designs such as the Cirrus SR-20, ENAER Namcu and Istravision ST-50 are all-composite. Executive aircraft now employ greater use of lightweight materials, leading to simpler, cheaper aircraft like the AASI Jetcruzer, StarKraft SK-700 and Visionaire Vantage.

The major change to this edition concerns the names of manufacturers. In Europe, Russia and the USA mergers have removed some of the most famous names in aviation. McDonnell Douglas has ceased to build aircraft under its own name, they all now appear under Boeing, along with Rockwell. Lockheed Martin now includes all aircraft made by FMA and General Dynamics. Northrop Grumman includes all aircraft of those two companies along with Fairchild and Vought. Raytheon now controls all Beech and Hawker production but continues to use the original names in marketing.

Outside the USA, Eurocopter is now the official title of all MBB and Aerospatiale helicopters. Westland now operates under the name GKN Westland. SIAI-Marchetti is now part of Aermacchi while South Africa's Atlas is now part of the Denel group. In Russia mergers threatened one of their most famous names MiG. Good marketing strategy led to the adoption of a new name for the group – MIG. No longer standing for Mikoyan i Guverich but Moscow Industrial Group, which includes several other companies including Kamov.

Aircraft that are in production or are being supported by the new companies, are listed by their new names with old names in parentheses. Aircraft like the Douglas DC-3 keep the name by which they are most commonly known.

In compiling this book I have received great assistance from Kevan Box, Mark Daly, Ian Drury, Joanne Fenwick, Jane Lawerence, Simon Michell and Gary Ransom.

David Alexander Rendall, 1998

COMBAT AIRCRAFT

Aermacchi MB-326 Italy

Operational trainer and ground attack aircraft

Length: 10.7 m (35 ft) Wingspan: 10.8 m (35 ft 7 in) Height: 3.7 m (12 ft 2 in)

Features: Low/straight wing; single engine; wingtip tanks

First flown in 1957, the MB-326 has been exported to twelve countries. It is built under licence in South Africa and Brazil. MB-326Ks are a single-seat development with internal cannon (top silhouette).

Variants and operators

MB-326: Argentina; Australia; Brazil (AT-26 Xavante); Paraguay; South Africa Atlas Impala; Togo; Zaire; Zambia. **MB-326K:** Dubai; Ghana; Tunisia; Zambia.

Accommodation

2 pilots

Armament

Two internal 30 mm DEFA cannon (MB-326K)
Hardpoints: six (two wet): six wing
Warload: 1,814 kg (4,000 lb)
AS.11, AS.12, Matra 550; bombs; rockets; minigun pods.

Aermacchi MB-339C Italy

Operational trainer and ground attack aircraft

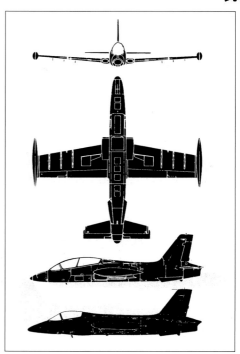

Based on the MB-326 the MB-339 can be recognized by its redesigned forward fuselage, with a sharper nose section and raised rear seat. A more powerful engine and redesigned flying controls give the MB-339 similar characteristics to fast jet fighters. Malaysian aircraft are specialist anti-ship versions.

Variants and operators
MB-339: Argentina; Eritrea; Ghana; Italy; Nigeria; Peru; New Zealand; UAE. **MB-339AM:** Malaya.

Accommodation
2 pilots

Armament
Hardpoints: six wing (two wet)
Warload: 1,814 kg (4,000 lb)
AIM-9L Sidewinder; Magic; AGM-65 Maverick; Marte Mk2 (Malaysian aircraft only); bombs, rockets, gun pods.

Features: Low/straight wing; single engine; sharp pointed nose

Length: 11.2 m (36 ft 9 in) Wingspan: 11.2 m (36 ft 9 in) Height: 4 m (13 ft 1 in)

Aermacchi (SIAI-Marchetti) S.211 Italy

Operational trainer / ground attack aircraft

Length: 9.5 m (31 ft 2 in) Wingspan: 8.4 m (27 ft 8 in) Height: 3.8 m (12 ft 5 in)

Features: High/swept wing; single engine; two-seats in tandem

Aermacchi acquired SIAI-Marchetti in 1997, and continues to promote the S.211 despite its obvious clash with the MB-339. Very similar in appearance to the IA-63 Pampa, the S.211 has a swept wing and longer tailpipe.

Variants and operators
S.211: Philippines; Singapore

Accommodation
2 pilots

Armament
Hardpoints: four wing (two wet)
Warload: 660 kg (1,455 lb)
Bombs; rockets; gun pods

Aero Vodochody L-29 Delfin Czech Republic

Operational trainer

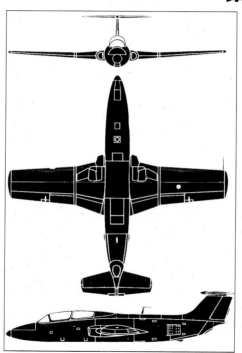

Length: 10.8 m (35 ft 5 in) Wingspan: 10.3 m (33 ft 9 in) Height: 3.1 m (10 ft 3 in)

The L-29 prototype flew in 1959, using a British built Viper engine. Production models had a Russian engine. Used extensively by former Soviet Bloc countries (3,665 were built). Today about 1,000 remain in service, 800 in Russia, where a replacement programme is underway.

Variants and operators

L-29: Azerbaijan; Bulgaria; Czech Republic; Egypt; Ghana; Mali; Russia; Slovakia; Vietnam; Uganda; Ukraine. **L-29R** reconnaissance version with wingtip tanks

Accommodation

2 pilots

Armament

Hardpoints: two (both wet)
Warload 200 kg (440 lb)
Light bombs, rockets, gun pods

Features: Mid/straight wing; single engine; T-Tail

Aero Vodochody L-39 Albatros Czech Republic

Operational trainer and ground attack aircraft

Length: 12.1 m (39 ft 9 in) Wingspan: 9.5 m (31 ft) Height: 4.8 m (15 ft 7 in)

Features: Low/straight wing; single engine; shoulder intakes

Since it first flew in 1968, the basic L-39 airframe has been re-designed to incorporate many Western features with new avionics and engines. The L-39ZO and ZA models have improved ground attack capabilities. The L-59 has a strengthened fuselage and uprated engine, recognized by its longer pointed nose.

Variants and operators

L-39: Afghanistan; Algeria; Cuba; Czech Republic; Ethiopia; Iraq; Russia; Vietnam. **L-39 ZA/ZO:** Algeria; Bangladesh; Bulgaria; Czech Republic; Germany; Iraq; Libya; Romania; Syria; Thailand. **L-59:** Egypt; Tunisia

Accommodation

2 pilots

Armament

Internal GSh-23 twin 23 mm cannon
Hardpoints: four (two wet)
Warload: 1,000 kg (2,205 lb)
AIM-9L Sidewinder; bombs; rockets

Aerospatiale (Fouga) CM 170 Magister France

Operational trainer and ground attack aircraft

Approaching half a century of service the Magister first flew in 1951. A navalised version the Zephyr, which incorporated arrester hook, catapult gear and rearwards sliding canopies, first flew in 1959. Built under licence in Finland, Israel and Germany a total of 921 were built, the last in 1969

Variants and operators

CM 170: Algeria; Bangladesh; Cameroon; El Salvador; France; Gabon; Ireland; Lebanon; Libya; Morocco; Senegambia. **CM 170 Super Magister:** France; Brazil **Tzukit:** Israel.

Accommodation

2 pilots

Armament

Two internal 7.62 mm machine guns
Hardpoints: two wing
Warload: 100 kg (220 lb)
AS.11; light bombs, rockets, gun pods

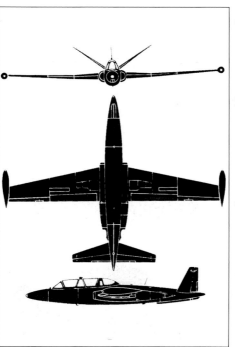

Length: 10 m (33 ft) Wingspan: 11.4 m (37 ft 5 in) Height: 2.8 m (9 ft 2 in)

Features: Mid/straight wing; Two engines; Butterfly tail

AIDC AT-3 Taiwan

Operational trainer and ground attack aircraft

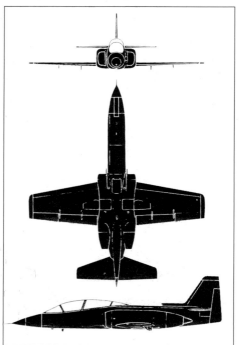

Length: 12.9 m (42 ft 2 in) Wingspan: 10.5 m (34 ft 3 in) Height: 4.4 m (14 ft 3 in)

Features: Low/straight wing; two engines; square intakes

Following its success in licence-building F-5 fighters, AIDC began work on a design of its own in 1975. First flown in 1980, 60 were built for the Taiwanese airforce. One prototype AT-3A single seater was built in 1989 as a simple dedicated ground attack fighter, no orders have yet been received. A two-seat close support version the AT-3B has also been trialed, with advanced Nav/attack systems.

Variants and operators
AT-3: Taiwan

Accommodation
2 pilots

Armament
Hardpoints: seven (two wet): one fuselage; four wing; two wingtip
Warload: 2,721 kg (6,000 lb)
Sky Sword 1; Hsiung Feng 2; bombs; rockets; gun pods

AIDC Ching Kuo Taiwan

Multi-role fighter

Developed from 1982 after America's refusal to sell fighters to Taiwan, the Ching Kuo first flew in 1989. Production continues although the USA has lifted restrictions on the purchase of F-16s, which it strongly resembles. (Note the air intakes are different and the Ching Kuo has two engines).

Variants and operators
Ching Kuo: Taiwan

Accommodation
1 pilot

Armament
Internal 20 mm M61A1 cannon
Hardpoints: nine (three wet) three fuselage; four wing; two wingtip
Warload: 3,901 kg (8,600 lb)
Sky Sword 1 and 2; Hsiung Feng 2; AGM-65 Maverick; bombs; rockets

Length: 13.2 m (43 ft 6 in) Wingspan: 8.5 m (28 ft) Height: 4.6 m (15 ft 3 in)

Features: Mid/swept wing; two engines; oval intakes

AMX Italy/Brazil

Ground attack fighter

Length: 12.5 m (41 ft 2 in) Wingspan: 9.9 m (32 ft 8 in) Height: 14 ft 11 in (4.5 m)

Features: High/swept wing; single engine; shoulder intakes

Developed by Alenia and Aermacchi of Italy and Embraer of Brazil, the AMX is replacing the G91R/Y and F-104G/S in Italy and MB-326 Xavante in Brazil. The AMX is a ground attack aircraft with a secondary air defence capability. Brazilian versions have two 30 mm DEFA 554 cannon while Italian aircraft have a 20 mm M61A1 cannon.

Variants and operators

AMX: Brazil (A-1), Italy **AMX-T:** Brazil, Italy

Accommodation

1 pilot

Armament

One internal 20 mm M61A1 or two 30 mm DEFA 554 cannon
Hardpoints: seven (two wet): one fuselage; four wing; two wingtip
Warload: 3800 kg (8377 lb)
Weapons: AIM-9L Sidewinder; Paveway; Exocet or Marte; bombs, rockets

Avioane IAR-93 / SOKO J-22 Orao Romania / Yugoslavia

Ground attack fighter / reconnaissance aircraft

A joint project between the Former Yugoslavia and Romania under the project name Yurom, it first flew in 1974. Yugoslav aircraft were built at the SOKO factory in Mostar, Bosnia Herzegovina, which was dismantled in 1992, production has not resumed. IAR-93As lacked the afterburner of the IAR-93B. NJ-22s are a Yugoslav built two-seat reconnaissance version.

Variants and operators
IAR-93A/B: Romania J-22/NJ-22 Orao:
Yugoslavia; Republic of Srpska

Accommodation
1 pilot

Armament
Two internal twin 23 mm GSh-23 cannon
Hardpoints: five (three wet): one fuselage; four wing
Warload: 2,500 kg (6,173 lb)
Weapons: Bombs, rockets, naval mines, limited Air-to-Air capability

Length: 13 m (42 ft 8 in) Wingspan: 9.3 m (30 ft 6 in) Height: 4.5 m (14 ft 10 in)

Features: High/swept wing; twin engines; small high intakes

Avioane IAR-99 Soim Romania

Operational trainer / ground attack fighter

Length: 11 m (36 ft 1 in) Wingspan: 9.8 m (32 ft 3 in) Height: 3.9 m (12 ft 9 in)

Features: Low/straight wing; single engine; cranked fin

Revealed at the 1983 Paris Air Show, the Soim first flew in 1985. The improved IAR-109 flew in 1992, but no orders were received and production appears to have finished.

Variants and operators
IAR-99: Romania

Accommodation
2 pilots

Armament
Twin 23 mm GSh-23 mm cannon in ventral pack
Hardpoints: four wing
Warload: 1,000 kg (2,204 lb)
Weapons: Infra Red AAMs, bombs, rockets, gun pods

BAe (English Electric) Canberra UK

Bomber and multi-role aircraft

Length: 20.3 m (66 ft 8 in) Wingspan: 20.6 m (67 ft 10 in) Height: 4.7 m (15 ft 8 in)

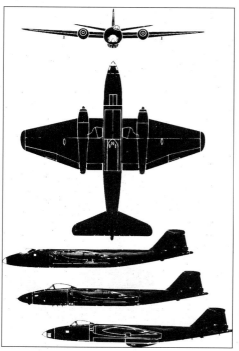

The oldest operational combat aircraft in service, the Canberra first flew in 1949. It is also the only combat aircraft with wooden parts: the forward part of the fin is made from plywood. Some 27 different marks of Canberra were built, seven marks and 85 aircraft remaining in service.

Variants and operators

B(I) Mk8/Mk56 (top): Argentina; Peru B(I) Mk58 (bottom) : India PR.Mk 9/57 (centre): UK T.Mk.54: Peru; India

Accommodation

2 pilots

Armament

Internal bomb bay
Hardpoints: two wing
Warload: (6,000 lb)
Weapons: AS.30; bombs; 20 mm gun pod

Features: Mid/straight wing; mid wing mounted engines; dihedral tailplane

21

BAe/Boeing GR. Mk7 Harrier UK/USA

STOVL ground attack fighter

Early GR.5 models had no FLIR blister on the upper nose, but all have now been upgraded. Royal Air Force Harriers now regularly deploy aboard Royal Navy carriers and have carried out lengthy deployments in support of UN missions.

Variants and operators

GR. Mk7(top): UK   T. Mk10(lower): UK

Accommodation

1 pilot

Armament

Two external 30 mm RO cannon
Hardpoints: nine (four wet): one fuselage;
eight wing
Warload: 4,899 kg (10,800 lb)
Weapons: AIM-9L Sidewinder; Paveway;
bombs; rockets

Features: High/swept wing; sharp anhedral wing; large semi-circular intakes

Length: 14.4 m (47 ft 1 in) Wingspan: 9.2 m (30 ft 4 in) Height: 3.5 m (11 ft 7 in)

BAe/Boeing T-45A Goshawk UK/USA

Naval carrier-borne trainer

Length: 10.9 m (35 ft 9 in) Wingspan: 9.4 m (30 ft 9 in) Height: 4.1 m (13 ft 4 in)

Developed from the BAe Hawk series, the Goshawk has a strengthened fuselage and landing gear and is being upgraded with a modern cockpit featuring multi-function displays to simulate modern combat aircraft.

Variants and operators
T-45A: USN

Accommodation
2 pilots

Armament
Hardpoints: three (two wet): one fuselage; four wing
Weapons: Training bombs; rockets

Features: Low/swept wing; side mounted air brakes; arrester hook

23

BAe Hawk 50/60/100 UK

Operational trainer / ground attack fighter

Length: 12.4 m (40 ft 9 in) Wingspan: 9.4 m (32 ft 7 in) Height: 3.4 m (13 ft)

Features: Low/swept wing; single engine; tandem cockpit

BAe has followed a wide ranging development process for its successful Hawk family, tailor making them to meet customer's requirements. The latest on offer is the Hawk 100 with lengthened nose incorporating FLIR and extra avionics and wingtip pylons for AAMs. The new NATO flying school in Canada will be equipped with the Hawk from 1999.

Variants and operators

Hawk T.Mk1: UK **Hawk 60 series:** Abu Dhabi; Dubai; Finland; Indonesia; Kenya; South Korea; Kuwait; Saudi Arabia; Switzerland; Zimbabwe **Hawk 100 Series:** Abu Dhabi; Australia; Indonesia; Malaysia; Oman; Qatar; South Africa

Accommodation

2 pilots

Armament

Hardpoints: five (two wet): one fuselage; four wing (+two wingtip on 100 series)
Warload: 3,000 kg (6,614 lb)
Weapons: AIM-9L Sidewinder; 30 mm ADEN cannon pod; bombs; rockets

BAe Hawk 200 UK

Multi-role lightweight fighter

Length: 10.9 m (35 ft 11 in) Wingspan: 9.4 m (30 ft 9 in) Height: 4.1 m (13 ft 6 in)

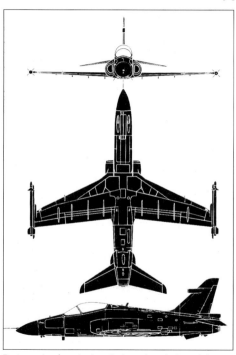

Developed as a private venture from the two-seat trainer, the Hawk 200 uses the extra space in the nose to house a AN/APG-66H radar, while keeping 80 per cent commonality with the original Hawk series. Both versions of the Hawk may be fitted with a new engine, giving greater payload and range.

Variants and operators
Hawk 200: Indonesia; Malaysia; Oman

Accommodation
1 pilot

Armament
Hardpoints: seven (two wet): one fuselage; four wing; two wingtip
Warload: 3,000 kg (6,614 lb)
Weapons: AIM-9L Sidewinder; AGM-65 Maverick; 30 mm ADEN cannon pod; bombs; rockets

Features: Low/swept wing; single engine; single cockpit

BAe Sea Harrier F/A.Mk2 UK

Carrier-borne VSTOL multi-role fighter

Length: 14.2 m (46 ft 6 in) Wingspan: 7.7 m (25 ft 3 in) Height: 3.7 m (12 ft 2 in)

The Royal Navy has replaced all its FRS.1s with the upgraded F/A.Mk2. The first 35 aircraft were re-manufactured from existing FRS.1s with 18 new-build F/A.Mk2s also being ordered. The main difference is the nav/attack system based around the Blue Vixen look-down shoot-down radar.

Features: High/swept wing; sharp anhedral wing; rounded nose cone

Variants and operators
F/A.Mk2: Royal Navy

Accommodation
1 pilot

Armament
Hardpoints: seven (two wet): three fuselage; four wing
Warload: 3,630 kg (8,000 lb)
Weapons: AIM-120 AMRAAM; AIM-9L Sidewinder; Sea Eagle; ALARM; bombs; rockets

BAe Sea Harrier FRS.Mk51 UK

Carrier-borne VSTOL multi-role fighter

Used by the Royal Navy in the Falklands war, the original Sea Harrier is now only flown by the Indian Navy. First flown in 1979, the Indian Navy began taking delivery in 1983. The sharply pointed nose containing the Blue Fox radar distinguishes it from the F\A.Mk2.

Variants and operators
FRS.Mk51: India

Accommodation
1 pilot

Armament
Hardpoints: seven (two wet): three fuselage; four wing
Warload: 3,630 kg (8,000 lb)
Weapons: Matra Magic; Sea Eagle; bombs; rockets

Length: 14.5 m (47 ft 7 in) Wingspan: 7.7 m (25 ft 3 in) Height: 3.7 m (12 ft 2 in)

Features: High/swept wing; sharp anhedral wing; pointed nose

BAe (BAC) Strikemaster UK

Operational trainer / lightweight ground attack fighter

Length: 10.3 m (33 ft 8 in) Wingspan: 11.2 m (36 ft 10 in) Height: 3.3 m (10 ft 11 in)

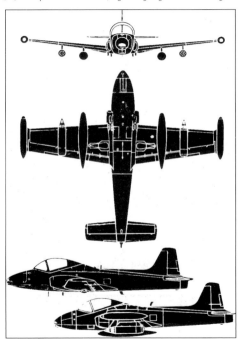

Developed from the unarmed Jet Provost in 1967, the Strikemaster has a more powerful engine enabling it to carry a useful weapons load.

Variants and operators

Mk 82: Oman **Mk 83:** Ecuador **Mk 90:** Sudan

Accommodation

2 pilots

Armament

Two internal 7.62 mm machine guns
Hardpoints: four wing (two wet)
Warload: 1,360 kg (3,000 lb)
Weapons: Bombs; rockets; gun pods

Features: Low/straight wing; Side-by-side cockpit; Wingtip tanks

Boeing B-52H Stratofortress USA

Strategic bomber

The B-52 has been flying for half the history of flight and shows no sign of disappearing. A proposal to re-engine them with four Rolls Royce RB211s is being studied. The 20 mm cannon in the tail is being removed.

Variants and operators
B-52H: USAF

Accommodation
2 pilots; 3 systems operators; 1 tail gunner

Armament
Internal bomb bay
Hardpoints: two wing
Warload: 24,750 kg (60,000 lb)
Weapons: AGM-86/129 cruise missiles; AGM-84 Harpoon; bombs; mines

Length: 49 m (160 ft 10 in) Wingspan: 56.4 m (185 ft) Height: 12.4 m (40 ft 8 in)

Features: High/swept wing; eight engines; bicycle undercarriage

Boeing/BAe AV-8B Harrier II USA/UK

Carrier-borne VSTOL multi-role fighter

Length: 14.5 m (47 ft 9 in) Wingspan: 9.2 m (30 ft 4 in) Height: 3.5 m (11 ft 7 in)

Features: High/swept wing; sharp anhedral wing; rounded radar radome

The Harrier II Plus (picture) was a private venture to fit the AN/APG-65 radar into an AV-8B (silhouette). The USMC, and the Spanish and Italian Navies ordered it as soon as trials proved successful. Despite its ability to carry AIM-120 AMRAAM making a true multi-role fighter it still lacks the 'F' (fighter) designation.

Variants and operators
AV-8B: Spain; USMC **AV-8B+:** Italy; Spain; USMC

Accommodation
1 pilot

Armament
Hardpoints: nine (four wet): three fuselage; six wing
Warload: 4,899 kg (10,800 lb)
Weapons: AIM-120 AMRAAM; AIM-9L Sidewinder; AGM-65 Maverick; 25 mm GAU-12/U cannon pod; Paveway; bombs; rockets

Boeing (Douglas) A-4 Skyhawk USA

Ground attack fighter

Length: 12.3 m (49 ft 4 in) Wingspan: 8.4 m (27 ft 6 in) Height: 4.6 m (15 ft)

The A4 was designed as the lightest carrier-borne attack aircraft capable of carrying the B57 nuclear bomb, and to use carrier elevators without the need for wing folding. Israel, Singapore and New Zealand have all carried out extensive modifications to their A-4s. New Zealand aircraft have a distinctive radar radome.

Variants and operators

A-4 (top): Argentina; Brazil; Indonesia; Israel; Kuwait; Malaysia **A-4K (middle):** New Zealand **A-4S- 1:** Singapore **TA-4 (bottom):** Israel; New Zealand

Accommodation

1 pilot

Armament

Two internal 20 mm Mk12 cannon
Hardpoints: five (two wet): one fuselage; four wing
Warload: (7,000 lb)
Weapons: AIM-9L Sidewinder, AGM-65 Maverick; bombs; rockets

Features: Small Delta with tail; dorsal hump; single engine

31

Boeing (McDonnell Douglas) F-4 Phantom II USA

Multi-role fighter

Length: 19.2 m (63 ft) Wingspan: 11.8 m (38 ft 7 in) Height: 5 m (16 ft 5 in)

Features: Low/swept wing; dihedral outer wing section; anhedral tail plane

Originally designed as a carrier-borne strike aircraft, the Phantom II has accepted a wide number of roles during its four decades of service. No longer used by US forces, 830 of the 5,000 built remain in service, with most operators looking to keep them well into the next century.

Variants and operators
F-4D: Iran; South Korea; F-4F: Germany F-4EJ: Japan F-4E: Egypt; Greece; Israel; Spain; Turkey

Accommodation
1 pilot; 1 systems operator

Armament
Internal 20 mm M61A1 cannon
Hardpoints: nine (three wet): one fuselage; four semi-recessed; four wing
Warload: 7,250 kg (16,000 lb)
Weapons: AIM-7 Sparrow; AIM-9L Sidewinder; AGM-45 Shrike; AGM-65 Maverick; bombs; rockets

Boeing (McDonnell Douglas) F-15 Eagle USA

Air superiority fighter

Length: 19.4 m (63 ft 9 in) Wingspan: 13 m (42 ft 9 in) Height: 5.6 m (18 ft 5 in)

First flown in 1972, the F-15 remains the premier air superiority fighter of the USAF, and several allied states. To be replaced by the F-22 Raptor from 2004, early A/B models are already being moved to desert graveyards. Can be fitted with conformal fuel tanks with four extra hardpoints for bombs.

Variants and operators

F-15C/D: USAF; Israel (Baaz); Saudi Arabia
F-15J: Japan

Accommodation

1 pilot

Armament

Internal 20 mm M61A1 cannon
Hardpoints: seven (three wet): one fuselage; four semi-recessed; two wing;
Warload: 10,705 kg (23,600 lb)
Weapons: AIM-7 Sparrow; AIM-9L Sidewinder; AIM-120 AMRAAM; bombs; rockets

Features: High/swept wing; twin tails; engines side by side

33

Boeing (McDonnell Douglas) F-15E Strike Eagle USA

Multi-role fighter

Length: 19.4 m (65 ft 4 in) Wingspan: 13 m (42 ft 9 in) Height: 5.6 m (18 ft 5 in)

Features: High/swept wing; twin tails; two-seats

34

McDonnell Douglas launched a ground attack version of the F-15 as a private venture in 1982, the programme getting the go-ahead from the USAF in 1984. Many improvements including standard fit conformal fuel tanks, new engines, Nav/attack pods under intakes and low-observable stealth kits.

Variants and operators
F-15E: USAF F-15I: Israel F-15S: Saudi Arabia
F-15H: Greece

Accommodation
1 pilot; 1 systems operator

Armament
Internal 20 mm M61A1 cannon
Hardpoints: thirteen (three wet): five fuselage;
eight wing
Warload: 11,13 kg (24,500 lb)
Weapons: AIM-7 Sparrow; AIM-9L Sidewinder;
AIM-120 AMRAAM ;AGM-65 Maverick; AGM-88
HARM; AGM-130; bombs; rockets

Boeing (McDonnell Douglas) F/A-18 Hornet USA

Carrier-borne multi-role fighter

Began life as the Northrop YF-17 in competition with the F-16 for the USAF light fighter contract. McDonnell Douglas developed it for the US Navy by strengthening the fuselage and landing gear and installing advanced avionics. Only the USN and USMC operates the Hornet from carriers, other customers use it as a land-based fighter.

Variants and operators
F/A-18A/B: Australia; Canada; Spain; USN; USMC **F/A-18C/D:** Kuwait; Malaysia; USN; USMC

Accommodation
1 pilot

Armament
Internal 20 mm M61A1 cannon
Hardpoints: nine (three wet): one fuselage; two semi-recessed; four wing; two wingtip
Warload: 7,031 kg (15,500 lb)
Weapons: AIM-7 Sparrow; AIM-9L Sidewinder; AIM-120 AMRAAM; AGM-65 Maverick; AGM-84E SLAM; AGM-84 Harpoon; AGM-88 HARM; bombs; rockets

Features: High/straight wing; long leading edge extensions; twin tails angled out

Length: 17 m (56 ft) Wingspan: 11.4 m (37 ft 6 in) Height: 4.7 m (15 ft 3 in)

Boeing (McDonnell Douglas) F/A-18E/F USA

Carrier-borne multi-role fighter

Length: 18.3 m (50 ft 1 in) Wingspan: 13.6 m (44 ft 8 in) Height: 4.8 m (16 ft)

Features: High/straight wing; dogtooth in wing; square intakes

McDonnell Douglas began studying ways of making the Hornet more stealthy, in order to fill the requirement for an A-6 replacement. The new Hornet boasts 'affordable' stealth features such as saw-toothed panels, realigned joints and angled antenna. More internal space was created with a longer fuselage and the wing area was increased.

Variants and operators
F/A-18E/F: USN

Accommodation
1 pilot

Armament
One internal lightweight cannon
Hardpoints: eleven (three wet): one fuselage; two semi-recessed; six wing; two wingtip
Warload: 4,082 kg (9,000 lb)
Weapons: AIM-9 Sidewinder; AIM-120 AMRAAM; AGM-65 Maverick; AGM-84E SLAM; AGM-84 Harpoon; AGM-88 HARM; JDAM; bombs; rockets

Boeing (Rockwell) B-1B Lancer USA

Strategic bomber

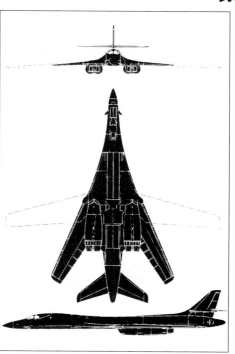

Length: 44.8 m (147 ft) Wingspan (spread):41 m (136 ft 8 in) Height: 10.4 m (34 ft)

The last B-1B was only delivered in 1988 and yet the USAF is already discussing withdrawing the first from service. Despite a radar cross section of 1 per cent that of the B-52 and a low-level capability, the B-1B looks as if it will disappear long before its venerable partner.

Variants and operators
B-1B: USAF

Accommodation
2 pilots; 2 systems operators

Armament
Three internal bomb bays
Hardpoints: six fuselage
Warload: 60,781 kg (134,000 lb)
Weapons: AGM-86 cruise missiles; AGM-69
SRAMs; bombs; mines

Features: Mid/swing wing: chin canards; ventral engine nacelles

37

Boeing (Rockwell) OV-10 Bronco USA

Counter Insurgency aircraft

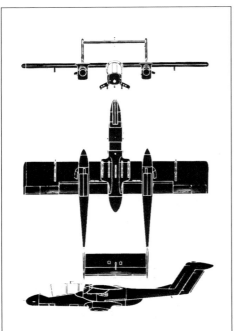

Length: 12.6 m (47 ft 4 in) Wingspan: 12.2 m (40 ft) Height: 4.6 m (15 ft 2 in)

Features: High/straight wing; twin boom tail;
two turboprops

The Bronco won the 1964 competition for the USAF Light Armed Reconnaissance Aircraft, and first flew in 1965. Now withdrawn from US service. The rear section of the fuselage can carry five paratroops or two stretchers.

Variants and operators
OV-10A: Colombia; Morocco; Philippines
OV-10C: Thailand **OV-10E/F:** Venezuela;
Indonesia

Accommodation
1 pilot; 1 observer

Armament
Hardpoints: five (one wet): five fuselage
Warload: 1,633 kg (3,600 lb)
Weapons: bombs; rockets; gun pods

Boeing (Rockwell) T-2B Buckeye USA

Carrier-borne operational trainer / light attack aircraft

Originally a North American design of 1956, the Buckeye is being replaced in USN service by the T-45A Goshawk. A total of 550 were built, the last in 1976. Greek T-2Es have a secondary ground attack role with extra weapons stations.

Variants and operators
T-2C: USN **T-2D:** Venezuela **T-2E:** Greece

Accommodation
2 pilots

Armament
Hardpoints: four wing
Warload: 1,588 kg (3,500 lb)
Weapons: bombs; rockets; gun pods

Features: Mid/straight wing; cheek intakes; two engines

39

CAC F-7 China

Interceptor / ground attack aircraft

Length: 13.9 m (45 ft 9 in) Wingspan: 7.1 m (27 ft 3 in) Height: 4.1 m (13 ft 5 in)

Features: Mid/small delta; nose intake; swept tail plane

A licence built version of the MiG-21, the J-7 has been constantly upgraded since it first flew in 1966, and can be considered a different aircraft. The latest J-7E version has a reduced sweep on the outboard half of the wing and increased wingspan. FF-7 is a two-seat operational trainer.

Variants and operators

J-7I: Albania; China; Tanzania **J-7II:** Bangladesh; China; Egypt; Iran; Myanmar (Burma); Pakistan; Sudan; Zimbabwe **J-7III:** China **F-7:** Egypt; Pakistan

Accommodation

1 pilot

Armament

Two internal 30 mm Type 30-1 cannon or One 23 mm Type 23-3 cannon
Hardpoints: five (three wet): one fuselage; four wing
Weapons: AIM-9L Sidewinder; PL-2, PL-5, bombs; rockets

Canadair CL-41 Tutor Canada

Operational trainer / light ground attack

Length: 9.7 m (32 ft) Wingspan: 11.1 m (36 ft 5 in) Height: 2.8 m (9 ft 3 in)

Begun as a private venture, the Tutor first flew in 1960. Malaysia took delivery of the CL-41G counter insurgency version, which are now in storage. Canadian aircraft are used solely for weapons training.

Variants and operators
CL-41: Canada

Accommodation
2 pilots

Armament
Hardpoints: six (six wet): two fuselage; four wing
Warload: 1,590 kg (3,500 lb)
Weapons: AIM-9 Sidewinder; bombs; rockets; gun pods

Features: Low/straight wing; T-tail; side-by-side cockpit

CASA C-101 Aviojet Spain

Operational trainer / ground attack aircraft

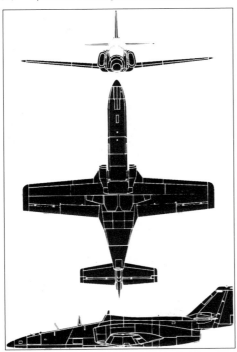

Length: 12.5 m (41 ft) Wingspan: 10.6 m (34 ft 9 in) Height: 4.3 m (13 ft 11 in)

Features: Low/straight wing; short tailpipe; single engine

First flown in 1977, a strengthened version with a more powerful engine arrived in 1983. ENAER of Chile assemble them under licence where they are known as A/T-36 Halcon. Very similar to the Argentine IA-63 Pampa the main difference being the Aviojet's low mounted wing.

Variants and operators
C-101: Spain C-101BB: Chile; Honduras
C-101CC: Chile (A/T-36), Jordan

Accommodation
2 pilots

Armament
Ventral 30 mm DEFA 553 cannon
Hardpoints: six wing
Warload: 2,250 kg (4,960 lb)
Weapons: AIM-9 Sidewinder; AGM-65 Maverick; bombs; rockets

Cessna A-37 Dragonfly USA

Basic trainer / counter insurgency aircraft

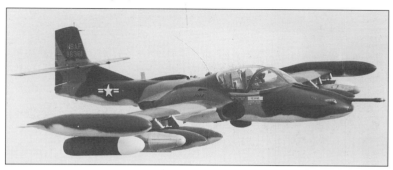

The USAF's first purpose built jet trainer, the T-37 was developed into the armed counter insurgency and forward air control A-37. The original T-37 retains a limited weapons capability.

Variants and operators

T-37: Chile; Colombia; Germany; Greece; South Korea; Pakistan; Thailand; Turkey; USAF **A-37:** Chile; Colombia; Dominican Republic; Ecuador; Guatemala; Honduras; South Korea; Peru; El Salvador; Thailand; Uruguay

Accommodation

2 pilots

Armament

Internal 7.62 mm Minigun
Hardpoints: eight wing (four wet)
Warload: 2,574 kg (5,680 lb)
Weapons: bombs; rockets; gun pods

Features: Mid/straight wing; broad fuselage; jetpipes in trailing edge root

Length: 8.6 m (28 ft 3 in) Wingspan: 10.9 m (35 ft 10 in) Height: 2.7 m (8 ft 10 in)

Denel (Atlas) Cheetah South Africa

Interceptor and reconnaissance aircraft

Length: 15.5 m (14 ft 9 in) Wingspan: 8.2 m (14 ft 9 in) Height: 4.5 m (14 ft 9 in)

Features: Tail-less delta; droop nose; canards

A rebuilt version of the Mirage III, Atlas received much assistance from IAI of Israel, leading to unsurprising similarities between the Cheetah and Kfir. One way to differentiate is the Kfir's pronounced step at the base of the fin. Produced in a single seat fighter (C and E models) and twin seat operational trainer (D) versions, exclusively for the South African Air Force.

Variants and operators
Cheetah: South Africa

Accommodation
1 pilot

Armament
Internal 30 mm DEFA cannon
Hardpoints: seven (two wet): three fuselage;
four wing
Warload: 6,000 kg (13,000 lb)
Weapons: V3B Kukri, V3C Darter; AS.30; bombs

Dassault/Dornier Alpha Jet France

Operational trainer / ground attack aircraft

A Franco-German trainer project that replaced the Anglo-French Jaguar programme. First flight came in 1973 and 504 had been built by 1991. Germany wanted their aircraft to have an operational war role, making the Alpha Jet one of the most powerfully armed trainers flying.

Variants and operators
Alpha Jet E: Belgium; Egypt; France; Ivory Coast; Morocco; Nigeria; Qatar; Togo **Alpha Jet A:** Portugal **Alpha Jet 2:** Egypt; Cameroon

Accommodation
2 pilots

Armament
Ventral 27 mm Mauser or 30 mm DEFA cannon
Hardpoints: five (four wet): one fuselage; four wing
Warload: 2,500 kg (5,510 lb)
Weapons: AIM-9 Sidewinder; Magic; AGM-65 Maverick; bombs; rockets

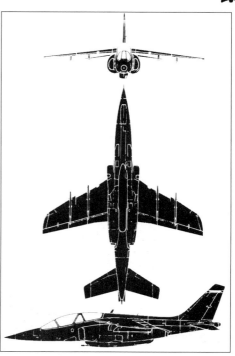

Length: 11.7 m (38 ft 5 in) Wingspan: 9.1 m (29 ft 10 in) Height: 4.2 m (13 ft 9 in)

Features: High/swept wing; dogtooth wing; two engines

45

Dassault Mirage III France

Interceptor / ground attack fighter

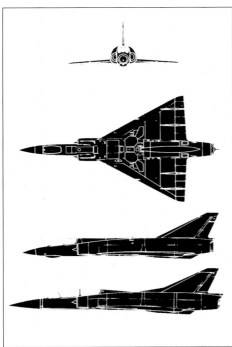

Length: 15 m (49 ft 3 in) Wingspan: 8.2 m (26 ft 11 in) Height: 4.5 m (14 ft 9 in)

Features: Tail-less delta; large radome; swept canards on some

First flown in 1956, the Mirage III remains in service with a number of smaller airforces; upgrades are expected to keep them in service well into the next century. The South African Cheetah is a re-manufactured Mirage III, but can be distinguished by its longer nose and smaller radome. Brazilian and Swiss models have swept canards on the intake.

Variants and operators

Mirage IIIE (top): Argentina; Brazil; Pakistan; South Africa **Mirage IIIS:** Switzerland **Mirage IIID (bottom):** Brazil, Pakistan; Switzerland

Accommodation

1 pilot

Armament

Two internal 30 mm DEFA cannon
Hardpoints: five (two wet): one fuselage; four wing
Warload: 4,000 kg (8,818 lb)
Weapons: Matra R.530; Magic; bombs; rockets

Dassault Mirage IV France

Strategic reconnaissance aircraft

Length: 23.5 m (77 ft 1 in) Wingspan: 11.8 m (38 ft 10 in) Height: 5.6 m (18 ft 6 in)

Based on the Mirage III design, the IV was scaled up in order to carry a nuclear weapon over longer distances. Since 1996 they have been used solely for strategic reconnaissance.

Variants and operators
Mirage IVP: France

Armament
No weapons carried

Accommodation
1 pilot; 1 systems operator

Features: Tail-less delta; two engines; two crew

Dassault Mirage V/50 France

Ground attack fighter

Length: 15.5 m (51 ft) Wingspan: 8.2 m (26 ft 11 in) Height: 4.5 m (14 ft 9 in)

Features: Tail-less delta; long nose; small radome

Developed from the Mirage III, the V was primarily a ground attack aircraft, with greater stores capability and no air-to-air radar. Israel received a number of Mirage Vs which they turned into the Nesher/Dagger and developed the Kfir. The Mirage 50 has a high rated engine and retains the large radome radar.

Variants and operators
Mirage V: Abu Dhabi; Argentina; Colombia; Egypt; Gabon; Libya; Pakistan; Peru; Zaire
Mirage 50: Chile; Venezuela **Dagger:** Argentina

Accommodation
1 pilot

Armament
Two internal 30 mm DEFA cannon
Hardpoints: Seven (two wet): three fuselage; four wing
Warload: 4,000 kg (8,818 lb)
Weapons: AIM-9 Sidewinder; Magic; bombs; rockets

Dassault Mirage F 1C France

Multi-role fighter

A departure from the basic Mirage line, the F 1C has a conventional wing giving greater control at low altitudes and low speeds. Exported under many different designations, South Africa is studying a new generic engine, developed with Russia, to be fitted to its F-1Cs and Cheetah's.

Variants and operators
Mirage F 1C: Ecuador; France; Greece; Iraq; Jordan; Kuwait; Libya; Morocco; South Africa; Spain

Accommodation
1 pilot

Armament
Two internal 30 mm DEFA cannon
Hardpoints: Seven (three wet): one fuselage; four wing; two wingtip
Warload: 4,000 kg (8,818 lb)
Weapons: AIM-9 Sidewinder; Magic; Matra Super 530; Armat; Exocet; AS 30L; PGMs; bombs; rockets

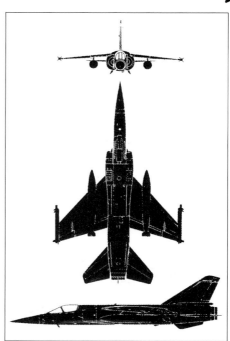

Length: 15.2 m (49 ft 11 in) Wingspan: 8.4 m (27 ft 6 in) Height: 4.5 m (14 ft 9 in)

Features: High/swept wing; single engine; fixed refuelling probe

Dassault Mirage 2000 France

Multi-role fighter

Length: 14.4 m (47 ft 1 in) Wingspan: 9 m (29 ft 11 in) Height: 5.2 m (17 ft)

Features: Tail-less delta; small canards; fixed re-fuelling probe

First flown in 1982, the Mirage 2000 has replaced the Mirage III and Mirage V in French service, and has been successfully exported as a Mirage replacement to existing customers. The canards on the intakes are shorter and longer than those on the Mirage III upgrades and Mirage look-a-likes.

Variants and operators
Mirage 2000: Abu Dhabi; Egypt; France; Greece; India; Peru; Qatar; Taiwan

Accommodation
1 pilot

Armament
Two internal 30 mm DEFA cannon
Hardpoints: nine (three wet): five fuselage; four wing
Warload: 6,300 kg (13,890 lb)
Weapons: Mica; Magic; AS.30; Exocet; bombs; rockets

Dassault Mirage 2000D/N France

Strike fighter

Developed from the basic Mirage 2000, the D model has a second crew member, fixings for precision guided weapons and terrain following avionics. The 2000N is equipped to carry the ASMP tactical nuclear stand off missile. Easily confused with Mirage 2000 twin-seat trainers, but has larger hardpoints.

Variants and operators
Mirage 2000D: France **Mirage 2000N:** France

Accommodation
1 pilot; 1 systems operator

Armament
Hardpoints: nine (three wet): five fuselage; four wing
Warload: 6,300 kg (13,890 lb)
Weapons: Magic; ASMP; APACHE; PGMs; bombs; rockets

Features: Tail-less delta; two crew; longer fuselage

Length: 14.6 m (47 ft 9 in) Wingspan: 9.1 m (29 ft 11 in) Height: 5.1 m (16 ft 10 in)

Dassault Rafale France

Multi-role land and carrier-borne fighter

Length: 15.3 m (50 ft 2 in) Wingspan: 10.9 m (35 ft 9 in) Height: 5.3 m (17 ft 6 in)

Features: Tail-less delta; moving canards; two engines

France's next-generation fighter, the Rafale is entering service with trials units, with full operational service planned for the end of century. The Rafale M is the navalised version, with arrester hook and strengthened undercarriage. A two-seat trainer, Rafale D, is also in production.

Variants and operators
Rafale C/D: France **Rafale M:** France

Accommodation
1 pilot

Armament
One internal 30 mm 791B cannon
Hardpoints: fourteen (three wet): six fuselage; six wing; two wingtip
Warload: 6,000 kg (13,228 lb)
Weapons: Mica; Magic; Exocet; AGM-65 Maverick; AGM-84 Harpoon; AGM-88 HARM; AS.30L; PGMs; bombs; rockets

Dassault Super Etendard France

Shipborne strike fighter

Developed from the earlier Etendard strike fighter, the Super Etendard retained 90 per cent commonality with the original, but had a more powerful engine and advanced nav-attack avionics. While the serviceability of Argentine aircraft is questionable, French aircraft have been upgraded to extended their service life.

Variants and operators
Super Etendard: Argentina; France

Accommodation
1 pilot

Armament
Two internal 30 mm DEFA cannon
Hardpoints: five (three wet): one fuselage; four wing
Warload: 2100 kg (4630 lb)
Weapons: Magic; Exocet; bombs; rockets

Features: Mid/swept wing; single engine; high tail

Length: 14.3 m (46 ft 11 in) Wingspan: 9.6 m (31 ft 6 in) Height: 3.9 m (12 ft 9 in)

Eurofighter 2000 Typhoon Germany/Italy/Spain/UK

Multi-role fighter

Length: 14.5 m (47 ft 7 in) Wingspan: 10.5 m (34 ft 5 in) Height: 4 m (13 ft 1 in)

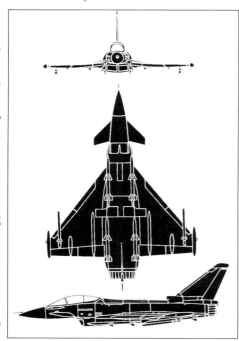

Features: Tail-less delta; movable canards; ventral square intakes

With seven pre-production prototypes flying, including two two-seat trainers, the troubled Eurofighter programme looks more stable than ever in its protracted history. Germany is still pushing for cost-saving measures which may be met by opening three rather than four separate production lines.

Variants and operators

Eurofighter 2000: requirement for 765 for Germany; Italy; Spain; UK

Accommodation

1 pilot

Armament

One internal 27 mm Mauser cannon
Hardpoints: thirteen (three wet): five fuselage; eight wing
Warload: 6,500 kg (14,330 lb)
Weapons: AIM-9 Sidewinder; AIM-120 AMRAAM; Apside; ASRAAM; ALARM; PGMs; bombs; rockets

HAL HJT-16 Kiran India

Operational trainer / ground attack aircraft

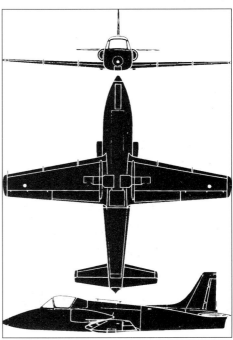

Early Mk I Kirans lacked the ability to carry weapons, but the later model Mk IA had two hardpoints. In 1976 HAL developed the Mk II with a Rolls Royce Orpheus engine and an extra two hardpoints to turn it into a counter-insurgency aircraft.

Variants and operators
Kiran Mk1: India **Kiran MkII:** India

Accommodation
2 pilots

Armament
Two internal 7.62 mm machine guns
Hardpoints: four wing (four wet)
Warload: (1,000 lb)
Weapons: bombs; rockets

Features: Low/straight wing; Prominent intakes; Side-by-side cockpit

IAI Kfir Israel

Multi-role fighter

Length: 15.6 m (51 ft 4 in) Wingspan: 8.2 m (25 ft 11 in) Height: 4.5 m (14 ft 11 in)

Features: Tail-less delta; swept canards; notch on tail fin

Struck by embargoes following the 1967 Six-Day war, Israel decided to develop a home-built fighter to reduce its dependence on the West. Israel copied the latest Mirage V and made improvements including the first use of canards. Two variants remain in service with their corresponding two-seat trainers C2/TC2 and C7/TC7, the C2s having smaller canards.

Variants and operators
Kfir C2: Ecuador; Israel; Sri Lanka
Kfir C7: Colombia; Israel

Accommodation
1 pilot

Armament
Two internal 30 mm DEFA cannon
Hardpoints: nine (three wet): five fuselage; four wing
Warload: 6,085 kg (13,415 lb)
Weapons: AIM-9 Sidewinder; Python 3/4; AGM-45 Shrike; AGM-65 Maverick; bombs; rockets

Kawasaki T-4 Japan

Operational trainer

Length: 13 m (42 ft 8 in) Wingspan: 9.9 m (32 ft 7 in) Height: 4.6 m (15 ft 1 in)

First flown in 1985, the T-4 was designed to replace the ageing T-33A T-bird and Fuji T-1. Although un-armed, three hardpoints enable it to carry ECM , target towing equipment and training weapons. Very similar to the Alpha Jet which has a much sharper nose section.

Variants and operators
T-4: Japan

Accommodation
2 pilots

Armament
Hardpoints: three (two wet): one fuselage; two wing
Weapons: training bombs, rockets

Features: High/swept wing; twin engines; rounded nose

57

Lockheed Martin Aircraft Argentina (FMA)
IA-58 Pucará Argentina

Counter insurgency aircraft

Length: 14.2 m (46 ft 9 in) Wingspan: 14.5 m (47 ft 6 in) Height: 5.4 m (17 ft 1 in)

Features: Low/straight wing; twin turboprop; T-tail

The Pucará entered service in 1976, having first flown in 1969. A single-seat version was built with increased internal armament and fuel, but the programme was suspended.

Variants and operators

IA-58: Argentina; Colombia; Sri Lanka; Uruguay

Accommodation

2 pilots

Armament

Two internal 20 mm Hispano cannon
Four internal 7.62 mm FN machine guns
Hardpoints: three (three wet): one fuselage; two wing
Warload: 1,500 kg (3,307 lb)
Weapons: bombs; rockets; gun pods

Lockheed Martin Aircraft Argentina (FMA)
IA-63 Pampa Argentina

Operational trainer / ground attack aircraft

Length: 4.3 m (14 ft 1 in) Wingspan: 9.7 m (31 ft 9 in) Height: 4.3 m (14 ft 1 in)

Argentina's first indigenous jet design, the Pampa first flew in 1987. A modified Pampa 2000 design competed unsuccessfully in the US JPATS competition, but other countries are now showing an interest. Very similar to the CASA Aviojet, the Pampa can be distinguished by its high mounted wing.

Variants and operators
IA-63: Argentina

Accommodation
2 pilots

Armament
Hardpoints: five: one fuselage; four wing
Warload: 1,160 kg (2,557 lb)
Weapons: bombs; rockets; gun pods

Features: High/swept wing; single engine; short tailpipe

59

Lockheed Martin AC-130U Spectre USA

Aerial Gunship

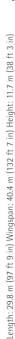

Length: 29.8 m (97 ft 9 in) Wingspan: 40.4 m (132 ft 7 in) Height: 11.7 m (38 ft 3 in)

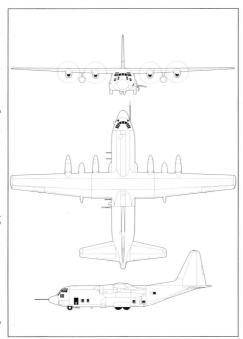

Features: High/straight wing; four turboprops; guns along port side

The latest development of the fighting Hercules, the AC-130U has been upgraded by Boeing (Rockwell). All weapons are now aimed independently, with greater accuracy. Its battle management centre makes it able to co-ordinate a variety of tasks and missions from combat-search-and-rescue to escort.

Variants and operators

AC-130U: USAF   AC-130H: USAF

Accommodation

2 pilots; 2 crew; 7 mission crew

Armament

One internal 105 mm Howitzer
One internal 40 mm Bofors cannon
One internal 25 mm GAU-12U cannon
(AC-130H Two internal 20 mm M61A1 cannon)
Hardpoints: four wing (four wet)
Weapons: AGM-114 Hellfire

Lockheed Martin F-16 Fighting Falcon USA

Multi-role fighter

Winner of the 1972 USAF lightweight fighter competition, the F-16 first flew in 1974, and more than 4,000 have been built, logging more than 5 million flight hours and an air combat score of 69-nil. Production will continue until 2010. Embraer of Brazil is discussing a possible licence built programme.

Variants and operators

F-16A/B: Belgium; Denmark; Egypt; Indonesia; Israel; Jordan; Netherlands; Norway; Pakistan; Portugal; Singapore; Taiwan; Thailand; USAF; Venezuela **F-16C/D:** Bahrain; Egypt; Greece; Israel; Korea; Singapore; Turkey; UAE; USAF; USN

Accommodation

1 pilot

Armament

One internal 20 mm M61A1 cannon
Hardpoints: nine (three wet): one fuselage; six wing; two wingtip
Warload: 4,320 kg (9,523 lb)
Weapons: AIM-7 Sparrow; AIM-9 Sidewinder; AIM-120 AMRAAM; Python3; AGM-45 Shrike; AGM-65 Maverick; AGM-88 HARM; Penguin Mk3; bombs; rockets

Length: 15 m (49 ft 4 in) Wingspan: 9.4 m (31 ft) Height: 5.1 m (16 ft 4 in)

Features: Mid/small delta; blended body; ventral intake

61

Lockheed Martin/Boeing F-22 Raptor USA

Air superiority stealth fighter

Length: 18.9 m (62 ft 1 in) Wingspan: 13.6 m (44 ft 6 in) Height: 5 m (16 ft 5 in)

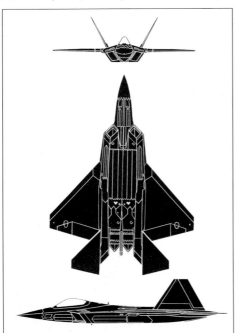

Features: Mid/swept diamond wing, twin angled tails; stealth features

Winner of the USAF Advanced Tactical Fighter competition, the F-22 is now called the Raptor. Production of the first of 750 aircraft has begun, and the first Raptors should reach the squadrons in 2004. A ground attack capability has been added, and a low cost derivative is being offered to several NATO nations.

Variants and operators
F-22A: USA

Accommodation
1 pilot

Armament
One internal 20 mm M61A2 cannon
Three internal weapons bays
Hardpoints: four wing (four wet)
Weapons: AIM-9 Sidewinder; AIM-120
AMRAAM; JDAM; AGM-88 HARM; Paveway

Lockheed Martin F-104 Starfighter USA

Interceptor / ground attack aircraft

First flown in 1954, the F-104 was based on experience gained in the Korean War. Designed to achieve altitude quickly and shoot down bombers, it is now flown at low level, carrying bombs. Italian interceptors were replaced by leased Tornado F.3s, Taiwanese aircraft being replaced by Ching Kuo.

Variants and operators
F-104G: Taiwan F-104S: Italy

Accommodation
1 pilot

Armament
One internal 20 mm M61A1 cannon
Hardpoints: nine (four wet): three fuselage; four wing; two wingtip
Warload: 3,402 kg (7,500 lb)
Weapons: AIM-7 Sparrow; AIM-9 Sidewinder; bombs; rockets

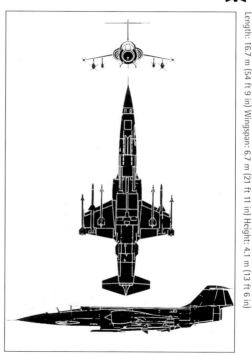

Length: 16.7 m (54 ft 9 in) Wingspan: 6.7 m (21 ft 11 in) Height: 4.1 m (13 ft 6 in)

Features: Mid/straight wing; narrow fuselage; T-tail

Lockheed Martin (General Dynamics)
F-111 Aardvark USA

Strike fighter

Length: 22.4 m (73 ft 6 in) Wingspan (spread): 19.2 m (63 ft) Height: 5.2 m (17 ft 1 in)

Features: High/swing wing; single tail; side-by-side cockpit

Being replaced in US service by the F-15E, the F-111 will soldier on in Australian service until 2020. Originally designed to carry out a wide variety of tasks from interceptor to bomber, from carriers or land, the 'vark found its niche low-level bombing from land.

Variants and operators
F-111C: Australia; EF-111A: USAF

Accommodation
1 pilot; 1 systems operator

Armament
One internal 20 mm M61A1 cannon
Internal bomb bay
Hardpoints: four wing (two wet)
Warloa6d: 13,610 kg (30,000 lb)
Weapons; Paveway; PGMs; bombs; mines

Lockheed Martin F-117A Stealth Fighter USA

Stealth bomber

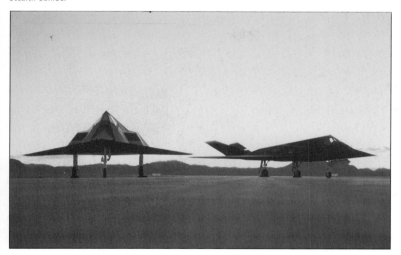

First seen in public in 1988, the F-117 had been flying since 1982. The USAF claims its weapons fit is the 'full range of tactical fighter ordnance' which can include any missile with an active seeker like HARM or Maverick and possibly Sidewinder giving it some fighter capability.

Variants and operators
F-117A: USAF

Accommodation
1 pilot

Armament
Internal bomb bay
Warload: approx 1,814 kg (4,000 lb)
Weapons: poss AIM-9 Sidewinder; PGMs; JDAM;
AGM-65 Maverick; AGM-88 HARM;

Length: 20.1 m (65 ft 11 in) Wingspan: 13.2 m (43 ft 4 in) Height: 3.8 m (12 ft 5 in)

Features: Low/swept wing; butterfly tail; stealth features

Lockheed Martin T-33 Shooting Star USA

Operational trainer

Length: 11.5 m (37 ft 8 in) Wingspan: 11.8 m (38 ft 10 in) Height: 3.5 m (11 ft 8 in)

Features: Low/straight wing; wingtip tanks; cheek intakes

The oldest aircraft in this section, the T-33 first flew as the P-80 in 1945. The T-33 came along in 1948. Known as the 'T-bird', it remains in service with a number of air forces. An armed version (AT-33) can carry light ordnance and is used for counter-insurgency missions.

Variants and operators

T-33: Bolivia; Canada; Ecuador; Greece; Iran; Japan; South Korea; Mexico; Pakistan; Paraguay; Thailand; Turkey; UruguayAT-33: Ecuador; Mexico; Paraguay; Uruguay

Accommodation

2 pilots

Armament

Early models have two internal 12.7 mm machine guns
Hardpoints: two wing
Weapons: bombs; rockets; gun pods

MIG-MAPO Advanced Trainer Russia

Operational trainer / ground attack aircraft

MIG is now owned by the MAPO consortium, who wisely kept the initials MIG even though they now stand for Moscow Industrial Group. Designed to replace the Aero L-29 and L-39 in Russian service, MIG-MAPO are also hoping it will secure export orders against the BAe Hawk series. It is also in competition with the Yakovlev-130

Variants and operators
Russian requirement for 250

Accommodation
2 pilots

Armament
Hardpoints: seven: one fuselage; four wing; two wingtip
Warload: 2,000 kg (4,410 lb)
Weapons: R-73E; R-77; AIM-9 Sidewinder; Kh-20; Kh-31; bombs; rockets

Features: Low/straight wing; two engines; cranked leading edge

Length: 11.3 m (37 ft 1 in) Wingspan: 10 m (32 ft 9 in) Height: 4.4 m (14 ft 6 in)

MIG-MAPO (Mikoyan) MIG-15 Fagot Russia

Operational trainer / ground attack fighter

Length: 11.1 m (36 ft 4 in) Wingspan: 10.1 m (33 ft 1 in) Height: 3.4 m (11 ft 2 in)

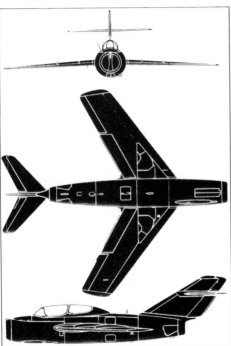

Features: Mid/swept wing; nose intake; high tail

First flown in 1947, the MiG-15 combined German aerodynamics and British engine-making. Still in widespread service as a trainer(UTI, see side view), the MiG-15 was also built in large numbers in China, Poland and the Czech Republic.

Variants and operators

MiG-15: Albania; Romania MiG-15 UTI: Albania; Angola; China; Congo; Guinea- Bissau; Guinea Republic; North Korea; Mali; Mozambique; Romania; Syria; Tanzania; Yemen

Accommodation

1 pilot

Armament

One internal 37 mm N cannon
Two internal 23 mm NS cannon
Hardpoints: two wing (both wet)
Weapons: bombs; rockets

MIG-MAPO (Mikoyan) MIG-17 Fresco Russia

Interceptor / ground attack fighter

Built around a more powerful engine than the MiG–15, the MiG-17 was larger and could reach mach 1. Licence-built in China and Poland, it was exported to many countries and remains in limited service.

Variants and operators

MiG-17: Algeria; Angola; Albania; Bulgaria; Congo; Cuba; Ethiopia; Guinea-Bissau; Guinea Republic; Madagascar; Mali; Mozambique; Romania; Syria

Accommodation

1 pilot

Armament

One internal 37 mm N cannon
Two internal 23 mm NS cannon
Hardpoints: two wing (both wet)
Warload: 500 kg (1,102 lb)
Weapons: bombs; rockets

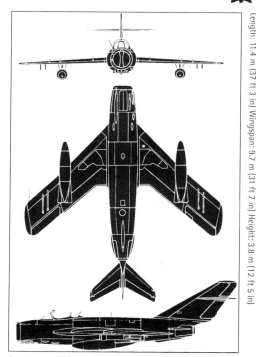

Length: 11.4 m (37 ft 3 in) Wingspan: 9.7 m (31 ft 7 in) Height: 3.8 m (12 ft 5 in)

Features: Mid/swept wing; nose intake; small nose radome

69

MIG-MAPO (Mikoyan) MIG-21 Fishbed Russia

Interceptor / ground attack fighter

Length: 15.7 m (51 ft 8 in) Wingspan: 7.2 m (23 ft 5 in) Height: 4.1 m (13 ft 5 in)

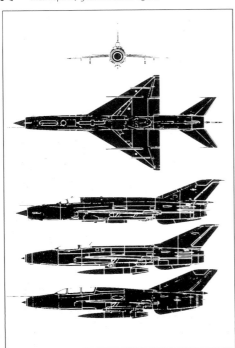

Features: Mid/small delta; swept tail plane; nose intake

The MiG-21 first flew in 1957, and with the numerous upgrades available looks likely to be around for many years. Major models are the Fishbed J (top) Fishbed C (middle) and Mongol two-seat trainer (bottom).

Variants and operators

MiG-21: Afghanistan; Algeria; Angola; Azerbaijan; Bulgaria; Congo; Croatia; Cuba; Czech Republic; Egypt; Ethiopia; Guinea Bissau; Guinea Republic; Hungary; India; Iraq; North Korea; Laos; Libya; Madagascar; Mali; Mongolia; Nigeria; Poland; Romania; Slovakia; Syria; Uganda; Vietnam; Yemen; Yugoslavia; Zambia

Accommodation

1 pilot

Armament

One internal 23 mm GSh-23 cannon
Hardpoints: five (three wet): one fuselage; four wing
Weapons: R-13A; bombs; rockets upgrades to allow wider range of western weapons

MIG-MAPO (Mikoyan) MIG-23 Flogger Russia

Interceptor / ground attack fighter

First flown in 1967, the MiG-23 entered service in 1970 and is being replaced in Russian service by the MiG-29 and Su-27. Numerous variants were built, main versions being the MiG-23UB two-seat trainer and MiG-23 MS export version with a smaller radome.

Variants and operators

MiG-23: Afghanistan; Algeria; Angola; Belarus; Bulgaria; Cuba; Czech Republic; Ethiopia; Hungary; India; Iraq; Kazakstan; North Korea; Libya; Poland; Romania; Russia; Sudan; Syria; Ukraine; Yemen

Accommodation

1 pilot

Armament

One internal 23 mm GSh-L cannon
Hardpoints: six (three wet): four fuselage; two wing
Warload: 3,000 kg (6,615 lb)
Weapons: R-23R; R-23T; R-60; bombs; rockets

Length: 15.6 m (51 ft 4 in) Wingspan(spread): 13.9 m (45 ft 10 in) Height: 4.8 m (15 ft 9 in)

Features: High/swing wing; single seat; single engine

71

MIG-MAPO MiG-25 Foxbat Russia

Interceptor / reconnaissance aircraft

Length: 23.8 m (78 ft 1 in) Wingspan: 14 m (45 ft 11 in) Height: 6.1 m (20 ft)

Features: High/swept wing; twin tails; single seat

Built around a pair of huge engines, the MIG-25 first flew in 1964 and was designed to combat the next generation of US supersonic bombers. When the USAF cancelled these Mach 3 bombers, the MiG-25 turned its hand to reconnaissance and defence suppression, as well as air defence.

Variants and operators

MiG-25: Algeria; Azerbaijan; India; Iraq; Kazakstan; Libya; Russia; Syria; Ukraine

Accommodation

1 pilot

Armament

Hardpoints: five (one wet): one fuselage; four wing
Weapons: R-40; R-60; R-23;

MIG-MAPO (Mikoyan)MiG-27 Flogger Russia

Ground attack fighter

Developed from the MiG-23, the MiG-27 has a more powerful engine and redesigned nose containing a laser designator in place of the radar. Russia is in the process of withdrawing them from frontline service.

Variants and operators
MiG-27: India; Iran; Kazakstan; Russia

Accommodation
1 pilot

Armament
One internal 23 mm GSh-23 cannon
Hardpoints: five (three wet): three fuselage; two wing
Warload: 4,000 kg (8,818 lb)
Weapons: R-3; R-13; Kh-23; Kh-29; bombs; rockets

Length: 17.1 m (56 ft) Wingspan(spread):13.9 m (45 ft 10 in) Height: 4.8 m (15 ft 9 in)

Features: High/swing wing; single seat; flat nose

MIG-MAPO MIG-29 Fulcrum Russia

Interceptor / ground attack fighter

Length: 14.9 m (48 ft 9 in) Wingspan: 11.4 m (37 ft 3 in) Height: 4.7 m (15 ft 6 in)

Features: Mid/swept wing; twin tails; ventral intakes

First seen in the Western press in 1986, the MIG-29 replaced a host of different fighter types when it came into service in 1983. The basic MIG-29 airframe is being upgraded by Russia to meet export customer demands.

Variants and operators

MiG-29: Algeria; Angola; Belarus; Bulgaria; Cuba; Hungary; India; Iraq; Kazakstan; North Korea; Moldova; Malaysia; Peru; Poland; Romania; Russia; Slovak Republic; Syria; Ukraine; Yemen; Yugoslavia

Accommodation

1 pilot

Armament

One internal 30 mm GSh-301 cannon
Hardpoints: seven (three wet): one fuselage; six wing
Warload: 3,000 kg (6,614 lb)
Weapons: R-60T; R-60 mK; R-27; R-73; bombs; rockets

MIG-MAPO MIG-31 Foxhound Russia

Strategic interceptor

Russia began improving the MIG-25 in 1975, and by 1979 it had become a totally different aircraft, designated MIG-31. Boasting the first operational airborne phased array radar, it can track and destroy incoming cruise missiles. Trials were carried out using anti-satellite Vympel missiles.

Variants and operators
MiG-31: Russia

Accommodation
1 pilot; 1 systems operator

Armament
One internal 23 mm GSh-6-23 cannon
Hardpoints: eight (two wet): four fuselage; four wing
Weapons: R-33; R-40; R-60; Vympel ASAT

Features: High/swept wing; twin tails; small canopies

75

Mitsubishi T2/F1 Japan

Operational trainer / ground attack fighter

Length: 17.3 m (56 ft 9 in) Wingspan: 7.9 m (25 ft 10 in) Height: 4.5 m (14 ft 8 in)

Features: High/swept wing; twin engines; dorsal hump

The two-seat T2 was Japan's first supersonic aircraft, and first flew in 1971. The F1 was developed from it in 1975 to meet a close air support requirement. Easily confused with the Jaguar, the F1 is recognizable by its large dorsal hump behind the cockpit.

Variants and operators

T2: Japan F1: Japan

Accommodation

1 or 2 pilots

Armament

One internal 20 mm JM61 cannon
Hardpoints: five (three wet): one fuselage; four wing
Warload: 2,721 kg (12,500 lb)
Weapons: AIM-9 Sidewinder; ASM-1; bombs; rockets

Mitsubishi F2 Japan

Multi-role fighter

A much modified F-16C, the F2 won the Japanese FS-X competition in 1987, with the first prototype flying in 1995. The first aircraft should reach squadron service in 2000. The F2 has a greater wingspan with more hardpoints than the F-16 and has a three piece canopy.

Variants and operators
F-2A: Japan

Accommodation
1 pilot

Armament
One internal 20 mm M61A1 cannon
Hardpoints: thirteen (three wet): one fuselage;
ten wing; two wingtip
Warload: 6,500 kg (10,326 lb)
Weapons: AIM-7 Sparrow; AIM-9 Sidewinder;
ASM-2; bombs; rockets

Features: Mid/delta wing; three piece canopy; underfuselage intake

77

NAMC Q-5 Fantan China

Ground attack fighter

Length: 15.4 m (50 ft 7 in) Wingspan: 9.7 m (31 ft 10 in) Height: 4.5 m (14 ft 9 in)

Developed from the MiG-19, the Q-5 has a totally redesigned forward fuselage, with side intakes in place of the nose intake. A-5 export versions have upgraded avionics and are Sidewinder-compatible.

Variants and operators
Q-5: China A-5: Bangladesh; North Korea; Myanmar (Burma); Pakistan

Accommodation
1 pilot

Armament
One internal 23 mm Norinco Type 23-2K cannon
Hardpoints: ten (four wet): four fuselage; six wing
Warload: 2,000 kg (4,410 lb)
Weapons: AIM-9 Sidewinder; PL-2; PL-7; C-801; bombs; rockets

Features: Mid/swept wing; sharp nose; two engines

Northrop Grumman (Vought) A-7 Corsair USA

Ground attack aircraft

Length: 14.1 m (46 ft 1 in) Wingspan: 11.8 m (38 ft 9 in) Height: 4.9 m (16 ft)

Delivered to the US Navy in 1966 and the USAF in 1968, the A-7 is no longer in service with US forces. Surplus A-7s are finding their way into the air forces of NATO countries, and the Thai Navy is receiving A-7s to make up its first fixed-wing strike capability.

Variants and operators
A-7E: Greece, Thailand A-7H: Greece A-7P: Portugal

Accommodation
1 pilot

Armament
One internal 20 mm M61A1 cannon
Hardpoints: eight (two wet): two fuselage; six wing
Warload: 6,805 kg (15,000 lb)
Weapons: AIM-9 Sidewinder; bombs; rockets

Features: High/swept wing; single engine; chin intake

79

Northrop Grumman (Fairchild) A-10 Thunderbolt USA

Close support aircraft

Length: 16.3 m (53 ft 4 in) Wingspan: 17.5 m (57 ft 6 in) Height: 4.5 m (14 ft 8 in)

Features: Low/straight wing; rear podded engines; twin tails

The A-10 first flew in 1972 and was selected by the USAF the year after. Titanium armour capable of surviving 23 mm cannon fire is used to protect the pilot and engines. A service life extension is required to keep them flying until 2028.

Variants and operators
A-10A: USAF OA-10A: USA

Accommodation
1 pilot

Armament
One internal 30 mm GAU-8 cannon
Hardpoints: seven (three wet): one fuselage; six wing
Warload: 7,257 kg (16,000 lb)
Weapons: AGM-65 Maverick; PGMs; bombs; rockets

Northrop Grumman B-2 Spirit USA

Strategic stealth bomber

At $865 million a piece the B-2 is the most expensive aircraft yet built. The original requirement for 133 has been cut by Congress to 20. The B-2's conventional strike capability is being upgraded with GPS technology to give a near-precision bombing capability.

Variants and operators
B-2: USA

Accommodation
2 pilots

Armament
Two internal bomb bays
Warload: 22,680 kg (50,000 lb)
Weapons: AGM-129 cruise missiles; B61, B83 nuclear weapons; GAM-113 penetration bombs; JDAM; mines

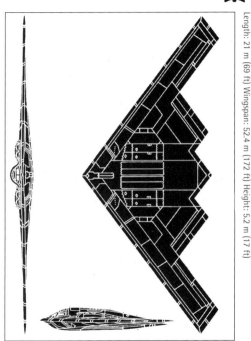

Length: 21 m (69 ft) Wingspan: 52.4 m (172 ft) Height: 5.2 m (17 ft)

Features: Tail-less flying wing; double-W trailing edge; stealth features

81

Northrop Grumman EA-6B Prowler USA

Carrier-borne electronic warfare aircraft

Length: 18.1 m (59 ft 10 in) Wingspan: 7.9 m (25 ft 10 in) Height: 5 m (16 ft 3 in)

Features: Mid/swept wing; four crew; fairing on tail fin

As the A-6 Intruder bows out of US Navy service, its close cousin the EA-6B will continue until replaced by modified F/A-18Fs. First flown in 1968, five years after the A-6 entered service, the Prowler will undergo a series of improvements to keep them operational until 2007.

Variants and operators
EA-6B: USN; USMC

Accommodation
2 pilots; 2 systems operators

Armament
Hardpoints: seven (five wet): one fuselage; six wing
Warload: 4,547 kg (10,025 lb)
Weapons: AGM-88 HARM; AN/ALQ-99F jamming pod

Northrop Grumman F-5 Tiger USA

Lightweight multi-role fighter

Despite it similarity to the T-38 Talon the F-5 was a totally different design. Built around the same two engines, taken from a canceled cruise missile, the F-5 was a no frills supersonic fighter that found great export success among NATO countries and US Allies. The RF-5E Tigereye has an enlarged nose with prominent camera lenses.

Variants and operators
F-5A/B: Botswana; Brazil; Greece; Morocco; Philippines; Saudi Arabia; Spain; Thailand; Turkey; Venezuela; Yemen **F-5E/F:** Bahrain; Brazil; Chile; Honduras; Indonesia; Iran; Jordan; Kenya; South Korea; Malaysia; Mexico; Morocco; Saudi Arabia; Singapore; Sudan; Switzerland; Taiwan; Thailand; Tunisia; Yemen **RF-5E:** Malaysia; Saudi Arabia; Singapore

Accommodation
1 pilot

Armament
Two internal 20 mm M39A2 cannon
Hardpoints: seven (three wet): one fuselage; four wing; two wingtip
Warload: 3,175 kg (7,000 lb)
Weapons: AIM-9 Sidewinder; AGM-65 Maverick; Durandal; bombs; rockets

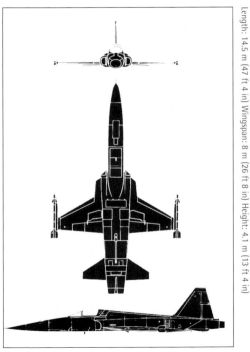

Length: 14.5 m (47 ft 4 in) Wingspan: 8 m (26 ft 8 in) Height: 4.1 m (13 ft 4 in)

Features: Low/swept wing; twin engines; single tail

83

Northrop Grumman (Vought) F-8 Crusader USA

Carrier-borne interceptor

Length: 16.6 m (54 ft 6 in) Wingspan: 10.1 m (35 ft 8 in) Height: 5 m (15 ft 9 in)

Features: High/swept wing; variable incidence wing; chin intake

First flown in 1955 the Crusader was the US Navy's first true supersonic fighter. The French Navy planned to replace them with the Rafale M in 1998, but programme delays mean they will have to continue until 2002.

Variants and operators
F-8E (FN): France

Accommodation
1 pilot

Armament
Four internal 20 mm Colt cannon
Hardpoints: two fuselage
Weapons: AIM-9 Sidewinder; Magic

Northrop Grumman F-14 Tomcat USA

Carrier-borne interceptor

Length: 19.1 m (62 ft 8 in) Wingspan (spread):19.5 m (64 ft 1 in) Height: 4.8 m (16 ft)

The big F-14 is being upgraded to keep it in service until sufficient F/A-18Fs and Joint Strike Fighters come into service. Next to the MIG-31, the Tomcat has the longest reach of any interceptor when using the AIM-54 Phoenix. F-14Ds have a bombing capability using precision guided munitions.

Variants and operators
F-14A: Iran; USN F-14B: USN F-14D: USN

Accommodation
1 pilot; 1 systems operator

Armament
One internal 20 mm M61A1 cannon
Hardpoints: ten (two wet): four fuselage; two on intakes; four wing
Warload: 6,577 kg (14,500 lb)
Weapons: AIM-7 Sparrow; AIM-9 Sidewinder; AIM-54 Phoenix; AIM-120 AMRAAM; JSOW; JDAM; AGM-88 HARM; SLAM; bombs; mines

Features: High/swing wing; twin tails; twin engines

85

Northrop Grumman T-38 Talon USA

Operational trainer

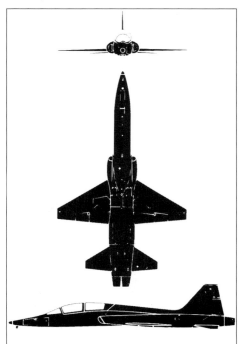

Length: 14.1 m (46 ft 4 in) Wingspan: 7.7 m (25 ft 3 in) Height: 3.9 m (12 ft 10 in)

Features: Low/swept wing; twin engines; twin seats

Not strictly speaking a combat aircraft, the T-38 was designed to simulate the characteristics of supersonic combat aircraft. First flown in 1959. NASA also operate T-38s for astronauts to maintain their flight readiness and as chase planes for the Space Shuttle.

Variants and operators
T-38C: Germany; Taiwan; Turkey; USAF; NASA

Accommodation
2 pilots

Armament
None fitted as standard

PAC K-8 Karakorum 8 China/Pakistan

Operational trainer / ground attack aircraft

A joint programme between China and Pakistan, the K-8 takes it name from the mountain range that separates the two countries. Pakistan decided against its own production run; all aircraft will be built in China.

Variants and operators
K-8: China; Pakistan

Accommodation
2 pilots

Armament
One ventral 23 mm cannon
Hardpoints: four wing (two wet)
Warload: 943 kg (2,080 lb)
Weapons: PL-7; bombs; rockets

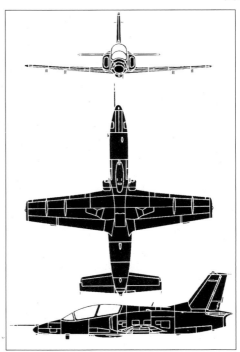

Length: 11.6 m (38 ft) Wingspan: 9.6 m (31 ft 7 in) Height: 4.2 m (13 ft 9 in)

Features: Low/straight wing; single engine; cranked tail fin

Panavia Tornado IDS Germany/Italy/UK

Multi-role fighter

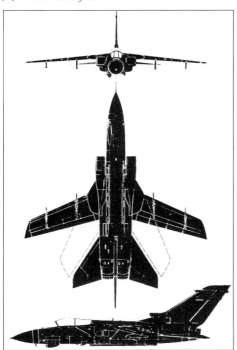

Features: High/swing wing; large single tail; twin engines

Optimized for the low-level penetration role, the Tornado first flew in 1974. Since entering service new roles include: German ECR electronic warfare aircraft; UK tactical reconnaissance GR.Mk1A and anti-ship GR.Mk1B. GR.Mk1As have no cannon and a series of optical lenses on the port side, ECRs carry the AGM-88 HARM and also lack cannon

Variants and operators

IDS: Germany; Italy; Saudi Arabia; UK **ECR:** Germany; Italy **GR.Mk1A/B:** UK

Accommodation

1 pilot; 1 systems operator

Armament

Two internal 27 mm Mauser cannon
Hardpoints: nine (four wet): three fuselage; six wing
Warload: 9,000 kg (19,840 lb)
Weapons: AIM-9 Sidewinder; AGM-65 Maverick; AGM-88 HARM; ALARM; Sea Eagle; Komoran; Paveway; JP223; bombs; rockets

Panavia Tornado ADV Germany/Italy/UK

Interceptor

Length: 18.7 m (61 ft 3 in) Wingspan(spread): 13.9 m (45 ft 7 in) Height: 5.6 m (19 ft 6 in)

A UK developed version of the IDS, the ADV has a longer forward fuselage to carry the Foxhunter radar and Skyflash AAMs. RAF aircraft deployed to Bosnia have begun carrying the outboard hardpoints from the IDS for carrying extra countermeasure pods.

Variants and operators
ADV F.Mk3: Italy; Saudi Arabia; UK

Accommodation
1 pilot; 1 systems operator

Armament
One internal 27 mm Mauser cannon
Hardpoints: ten (two wet): four fuselage; six wing
Warload: 8,500 kg (18,740 lb)
Weapons: Skyflash; Apside; ; AIM-9 Sidewinder; AIM-120 AMRAAM

Features: High/swing wing; large single tail; longer fuselage

89

Saab Draken Sweden

Interceptor / reconnaissance aircraft

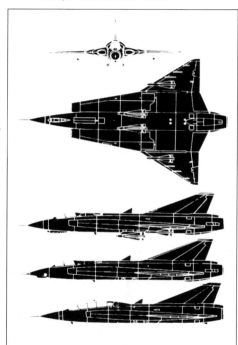

Length: 15.4 m (50 ft 4 in) Wingspan: 9.4 m (30 ft 10 in) Height: 3.9 m (12 ft 9 in)

Features: Mid/double delta; single tail; single engine

Europe's first supersonic fighter, the Draken first flew in 1955. The Draken is beginning to be replaced by the Gripen in the interceptor role and has been withdrawn from Danish service.

Variants and operators
J35: Austria; Finland; Sweden

Accommodation
1 pilot

Armament
One internal 30 mm ADEN cannon
Hardpoints: six (four wet): two fuselage; four wing
Weapons: Rb27 Falcon; Rb24 Sidewinder; bomb; rockets

Saab Viggen Sweden

Multi-role fighter

Designed to operate from rough field strips and stretches of highway, the Viggen could be described as the only modern biplane fighter as the forward delta also provide substantial lift. When it appeared in 1967 its tandem delta design was revolutionary, and much copied since.

Variants and operators
AJS37: Sweden

Accommodation
1 pilot

Armament
One ventral 30 mm Oerlikon cannon
Hardpoints: seven (one wet): three fuselage; four wing
Weapons: Rb71 Skyflash; Rb24 Sidewinder; bombs; rockets

Features: Tandem delta; single engine; dorsal hump

91

Saab Gripen Sweden

Multi-role fighter

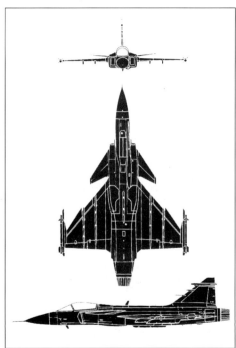

Length: 14.1 m (46 ft 3 in) Wingspan: 8.4 m (27 ft 6 in) Height: 4.5 m (14 ft 9 in)

Features: Mid/tail-less delta; movable canards; single engine

Now marketed through BAe, the Gripen is the first of Europe's fifth generation fighters to enter service. Hungary has begun building components for the Gripen, which could lead to an order to replace MiG-21s and even MiG-29s.

Variants and operators
JAS 39: Sweden; South Africa

Accommodation
1 pilot

Armament
One internal 27 mm BK27 cannon
Hardpoints: seven (three wet): one fuselage; four wing; two wingtip
Warload: approx 4,500 kg (9,920 lb)
Weapons: Rb74 Sidewinder; AIM-120 AMRAAM; Mica; Rb75 Maverick; RbS 15F; bombs; rockets

Saab 105 Sweden

Operational trainer / ground attack aircraft

First flown in 1963, the 105 is unique in that it is used throughout every stage of training from primary to tactical, and then has a secondary ground attack role. The original Turbomeca engines are being replaced with Williams/Rolls FJ44-1C turbojets keeping them in service until 2010.

Variants and operators
105: Sweden 105OE: Austria

Accommodation
2 pilots

Armament
Hardpoints: six wing
Weapons: Rb74 Sidewinder; Rb75 Maverick; bombs; rockets; gun pods

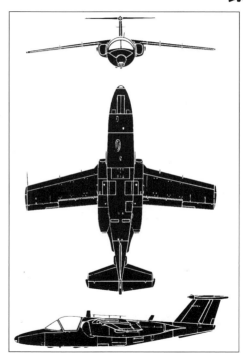

Features: High/swept wing; T-tail; side-by-side cockpit

93

SAIG J-8 Finback China

Multi-role fighter

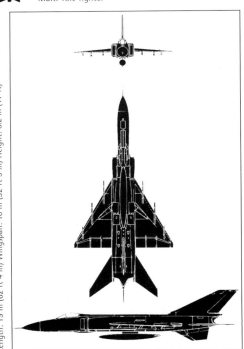

Length: 19 m (62 ft 4 in) Wingspan: 10 m (32 ft 9 in) Height: 5.2 m (17 ft)

Features: Mid/delta wing; swept tail plane; two engines

Despite its obvious Russian influences, the J-8 was an indigenous Chinese design, taking its first flight in 1969. The original J-8I had a nose intake while the J-8II (picture) had a solid nose, radar and MiG-23 side intakes.

Variants and operators
J-8I: China   J-8II: China

Accommodation
1 pilot

Armament
One internal 23 mm GSh-23 cannon
Hardpoints: seven (one wet): one fuselage; six wing
Weapons: PL-2; PL-7; bombs; rockets

SEPECAT **Jaguar** France/UK

Ground attack fighter

Length: 15.5 m (50 ft 11 in) Wingspan: 8.7 m (28 ft 6 in) Height: 4.9 m (16 ft)

Begun in 1965 as an operational trainer, the Jaguar evolved into a ground attack fighter. Some Indian licence-built versions are equipped with Agave radar for an anti-shipping role using Exocet.

Variants and operators

Jaguar: France; UK **Jaguar International:**
Ecuador; India; Nigeria; Oman

Accommodation

1 pilot

Armament

Two internal 30 mm ADEN or DEFA cannon
Hardpoints: seven (three wet): one fuselage; four wing; two over wing
Warload: 4,763 kg (10,500 lb)
Weapons: AIM-9 Sidewinder; Magic; Exocet (India); bombs; rockets

Features: High/swept wing; twin engines; single tail

95

SOKO G-2 Galeb Yugoslavia

Operational trainer / ground attack aircraft

Length: 10.3 m (33 ft 11 in) Wingspan: 10.5 m (34 ft 4 in) Height: 3.3 m (10 ft 9 in)

Features: Low/straight wing; wingtip tanks; single engine

Despite the fact that much of its tooling was removed to Utva in the Federal Yugoslavia, SOKO has begun to rebuild its Mostar factory. The G-2 Galeb, SOKOs first jet design, finished production in 1984, several G-2s and single seat J-1s (silhouette) found their way into the arsenals of the warring sides.

Variants and operators
G-2: Croatia; Libya; Republic of Srpska; Yugoslavia **J-1 Jastreb:** Republic of Srpska; Yugoslavia; Zambia

Accommodation 2 pilots

Armament
Two internal 12.7 mm machine guns
Hardpoints: two wing
Warload: 300 kg (660 lb)
Weapons: bombs; rockets; gun pods

SOKO G-4 Super Galeb Yugoslavia

Operational trainer / ground attack aircraft

Production of the G-4 ceased when the factory was dismantled in 1992. Most G-4s ended up in the Federal Yugoslav airforce, where they where upgraded to carry AAMs and Maverick missiles. First flown in 1980, it is uncertain whether Federal Yugoslavia has the facilities to develop the G-4 further.

Variants and operators
G-4: Bosnia-Herzegovina; Myanmar (Burma); Yugoslavia

Accommodation
2 pilots

Armament
One ventral 23 mm GSh-23 cannon
Hardpoints: five (three wet): one fuselage; four wing
Warload: 2,053 kg (4,526 lb)
Weapons: R-60; AGM-65 Maverick; bombs; rockets

Length: 12.5 m (40 ft 2 in) Wingspan: 9.9 m (32 ft 5 in) Height: 4.3 m (14 ft 1 in)

Features: Low/swept wing; ventral fin; single engine

Sukhoi Su-7 Fitter A Russia

Ground attack fighter

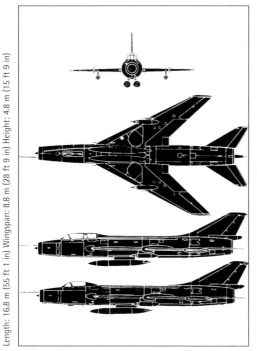

First flown in 1955, the Su-7 began life as an interceptor but was primarily used as a ground attack fighter. To give it a short field capability Su-7s could be fitted with rocket assisted take-off equipment. Withdrawn from European service.

Variants and operators

Su-7: Afghanistan; Algeria; North Korea

Accommodation

1 pilot

Armament

Two 30 mm NR-30 cannon
Hardpoints: six (two wet): two fuselage; four wing
Warload: 1,000 kg (2,205 lb)
Weapons: bombs; rockets

Features: Mid/swept wing; nose intake; single engine

Length: 16.8 m (55 ft 1 in) Wingspan: 8.8 m (28 ft 9 in) Height: 4.8 m (15 ft 9 in)

Sukhoi Su-17/22 Fitter D/K Russia

Ground attack aircraft

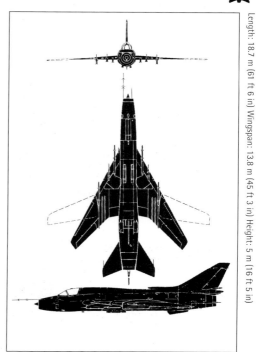

The first prototype was a straightforward conversion of a fixed wing Su-7 in 1966. Since then it has been developed into the Su-20 and 22 export versions and has dedicated ground attack avionics.

Variants and operators

Su-17: Russia; Ukraine **Su-20:** Algeria; Poland
Su-22: Afghanistan; Angola; Bulgaria; Czech Republic; Iraq; Libya; Peru; Poland; Slovak Republic; Syria; Vietnam; Yemen

Accommodation

1 pilot

Armament

Two internal 30 mm NR-30 cannon
Hardpoints: nine (four wet): five fuselage; four wing
Warload: 3,175 kg (7,000 lb)
Weapons: R-3; R-30; R-60; Kh-23; AS-9; Kh-25; bombs; rockets

Features: Low/swing wing; nose intake; single engine

Length: 18.7 m (61 ft 6 in) Wingspan: 13.8 m (45 ft 3 in) Height: 5 m (16 ft 5 in)

99

Sukhoi Su-24 Fencer Russia

Strike bomber / reconnaissance aircraft

Length: 24.5 m (80 ft 5 in) Wingspan (spread): 17.6 m (57 ft 10 in) Height: 4.9 m (16 ft 3 in)

Features: High/swing wing; square intakes; side-by-side cockpit

The first prototype flew in 1967 with fixed delta wings and four auxiliary jets to assist take off. By the time production began in 1970 the auxiliary jets had gone and a variable geometry wing was installed. Iran inherited Iraqi Su-24s during the 1991 Gulf War and put them into service. The Su-24 MR reconnaissance version has a shorter nose section and central recce pod.

Variants and operators

Su-24: Azerbaijan; Belarus; Iran; Kazakstan; Libya; Russia; Syria; Ukraine **Su-24 MR:** Belarus; Kazakstan; Russia; Ukraine

Accommodation

1 pilot; 1 systems operator

Armament

One internal 23 mm Gatling cannon
Hardpoints: nine (four wet): five fuselage; four wing
Warload: 8,000 kg (17,635 lb)
Weapons: TN-1000, TN-1200 nuclear weapons; Kh-23; Kh-25; AS-11; AS-12; AS-13; Kh-29; bombs

Sukhoi Su-25 Frogfoot Russia

Ground attack aircraft

First flown in 1975, the Su-25 was thrown into the Afghan war before reaching full operational status. A number of changes were made with experience from Afghanistan, most notably the larger dorsal hump with an extra tonne of fuel in the Su-25T (bottom).

Variants and operators
Su-25: Afghanistan; Angola; Azerbaijan; Belarus; Bulgaria; Czech Republic; Georgia; Iran; Iraq; Kazakstan; North Korea; Peru; Slovak Republic; Ukraine

Accommodation
1 pilot

Armament
One internal 30 mm AO-17A cannon
Hardpoints: eight wing (four wet)
Warload: 4,400 kg (9,700 lb)
Weapons: R-3; R-60; Kh-23; Kh-25; Kh-29; bombs; rockets

Length: 15.5 m (50 ft 11 in) Wingspan: 14.4 m (47 ft 1 in) Height: 4.8 m (15 ft 9 in)

Features: High/straight wing; twin engines; single tail

Sukhoi Su-27 Flanker Russia

Interceptor / ground attack fighter

Features: Mid/swept wing; twin tails; ventral intakes

Although NATO reporting names are not used by Russian forces, such was the Su-27's impact on Western observers that Sukhoi now markets it under the name 'Flanker'. The Su-27S was developed for Russian Frontal Aviation with increased ground attack capability.

Variants and operators
Su-27: Belarus; China; Kazakstan; Russia; Ukraine; Vietnam **Su-27S:** Russia

Accommodation
1 pilot

Armament
One internal 30 mm GSh-301 cannon
Hardpoints: ten (two wet): four fuselage; four wing; two wingtip
Warload: 4,000 kg (8,818 lb)
Weapons; R-27R; R-27T; R-60; R-73; R-33; bombs; rockets

Sukhoi Su-30 Flanker Russia

Multi-role fighter

Length: 21.9 m (71 ft 11 in) Wingspan: 14.7 m (48 ft 2 in) Height: 5.9 m (20 ft 10 in)

Retains all the air-to-air capability of the Su-27, but has a precision attack capability, and is optimized for long (10 hour) missions. India has ordered 28 standard models and 12 with vectored-thrust nozzles. All Indian aircraft will eventually be retrofitted with vectored-thrust.

Variants and operators
Su-30: Russia **Su-30 MKI:** India

Accommodation
1 pilot; 1 systems operator

Armament
One internal 30 mm GSh-301 cannon
Hardpoints: twelve (two wet): four fuselage; six wing; two wingtip
Warload: 8,000 kg (17,635 lb)
Weapons: R-27; R73; R-77; Kh-29; Kh-31; D-9 m; Kh-59; bombs; rockets

Features: Mid/swept wing; twin tails; two-seats

Sukhoi Su-33/35/37 Flanker Russia

Multi-role fighter / carrier-borne fighter

Length: 22.2 m (72 ft 10 in) Wingspan: 15.2 m (49 ft 8 in) Height: 6.4 m (20 ft 10 in)

Features: Mid/swept wing; forward canards; twin tails

The Su-33 was designed to operate from the aircraft carrier *Kuznetzov* and was the first to sport canards. Sukhoi is chasing export orders for its Flanker family and have developed a ground-based version the Su-35 and an advanced version with thrust vectoring the Su-37.

Variants and operators
Su-33: Russia Su-35: Russia

Accommodation
1 pilot

Armament
One internal 30 mm GSh-301 cannon
Hardpoints: fourteen (two wet): six fuselage; six wing; two wingtip
Warload: 8,000 kg (17,635 lb)
Weapons: R-27; R-40; R-60; R-73; R-77; Kh-25; Kh-29; Kh-31; Kh-59; PGMs; bombs; rockets

Sukhoi Su-34 Flanker Russia

Strike bomber

A radical development of the basic Su-27 airframe, the Su-34 boasts advanced nav-attack avionics in the flat nose; rearwards-facing radar controlling defensive missiles in the tail; and a toilet and galley in the rear cockpit. The Su-32FN is a maritime attack development. It is intended to replace the Su-24 by 2005.

Variants and operators
Su-34: Russia Su-32FN: Russia

Accommodation
1 pilot; 1 systems operator

Armament
One internal 30 mm GSh-301 cannon
Hardpoints: twelve (two wet): four fuselage; six wing; two wingtip
Warload: 8,000 kg (17,635 lb)
Weapons: R-73; R-27; Kh-29; Kh-59; Kh-35; Kh-41; PGMs; bombs; rockets

Features: Mid/swept wing; side-by-side cockpit; twin tails

Length: 25.5 m (82 ft 8 in) Wingspan: 14.7 m (48 ft 2 in) Height: 6.2 m (20 ft 4 in)

Tupolev Tu-16 Badger Russia

Maritime strike / electronic warfare aircraft

Features: Mid/swept wing; glass nose; wingroot engines

Length: 34.8 m (114 ft 2 in) Wingspan: 32.9 m (108 ft 3 in) Height: 10.4 m (34 ft)

First flown in 1952, the Tu-16 was held back from production because of excessive weight problems. China licence-builds exact copies under the designation H-6. Now used only for maritime strike and EW in Ukraine.

Variants and operators
Tu-16: Iraq; Ukraine **H-6:** China

Accommodation
2 pilots; 3 systems operators; 1 tail gunner

Armament
Three 23 mm gun turrets in dorsal, ventral and tail positions
Internal bomb bay
Hardpoints: two wing
Warload: 9,000 kg (19,800 lb)
Weapons: AS-6; bombs

Tupolev Tu-22 Blinder Russia

Strategic bomber / maritime strike

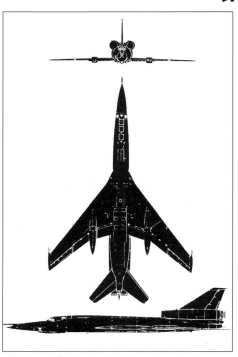

Development began in 1956 as a purpose built stand-off missile carrier with a supersonic dash capability. When it was first seen in 1961, it was carrying a Kh-22 Kitchen missile. Iraq is believed to have some although their serviceability is questionable.

Variants and operators
Tu-22: Iraq; Libya; Ukraine

Accommodation
1 pilot; 1 systems operator; 1 rear gunner

Armament
One 23 mm NR-23 cannon in tail
Internal bomb bay
Warload: 12,000 kg (26,455 lb)
Weapons: Kh-22; bombs

Length: 42.6 m (139 ft) **Wingspan:** 23.5 m (77 ft 1 in) **Height:** 10 m (32 ft 9 in)

Features: Low/swept wing; two tail engines; sponsons on wing

Tupolev Tu-22M Backfire Russia

Strategic bomber / maritime strike aircraft

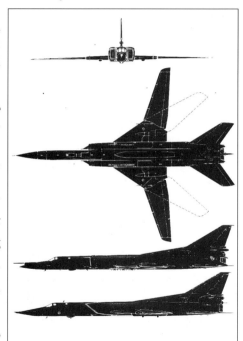

Length: 42.4 m (139 ft) Wingspan (spread):34.3 m (112 ft 5 in) Height: 11.1 m (36 ft 3 in)

Features: Low/swing wing; twin engines; large side intakes

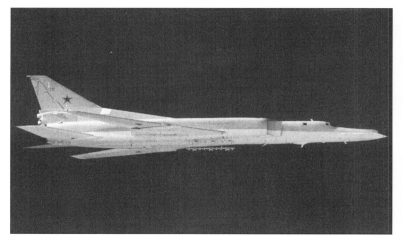

First observed in 1970, the Tu-22M is being upgraded to keep it in service into the next century, and new weapons are also being studied. It forms the backbone of Russia's strategic bomber force with over 250 in service. Early models had straight cut intakes (top).

Variants and operators
Tu-22M: Russia; Ukraine

Accommodation
2 pilots; 2 systems operators

Armament
One 23 mm GSh-23 cannon in tail
Internal bomb bay
Hardpoints: two wing
Warload: 24,000 kg (52,910 lb)
Weapons: Kh-22; Kh-15; bombs; mines

Tupolev Tu-95/142 Bear Russia

Strategic bomber / reconnaissance aircraft

The Tu-95 is known by its NATO reporting name inside Russia: on its first appearance at a Western airshow the author asked the crew what they called the Tu-95, they smiled and said 'it couldn't be anything other than a Bear'. The anti-submarine version, also in use by India, is designated Tu-142 and has a glass nose (top).

Variants and operators
Tu-95: Russia; Ukraine **Tu-142:** India; Russia

Accommodation
2 pilots; 4 mission crew; 1 rear gunner

Armament
One 23 mm GSh-23 cannon in tail
Internal bomb bay
Hardpoints; four wing
Warload: 11,340 kg (25,000 lb)
Weapons: Kh-55; Kh-22; bombs; mines; ASW
torpedoes; depth charges

Features: Mid/swept wing; four turboprops; glass or solid nose

Length: 49.5 m (162 ft 5 in) Wingspan: 51.1 m (167 ft 8 in) Height: 12.1 m (39 ft 9 in)

Tupolev Tu-160 Blackjack Russia

Strategic bomber

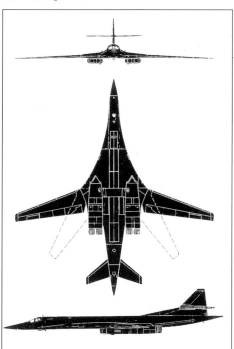

Length: 54.1 m (177 ft 6 in) Wingspan(spread):55.7 m (182 ft 9 in) Height: 13.1 m (43 ft)

Features: Low/swing wing; blended fuselage; ventral engines

Ukraine is in the process of handing back its Tu-160s to Russia. First flown in 1981, the Tu-160 looks very similar to the B-1B of about the same vintage, but is almost 10 m longer. Despite the fact that it remains Russia's most advanced strategic bomber production was ceased after only 36 were built.

Variants and operators
Tu-160: Russia; Ukraine

Accommodation
2 pilots; 2 systems operators

Armament
Internal bomb bay
Warload: 16,300 kg (36,000 lb)
Weapons: Kh-15; Kh-55; Kh-101; bombs

Yakovlev/Aermacchi Yak-130 Russia/Italy

Operational trainer / ground attack aircraft

Pitted against the MiG-AT for the Russian trainer competition, Yakovlev is developing the Yak-130 alongside Aermacchi of Italy. Yakovlev hopes partnership with an established Western manufacturer will bring export orders. The Slovak Republic has already shown interest.

Variants and operators
Yak-130: Russia

Accommodation
2 pilots

Armament
Hardpoints: seven (two wet): three fuselage; four wing
Warload: 3,000 kg (6,614 lb)
Weapons: AIM-9 Sidewinder; R-73; AGM-65 Maverick; Kh-25; bombs; rockets

Length: 11.9 m (39 ft) Wingspan: 10.6 m (34 ft 11 in) Height: 4.7 m (15 ft 5 in)

Features: Mid/swept wing; winglets; twin engines

COMBAT SUPPORT AIRCRAFT

Aérospatiale (Nord) N262 Frégate France

Light transport

The Frégate first flew in 1962, and although still used by the French air force today, it achieved no significant export orders. Built in four marks, the only major difference being the engines and role. The 262E is a navigation and flight engineer training and inshore patrol aircraft.

Variants and operators
N262: Burkina Faso; France; Gabon

Payload
Cargo: 3,075 kg (6,679 lb)
Accommodation: 2 pilots; 1 crew; 26 passengers

Features: Straight/high wing; twin turboprop; low tailplane

113

Airtech/CASA CN-235M Indonesia/Spain

Light tactical transport / maritime patrol aircraft

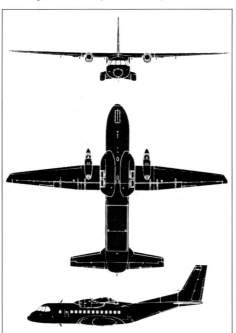

Length: 21.4 m (70 ft 2 in) Wingspan: 25.8 m (84 ft 8 in) Height: 8.2 m (26 ft 10 in)

Features: High/swept wing; twin turboprops; rear loading ramp

A joint venture between CASA of Spain and IPTN of Indonesia, the CN-235 first flew in 1983. Built in both civil and military versions, it is in military markets that it has found greater success. Turkey began its own licence-built production line in 1992. The maritime patrol version carries Harpoon or Exocet missiles and has a large ventral radar.

Variants and operators

CN-235M: Abu Dhabi; Brunei; Croatia; Indonesia; Malaya; Botswana; Chile Ecuador; France; Gabon; Ireland; Morocco; Oman; Panama; Papua New Guinea; Saudi Arabia; South Africa; South Korea; Spain; Thailand; Turkey

CN-235MP: Brunei; Indonesia; Malaysia; UAE

Payload

Cargo: 6,000 kg (13,227 lb)
Accommodation: 2 pilots; 2 crew; 48 troops; 44 paratroops; 24 stretchers

Alenia **G222** Italy

Light tactical transport

First flown in 1970, the G222 was originally a Fiat/Aeritalia design built in collaboration between Aermacchi, Piaggio, CIRSEA and IAM. Italy also operates radio/radar calibration versions and a specialised electronic warfare version, the 222VS. A firefighting version has also been built for the Italian Air Force.

Variants and operators

G222: Argentina; Congo; Italy; Libya; Nigeria; Somalia; Thailand; UAE; Venezuela **C-27A:** USA

Payload

Cargo: 9,000 kg (19,840 lb)
Accommodation: 2 pilots; 2 crew; 53 troops; 40 paratroops; 32 stretchers

Features: High/straight wing; twin turboprops; short fuselage

115

Antonov An-12 Cub Ukraine

Medium tactical transport

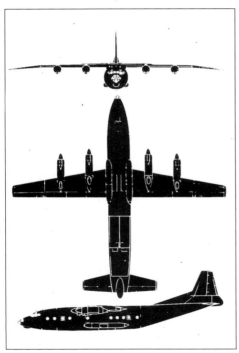

Length: 33.1 m (108 ft 7 in) Wingspan: 38 m (124 ft 8 in) Height: 10.5 m (34 ft 6 in)

Features: High/straight wing; Four turboprops; glass nose

First flown in 1958, the An-12 was a development of the civil An-10 airliner. The Chinese Y-8 is a licence-built version, the only major differences are the avionics and manufacturing techniques. Russia and Ukraine employ a number of specialist electronic warfare and intelligence versions with a wide range of antennas and blisters.

Variants and operators

An-12: Afghanistan; Angola; Belarus; Czech Republic; Ethiopia; Iraq; Kazakhstan; Russia; Slovakia; Ukraine; Yemen **Y-8:** China; Myanmar (Burma); Sri Lanka; Sudan

Payload

Cargo: 20,000 kg (61,730 lb)
Accommodation: 2 pilots; 3 crew; 90 troops; 60 paratroops

Armament

Twin 23 mm tail gun

Antonov An-22 Antheus, Cock Ukraine

Heavy strategic transport

First flown in 1965, production ended in 1974, and only around 45 remain in service. Operated by Aeroflot on behalf of the Russian air force, the An-22 can be adapted to carry piggy-back loads on top of the fuselage. These aircraft have a third tail fin.

Variants and operators
An-22: Russia

Payload
Cargo: 80,000 kg (176 350 lb)
Accommodation: 2 pilots; 3 crew; 29 passengers

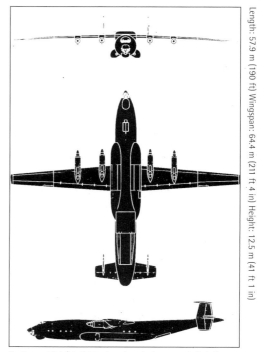

Length: 57.9 m (190 ft) Wingspan: 64.4 m (211 ft 4 in) Height: 12.5 m (41 ft 1 in)

Features: High/straight wing; four turboprops; twin tail

117

Antonov An-24 Coke Ukraine

Light tactical transport

Length: 23.8 m (78 ft 1 in) Wingspan: 29.9 m (95 ft 9 in) Height: 8.5 m (28 ft 1 in)

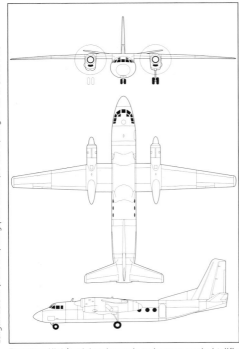

Features: High/straight wing; twin turboprop; cranked tailfin

First flown in 1960, the original 'Coke' was developed for Russia's internal commuter airlines. Designed to operate from small airfields, the An-24 was easily adapted for military purposes. Built under licence in China as the Y-7, which can be recognized by its winglets. Firefighting variants are operated in Russia.

Variants and operators

An-24: Belarus; Bulgaria; Cambodia; Congo; Cuba; Czech Republic; Guinea-Bissau; Guinea Republic; Hungary; Kazakhstan; North Korea; Lithuania; Mali; Mongolia; Romania; Russia; Slovakia; Sudan; Syria; Ukraine; Yemen

Payload

Cargo: 5,500 kg (12,125 lb)
Accommodation: 2 pilots; 3 crew; 38 troops; 30 paratroops; 24 stretchers

Antonov An-26 Curl Ukraine

Light tactical transport

Length: 23.8 m (78 ft 1 in) Wingspan: 29.9 m (95 ft 9 in) Height: 8.5 m (28 ft 1 in)

The An-24 proved such a success in military service that Antonov redesigned the tail unit to accommodate a rear loading ramp and improved cargo capabilities. The new aircraft was first seen at the Paris Air Show in 1969. The An-26 has a large observation blister on the left side of the fuselage.

Variants and operators

An-26: Afghanistan; Algeria; Angola; Belarus; Benin; Bulgaria; Cape Verde; Chad; China; Congo; Cuba; Czech Republic; Ethiopia; Hungary; Iraq; Kazakhstan; Libya; Lithuania; Madagascar; Mali; Mongolia; Mozambique; Nicaragua; Poland; Romania; Russia; Slovakia; Syria; Ukraine; Uzbekistan; Vietnam; Yemen; Yugoslavia; Zambia

Payload

Cargo: 5,500 kg (12,125 lb)
Accommodation: 2 pilots; 2 crew; 40 troops, 38 paratroops, 24 stretchers

Armament

Bomb racks under the wings

Features: High/straight wing; twin turboprop; rear loading ramp

Antonov An-32 Cline Ukraine

Light tactical transport

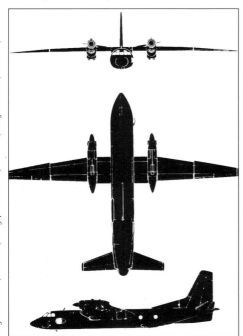

Length: 23.6 m (77 ft 8 in) Wingspan: 29.2 m (95 ft 9 in) Height: 8.7 m (28 ft 8 in)

Features: High/swept wing; overwing twin turboprops; rear loading ramp

The latest development of the An-24 / An-26 family, the An-32 first appeared in 1977. The aircraft was developed to carry heavy loads from unprepared airstrips. By placing the engines above the high-lift wing, the props are kept clear of the ground and intakes clear of debris.

Variants and operators

An-32: Afghanistan; Angola; Bangladesh; Croatia; Cuba; Equatorial Guinea; Ethiopia; India; Kazakstan; Peru; Russia; Ukraine

Payload

Cargo: 6,700 kg (14,770 lb)
Accommodation: 2 pilots; 2 crew; 50 troops; 42 Paratroops

Antonov An-70 Ukraine

Medium tactical transport

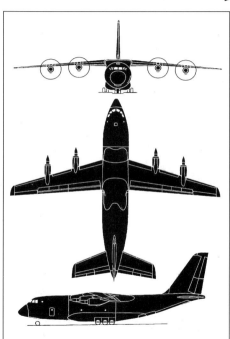

Developed as a replacement for the An-12 series, the An-70 first flew in 1994. The first propfan powered aircraft, the An-70 will be built in both military and civil versions, and an export version powered by CFM turbofans is also expected.

Variants and operators

An-70: Ukraine

Payload

Cargo: 47,000 kg (103,615 lb)
Accommodation: 2 pilots; 1 crew; 300 troops; 206 stretchers

Length: 40.7 m (133 ft 7 in) Wingspan: 44.1 m (144 ft 6 in) Height: 16.4 m (53 ft 9 in)

Features: High/swept wing; four propfans; low tail

121

Antonov An-72/74 Coaler Ukraine

Light tactical transport

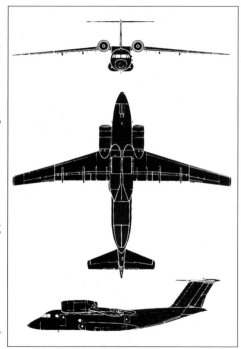

Length: 28.1 m (92 ft 1 in) Wingspan: 31.9 m (104 ft 7 in) Height: 8.7 m (28 ft 8 in)

Features: High/swept wing; overwing twin turbofans; T-tail

First flown in 1977, the An-72 was designed for STOL operations. Placing the engines above the wing improves lift and keeps them clear of debris. An-72 is the military designation, An-74 civil. An-72Ps are modified for maritime patrol, with weapons stations either side of the mainwheel housing and under the rear loading ramp.

Variants and operators
An-72/74: Kazakhstan; Peru; Russia; Ukraine; Iran **An-72P:** Ukraine; Russia

Payload
Cargo: 10,000 kg (22,045 lb)
Accommodation: 2 pilots; 2 crew; 68 troops; 57 paratroops; 24 stretchers

Armament
(An-72P) one 23 mm GSh-23L cannon
Bombs; rockets

Antonov An-124 Condor Ukraine

Heavy strategic transport

The holder of 20 payload, altitude and distance world records, the An-124 first flew in 1982, and is still the world's largest production aircraft. Also operated by civilian cargo airlines, it can load cargo from a wide range of airfields with limited facilities due to its rugged military design.

Variants and operators
An-124: (military) Russia; Ukraine

Payload
Cargo: 150,000 kg (330,700 lb)
Accomodation: 2 pilots; 4 crew; 451 passengers

Features: High/swept wing; four turbofans; chin radar

Length: 69.1 m (226 ft 8 in) Wingspan: 73.3 m (240 ft 5 in) Height: 21.1 m (69 ft 2 in)

123

Antonov An-225 Mirya Cossack Ukraine

Super heavy strategic transport

Length: 84 m (275 ft 7 in) Wingspan: 88.4 m (290 ft) Height: 18.2 m (59 ft 8 in)

Features: High/swept wing; six turbofans; twin tails

Only one Mriya (Dream) has been built, making its first flight in 1988. Designed to carry outsized loads such as the Buran space shuttle, the Mriya remains the largest aircraft in the world. Developed from the An-124 but lacking the rear loading ramp, it has two extra engines.

Variants and operators

An-225: Russia

Payload

Cargo: 250,000 kg (551,150 lb)
Accommodation: 2 pilots; 4 crew; 70 passengers

BAe (HS) Nimrod UK

Maritime patrol aircraft

Currently undergoing an upgrade programme to keep it in service until 2025, the Nimrod first flew in 1967. Two versions are in service with the Royal Air Force: the standard MR. Mk 2 and R. Mk 1 electronic reconnaissance aircraft. The R. Mk 1 can be recognized by its lack of MAD boom in the tail.

Variants and operators
MR. Mk 2: UK R. Mk 1: UK

Accomodation
2 pilots; 5 crew; 4 systems operators

Armament
Internal bomb bay
Hardpoints: two wing
Warload: 6,120 kg (13,500 lb)
Weapons: AIM-9 Sidewinder; AGM-84 Harpoon; torpedoes; mines

Features: Mid/swept wing; wingroot engines; double bubble cross section

BAe (BAC/Vickers)VC10 UK

Air-to-air tanker / transport

Length: 48.4 m (158 ft 8 in) Wingspan: 44.5 m (146 ft 2 in) Height: 12 m (39 ft 6 in)

Features: Low/swept wing; four tail mounted turbofans; swept T-tail

The VC10 first flew in 1962. Designed to operate from airfields with limited resources and in tropical climates, the VC10 is a very rugged design with an enviable safety record. No longer in operation as an airliner. In RAF service, 'C' models are the original transports upgraded to serve as dual-role tankers, 'K' models are converted airliners.

Variants and operators
C. Mk 1(K): UK **K.Mk 2/3/4:** UK

Payload
Cargo: 18,039 kg (39,769 lb)
Accommodation: 2 pilots; 2 crew; 151 passengers max

Beriev Be-12 Chaika 'Mail' Russia

Maritime patrol amphibian

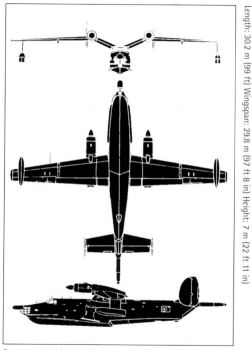

First flown in 1960, the Chaika (Seagull) was designed to replace the Be-6 flying boat from which it inherited the basic configuration. The Chaika was powered by turboprops rather than the Be-6's piston engines but retained the same cranked wing and single-stepped hull. Beriev has converted a small number to firefighters for the Russian Federal Service for Forestry

Variants and operators
Be-12: Russia; Ukraine

Accommodation
2 pilots; 3 crew

Armament
Internal bomb bay in tail
Hardpoints: four wing
Weapons: torpedoes; mines; depth charges

Features: High/cranked wing; twin tails; glazed nose

Length: 30.2 m (99 ft) Wingspan: 29.8 m (97 ft 8 in) Height: 7 m (22 ft 11 in)

Beriev A-40 Albatross 'Mermaid' Russia

Maritime patrol amphibian

Length: 43.8 m (143 ft 10 in) Wingspan: 41.6 m (136 ft 6 in) Height: 11.1 m (35 ft 3 in)

Features: High/swept wing; high fuselage mounted engines; T-tail

The A-40 is not only the largest amphibian ever put into production, but is also the only turbofan-powered amphibian in service. Designed to operate in the Pacific in cargo, search-and-rescue, anti-submarine warfare and maritime patrol missions, it has set a number of world records.

Variants and operators
A-40: Russia

Accommodation
2 pilots; 3 crew; 3 observers

Payload
Cargo: 6,500 kg (14,330 lb)

Armament
Internal bomb bay in tail
Weapons: torpedoes; mines; depth charges

128

Boeing E-3 Sentry USA

Airborne Warning and Control System (AWACS)

The most widely used AWACS aircraft in the world, the Sentry is now in service with five air forces. The first entered service in 1977 with the USAF, and a total of 68 have been built for all customers. NATO aircraft are operated by aircrew from every NATO country except the UK.

Variants and operators

E-3A: NATO; Saudi Arabia E-3B/C: USA E-3D: UK E-3F: France

Payload

AN/APY-1/2 airborne surveillance radar
Accommodation: 2 pilots; 2 crew; 13 mission crew

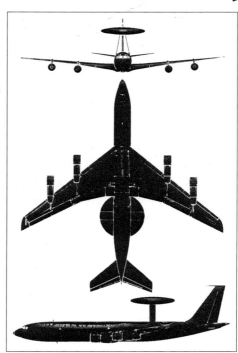

Length: 46.6 m (152 ft 11 in) Wingspan: 44.4 m (145 ft 9 in) Height: 12.7 m (41 ft 9 in)

Features: Low/swept wing; four turbofans; radar rotordome

129

Boeing E-4B USA

National emergency command post

Length: 70.5 m (231 ft 4 in) Wingspan: 59.6 m (195 ft 8 in) Height: 19.3 m (63 ft 5 in)

Features: Low/swept wing; four turbofans; dorsal hump

First flown in 1973, E-4Bs enable the President and Vice-president of the United States, to remain in contact with every branch of the US government and armed forces should ground facilities be destroyed. Communications equipment, state rooms, living quarters and briefing rooms fill three decks, and are resistant to nuclear blast, radiation and ECM. Not to be confused with the presidential transport, Air Force One, which lacks the command and control facilities.

Variants and operators
E-4B: USA

Payload
HF,MF, VHF,UHF, Satellite communications
Accommodation: 2-4 pilots; 2-4 aircrew; 94 mission crew

Boeing E-767 AWACS USA

Airborne Warning and Control System (AWACS)

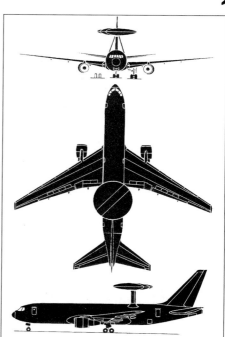

The successor to the E-3 Sentry AWACS. Boeing is offering the 767 in a number of other military versions including tankers and communications aircraft. The E-767 first flew in 1994 and has attracted only one customer: Japan. However, four other countries have so far shown an interest.

Variants and operators

-767: Japan

Payload

AN/APY-2 surveillance radar
Accommodation: 2 pilots; 18 mission crew

Features: Low/swept wing; twin turbofans; radar rotordome

Length: 48.5 m (159 ft 2 in) Wingspan: 47.6 m (156 ft 1 in) Height: 15.8 m (52 ft)

Boeing KC-135 Stratotanker USA

Air-to-air tanker / transport

Length: 41.5 m (136 ft 3 in) Wingspan: 39.9 m (130 ft 10 in) Height: 11.7 m (38 ft 4 in)

Features: Low/swept wing; four turbofans; extendible boom under tail or hose and drogue under wing

The KC-135 has been the mainstay of USAF aerial refuelling since 1957. Over 750 aircraft were built and have been upgraded to keep them in service until 2020. Boeing is offering the 767 as a replacement in the tanker role, when the airframes become too old to upgrade further. Civil 707s have been converted to tankers in many countries; these use a hose and drogue system, not the KC-135's extending boom.

Variants and operators

KC-135: France; Singapore; Turkey; USA **707**
Conversions: Australia; Brazil; Canada; Israel; Italy; Morocco; Spain; South Africa; Venezuela

Payload

Fuel: 92,210 kg (203,288 lb)
Accommodation: 2 pilots; 3 crew

Boeing RC-135S Cobra Ball USA

Ballistic missile reconnaissance aircraft

Cobra Balls were used to track Russian and Chinese ballistic missile tests during the Cold War. The USAF were going to retire them but the proliferation of ballistic missiles to third world nations has created a new role for them. The RC-135X Cobra Eye is used to track missiles in space and has one black wing to reduce glare.

Variants and operators
RC-135S: USAF RC-135X: USAF

Payload
Television and powerful imaging equipment
Accomodation: unknown number of mission specialists

Length: 49.9 m (164 ft) Wingspan: 44.4 m (145 ft 9 in) Height: 12.9 m (42 ft 6 in)

Features: Low/swept wing; four turbofans; large circular windows

Boeing RC-135U Combat Sent USA

Signals intelligence aircraft

RC-135U Combat Sent aircraft are used to collect very fine-grain electronic emissions from surface-to-air missile sites, radars and tracking stations to provide the intelligence needed to build US jamming and ECM equipment. The air intake under the nose provides air to cool the mass of electronic equipment in the fuselage.

Variants and operators
RC-135U: USAF

Payload
Highly classified electronic intelligence systems
Accomodation: unknown number of mission specialists

Features: Low/swept wing; four turbofans; chin intake

Length: 46.6 m (152 ft 11 in) Wingspan: 44.4 m (145 ft 9 in) Height: 12.9 m (42 ft 6 in)

Boeing RC-135V Rivet Joint USA

Electronic intelligence aircraft

Length: 49.9 m (164 ft) Wingspan: 44.4 m (145 ft 8 in) Height: 12.9 m (42 ft 6 in)

The workhorse of the USAF SIGINT fleet the Rivet Joint is used to gather information on air defence and communications systems. Upgrades will provide powerful laser tracking equipment and infra-red search facilities to enable it to locate ballistic missile launchers and direct airstrikes onto them.

Variants and operators
RC-135V: USAF

Payload
Highly classified electronic intelligence systems
Accomodation: unknown number of mission specialists

Features: Low/swept wing; four turbofans; large side fairings

135

Boeing C-17 Globemaster II USA

Strategic heavy transport

Length: 53 m (174 ft) Wingspan: 51.7 m (169 ft 10 in) Height: 16.8 m (55 ft 1 in)

Features: High/swept wing; four turbofans; winglets

First flown in 1991, the C-17 was originally a McDonnell Douglas design, but has now taken the Boeing name following the merger of McDonnell Douglas and Boeing. The C-17 was designed to carry bulk loads such as the M1 Abrams main battle tank. It can carry up to three AH-64 Apache helicopters and is the only aircraft capable of airdropping heavy armoured vehicles like the M2 Bradley.

Variants and operators
C-17: USAF

Payload
Cargo: 77,290 kg (170,400 lb)
Accommodation: 2 pilots; 2 crew; 154 troops;
102 paratroops; 48 stretchers

Boeing (McDonnell Douglas) KC-10 Extender USA

Air-to-air tanker / transport

Length: 55.3 m (182 ft 7 in) Wingspan: 50.4 m (165 ft 4 in) Height: 17.7 m (58 ft 1 in)

Developed from the civil DC-10, the KC-10 began operating with the USAF in 1981. Capable of refuelling with a boom or hose and drogue, the KC-10 can also carry a substantial cargo on standard pallets. The fleet is currently being upgraded with GPS and improved avionics to extend service life.

Variants and operators
KC-10: USAF
KDC-10: Netherlands

Payload
Fuel: 158,291 kg (348,973 lb)
Cargo: 110,945 kg (244,591 lb)
Accommodation: 2 pilots; 3 crew

Features: Low/swept wing; three turbofans; extendible refuelling boom in tail

CASA C-212 Aviocar Spain

Light tactical transport

Length: 15.1 m (49 ft 8 in) Wingspan: 19 m (62 ft 4 in) Height: 6.3 m (20 ft 8 in)

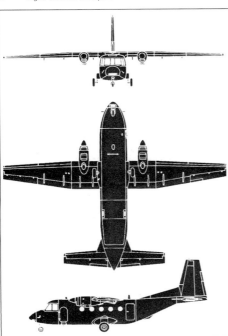

Features: High/straight wing; twin turboprops; square fuselage

Designed to replace the World War II vintage Junkers Ju-52s in Spanish service, the Aviocar has found export success as a general purpose utility aircraft. Tasks include maritime patrol, with an extended nose cone, housing a search radar, Sigint and ECM.

Variants and operators

C-212: Chile; Indonesia; Jordan; Portugal; Spain
C-212-200: Angola; Argentina; Bolivia; Chad; Colombia; Indonesia; Mexico; Panama; Paraguay; Spain; Sweden; UAE; Venezuela; Zaire; Zimbabwe
C-212ASW: Mexico; Portugal; Spain; Sweden

Payload

Cargo: 2,700 kg (5,952 lb)
Accommodation: 2 pilots; 1 crew; 26 troops; 23 paratroops; 12 stretchers

Cessna O-2 Skymaster USA

Light observation aircraft

Now withdrawn from the USAF, the O-2 first flew in 1961. Apart from military versions, several civil variants have been produced in small numbers known as the Cessna 337. Used as a forward control aircraft in military service, the first 195 had fixed landing gear, the remaining 1,300 retractable.

Variants and operators

O-2: Burkina Faso; Chile; Mexico; Paraguay; Sri Lanka; Venezuela; Zimbabwe

Accommodation

2 pilots

Armament

Hardpoints: two wing
Weapons: marking rockets; gun pods

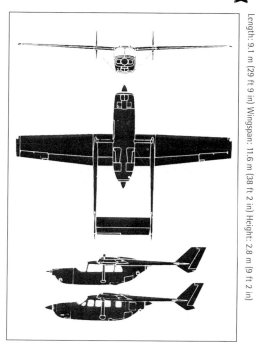

Features: High/straight wing; fore and aft engines; twin boom tail

Length: 9.1 m (29 ft 9 in) Wingspan: 11.6 m (38 ft 2 in) Height: 2.8 m (9 ft 2 in)

Dassault (Breguet) Alizé France

Carrier-borne anti-submarine aircraft

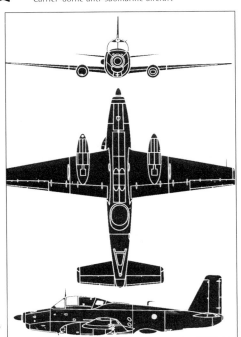

Length: 13.8 m (45 ft 5 in) Wingspan: 15.6 m(51 ft 2 in) Height: 5 m (16 ft 5 in)

Features: Low/straight wing; single turboprop; wheel fairings in wing

First flown in 1956, the Alizé will continue in service aboard the new nuclear-powered French carriers of the Charles de Gaulle class until a replacement can be found. The radar dome in the rear fuselage can be lowered for operation and raised for landing/take off.

Variants and operators
Alizé: France; India

Accommodation
1 pilot; 2 crew

Armament
Internal bomb bay
Hardpoints: two wing
Weapons: torpedoes; depth charges; mines; rockets

Dassault (Breguet) Atlantic France

Maritime patrol aircraft

First flown in 1961 the Atlantic can carry a crew of 12 on 18 hour patrols without refueling. A rest area is provided and for very long patrols a complete second crew can be carried. The Atlantique 2, used by the French Navy, can carry anti-ship missiles on four underwing hardpoints and has no dome on top of the tailfin

Variants and operators
Atlantic: Germany; Italy; Pakistan **Atlantique 2:** France

Accommodation
2 pilots; 3 crew; 8 mission crew

Armament
Internal bomb bay
Hardpoints: four wing (Atlantique 2)
Warload: 18,551 kg (40,900 lb)
Weapons: torpedoes; bombs; depth charges; mines

Features: Low/straight wing; twin turboprops; glazed nose

141

de Havilland Canada DHC-4A Caribou Canada

Light STOL tactical transport

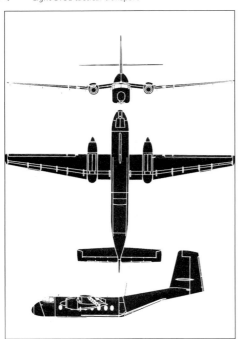

Length: 12.8 m (41 ft 10 in) Wingspan: 17.7 m (58 ft) Height: 3.8 m (12 ft 7 in)

Features: High/straight wing; twin piston engines; swept trailing edge.

A Short Take-Off and Landing transport, the Caribou was designed in conjunction with the Canadian Department of Defence in 1957. The first flight took place in 1958. Some ex-USAF Caribous have found their way into civil hands. The DHC-4T has been fitted with two turboprops and has longer engine nacelles to accommodate them.

Variants and operators
DHC-4: Australia; Cameroon; Costa Rica; Malaysia; Thailand

Payload
Cargo: 12,928 kg (28,500 lb)
Accommodation: 2 pilots; 2 crew; 32 troops; 26 paratroops; 22 stretchers

de Havilland Canada DHC-5 Buffalo Canada

Light STOL tactical transport

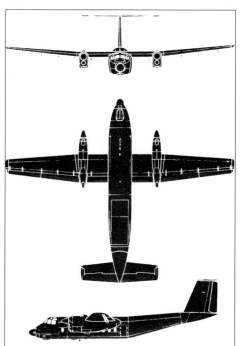

Developed from the Caribou, the Buffalo was funded by both the US and Canadian governments. Powered by General Electric turboprops and with a re-designed tail the Buffalo first flew in 1967. Production ceased in 1986.

Variants and operators

Buffalo: Brazil; Cameroon; Canada; Ecuador; Egypt; Kenya; Mexico; Sudan; Tanzania; Togo; UAE; USN; Zaire; Zambia

Payload

Cargo: 8,164 kg (18,000 lb)
Accommodation: 2 pilots; 2 crew; 41 troops; 35 paratroops; 24 stretchers

Features: High/straight wing; twin turboprops; T-tail

143

Douglas DC-3 USA

Light transport

Features: Low/swept wing; twin piston engines; semi-retractable landing gear

The DC-3 first flew in 1935 and is still in widespread service 63 years later. A total of 12,629 aircraft were built in the USA, Russia and Japan. South Africa has begun upgrading its DC-3s with twin turboprops and maritime patrol equipment. Upgrade programmes and dedicated DC-3 support companies exist to keep it in service for another generation.

Variants and operators

DC-3: Chad; Colombia; Dominican Republic; Greece; Guatemala; Haiti; Honduras; Indonesia; Israel; Madagascar; Mexico; Paraguay; South Africa; Taiwan; Thailand; Turkey; Zaire

Payload

Cargo: 3,784 kg (8.784 lb)
Accommodation: 2 pilots; 2 crew; 21 troops

Dornier Do-228 ASW Germany

Maritime patrol aircraft

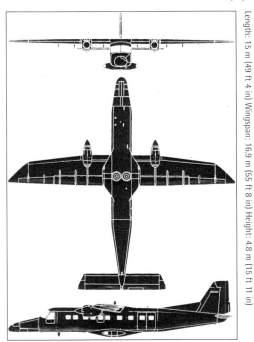

Originally a Dornier design, military versions of the 228 have been spurred on by India which is planning to licence-build, anti-ship, and anti-submarine versions. Germany has developed pollution surveillance and fishery protection versions for coast guard units in Europe and the Far East.

Variants and operators
228 MPA: India; Falkland Islands; Finland; Thailand **228Utility:** Germany; India; Italy; Malawi; Mauritius; Niger; Nigeria **228PS:** Netherlands; Germany

Payload
Cargo: 2,201 kg (4,852 lb)
Accommodation: 2 pilots; 2 crew or 19 troops
Hardpoints: four wing
Weapons: bombs; rockets; depth charges

Length: 15 m (49 ft 4 in) Wingspan: 16.9 m (55 ft 8 in) Height: 4.8 m (15 ft 11 in)

Features: High/straight wing; twin turboprops; swept wing tips

145

Fokker F27/F50 Maritime Netherlands

Maritime patrol aircraft

Length: 25.2 m (82 ft 10 in) Wingspan: 29 m (95 ft 1 in) Height: 8.3 m (27 ft 3 in)

Features: High/straight wing; twin turboprops; ventral radar

Basic military versions of the F27 and F50 include the unarmed coastguard/maritime patrol aircraft, and the armed Maritime Enforcer for anti-ship and anti-submarine missions. Two more versions are under development: the Kingbird, with a sideways-looking airborne early warning radar, and the Sentinel, with a synthetic aperture radar and electro-optics for border surveillance.

Variants and operators

F27 Maritime: Finland; Iceland; Netherlands; Philippines; Spain; Angola **F27 Maritime Enforcer:** Thailand **F50 Maritime Enforcer:** Singapore

Accommodation

2 pilots; 6 mission crew

Armament

Hardpoints: eight (two wet): two fuselage; six wing
Warload: 8,200 kg (18,078 lb)
Weapons: AM39 Exocet; AGM-65 Maverick; AGM-84 Harpoon; Sea Skua; torpedoes; depth charges; mines

HAMC SH-5 China

Maritime patrol amphibian

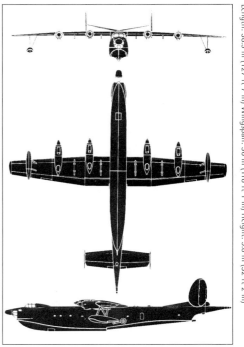

Design work began in 1970, but the cultural revolution delayed the programme. First flown in 1977, only a few have been delivered, but carry out a number of roles including anti-submarine, anti-ship, minelaying; cargo; search and rescue and aerial firefighter.

Variants and operators
SH-5: China

Accommodation
2 pilots; 3 crew; 3 mission crew

Armament
Internal bomb bay
Hardpoints: four wing
Warload: 6,000 kg (13,228 lb)
Cargo: 10,000 kg (22,045 lb)
C-101 missiles; torpedoes; mines; depth charges; bombs

Length: 38.9 m (127 ft 7 in) Wingspan: 36 m (118 ft 1 in) Height: 9.8 m (32 ft 2 in)

Features: High/straight wing; four turboprops; twin tails

IAI Arava Israel

Light STOL transport

Length: 13.5 m (44 ft 2 in) Wingspan: 21.6 m (70 ft 11 in) Height: 5.2 m (17 ft 1 in)

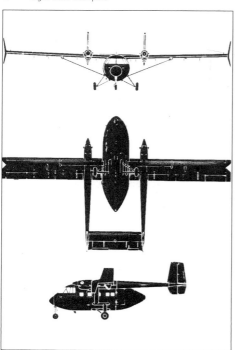

Features: High/straight wing; twin turboprops; twin boom tail

First flown in 1969, the Arava was originally certified as a civil aircraft. However, it has found greater success as a military special missions and utility aircraft. It can be fitted with fuselage-mounted machine gun pods or rockets, and the tail cone of the fuselage can be detached to enable a jeep to be loaded.

Variants and operators

Arava: Bolivia; Cameroon; Colombia; Ecuador; El Salvador; Guatemala; Honduras; Israel; Mexico; Swaziland; Thailand; Venezuela

Payload

Cargo: 2,494 kg (5,500 lb)
Accommodation: 2 pilots; 24 troops; 16 paratroops

IAI Phalcon Israel

Airborne early warning aircraft

Length: 46.6 m (152 ft 11 in) Wingspan: 44.4 m (145 ft 9 in) Height: 12.9 m (42 ft 6 in)

Converted from a standard Boeing 707, the Phalcon was designed around a modular radar and avionics system which could be fitted to other similar-sized aircraft. South Africa is reported to have installed parts of this system on their 707 tankers. An Airbus-based version for Australia and 767-based version for Korea are being studied.

Variants and operators
Phalcon: Chile

Payload
Elta EL/2075 phased array radar
Elta EL/K-7031 comms system
Accomodation: unknown number of mission specialists

Features: Low/swept wing; fuselage mounted radar; large nose radome

149

Ilyushin Il-20 Coot Russia

Electronic intelligence aircraft

Length: 24 m (79 ft) Wingspan: 37.4 m (122 ft 9 in) Height: 10.2 m (33 ft 4 in)

Features: Low/straight wing; four turbofans; ventral canoe

First seen in the West in 1978, the Il-20 was developed from the standard Il-18 airliner. A sideways-looking radar is housed in the ventral canoe, and a wide range of signals intelligence sensors and optics in the side fairings.

Variants and operators

Il-20: Russia; Ukraine

Payload

Signals intelligence systems
Accomodation: unknown number of mission specialists

Ilyushin Il-38 May Russia

Maritime patrol aircraft

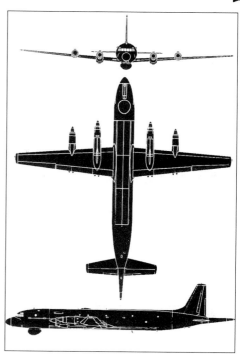

A further development of the Il-18 Coot, the Il-38 was first reported in 1970. The fuselage was lengthened and wings moved forward to counter the weight of the weapons bays. A crew of nine can carry out patrols of 12 hours, but it lacks an air-to-air refueling capability.

Variants and operators
Il-38: India; Russia; Ukraine

Accomodation
Unknown number of mission specialists

Armament
Two internal bomb bays
Torpedoes; mines; depth charges

Length: 39.6 m (129 ft 10 in) Wingspan: 37.4 m (122 ft 9 in) Height: 10.2 m (33 ft 4 in)

Features: Low/straight wing; four turboprops; ventral radome

Ilyushin/Beriev A-50 Mainstay Russia

Airborne early warning and control aircraft

Length: 46.6 m (152 ft 10 in) Wingspan: 50.5 m (165 ft 8 in) Height: 14.8 m (48 ft 5 in)

Features: High/swept wing; four turbofans; radar rotordome

Entered service in 1984, the Mainstay was developed from the Il-76 transport keeping its glazed nose. An upgraded version with the more powerful Vega Shmel-M radar was seen at the Moscow air show in 1995. Iraq converted a number of Il-76 transports along similar lines. Their status is uncertain but they can be recognized by two large ventral strakes.

Variants and operators
A-50: Russia Baghdad 1: Iraq

Payload
Liana or Shmel-M airborne radar
Accomodation: unknown number of mission specialists

Ilyushin Il-76 Candid Russia

Heavy tactical transport

First flown in 1971, the Candid remains in production in Tashkent, Uzbekistan. An upgraded version with lengthened fuselage and uprated engines is being marketed, other variants include the Il-76SK airborne command post, with no glazed nose and dorsal canoe and Il-78 M Midas aerial tanker.

Variants and operators

Il-76: Algeria; Belarus; India; Iran; Iraq; Kazakhstan; North Korea; Libya; Russia; Syria; Ukraine; Yemen **Il-78:** Russia; Ukraine **Il-76SK:** Russia

Payload

Cargo: 52,000 kg (114,640 lb)
Fuel (Midas): 90,000 kg (198,412 lb)
Accommodation: 2 pilots; 5 crew; 140 troops; 125 paratroops

Length: 46.6 m (152 ft 10 in) Wingspan: 50.5 m (165 ft 8 in) Height: 14.7 m (48 ft 5 in)

Features: High/swept wing; four turbofans; glazed nose

153

Ilyushin Il-86 Camber Russia

Airborne command post

Length: 59.5 m (195 ft 4 in) Wingspan: 48.1 m (157 ft 8 in) Height: 15.8 m (51 ft 10 in)

Features: Low/swept wing; four turbofans; dorsal canoe

First seen in 1992, the Il-86 operates in the same fashion as the E-4B. It is shielded against nuclear blast and electromagnetic pulse – hence the lack of windows. The dorsal canoe carries satellite comms and a very long trailing wire antenna. The pods under the wings appear to be generators.

Variants and operators

Il-86: Russia

Payload

Comprehensive suite of Sat, HF,MF,VHF, UHF communications
Accomodation: unknown number of mission specialists

Kawasaki C-1A Japan

Medium tactical transport

Length: 29 m (95 ft 1 in) Wingspan: 30.6 m (100 ft 4 in) Height: 9.9 m (32 ft 9 in)

First flown in 1970, the C-1A was designed to replace the Japanese Air Self Defence Force's World War II vintage C-46 transports. One aircraft was finished as an ECM training aircraft and was designated EC-1; it can be recognized by its bulbous nose radome.

Variants and operators
C-1A: Japan EC-1: Japan

Payload
Cargo: 11,900 kg (26,235 lb)
Accommodation: 2 pilots; 3 crew; 60 troops; 45 paratroops; 36 stretchers

Features: High/swept wing; twin turbofans; swept T-tail

Lockheed Martin C-5 Galaxy USA

Heavy strategic transport

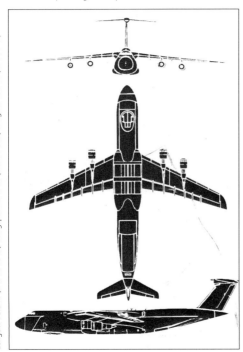

Length: 75.5 m (247 ft 10 in) Wingspan: 67.8 m (222 ft 8 in) Height: 19.8 m (65 ft 1 in)

Features: High/swept wing; four turbofans; swept T-tail

The largest aircraft in the world when it first flew in 1968, the C-5 now ranks behind Antonov's An-124 and An-225. All C-5s have now been upgraded with a stronger wing to increase their service life. Capable of carrying two M1 Abrams MBTs or six AH-64 Apache helicopters, the C-5 can carry up to 360 troops, but is usually employed in moving equipment.

Variants and operators
C-5: USAF

Payload
Cargo: 118,387 kg (261,000 lb)
Accommodation: 2 pilots; 3 crew; 360 troops

Lockheed Martin C-130H Hercules USA

Medium tactical transport

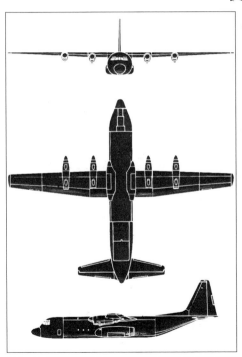

Over 2,000 Hercules have been built since the aircraft first flew in 1954. The huge range of missions carried out by C-130s prohibits a full description of every variant, but includes air data gathering, Antarctic transport on skis, combat search and rescue, aerial tanker, surveillance, maritime patrol and recovering space capsules.

Variants and operators

C-130: Algeria; Argentina; Australia; Belgium; Bolivia; Brazil; Cameroon; Canada; Chad; Chile; Colombia; Denmark; Ecuador; Egypt; France; Gabon; Greece; Honduras; Indonesia; Iran; Israel; Italy; Japan; Jordan; South Korea; Libya; Malaysia; Mexico; Morocco; Netherlands; New Zealand; Niger; Nigeria; Norway; Oman; Pakistan; Peru; Philippines; Portugal; Saudi Arabia; Singapore; South Africa; Spain; Sudan; Sweden; Taiwan; Thailand; Tunisia; Turkey; UAE; UK; USA; Uruguay; Venezuela; Yemen; Zaire

Payload

Cargo: 17,645 kg (38,900 lb)
Fuel (KC-130): 20,865 kg (46,000 lb)
Accommodation: 2 pilots; 3 crew; 92 troops; 64 paratroops; 74 stretchers

Features: High/straight wing; four turboprops; large nose radium

157

Lockheed Martin C-130J Hercules USA

Medium tactical transport

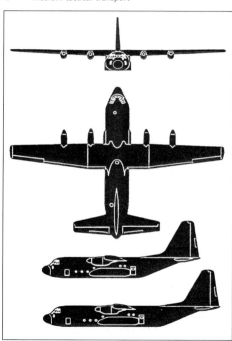

Length: 34.3 m (112 ft 9 in) Wingspan: 40.4 m (132 ft 7 in) Height: 11.8 m (38 ft 10 in)

Features: High/straight wing; four turboprops; scimitar propellers

This latest development of the C-130 first flew in 1996. Designed to operate more cost-effectively, the C-130J has a modern avionics suite and revised two man flight deck, more powerful engines fitted with Dowty six blade composite propellers with a distinctive scimitar shape. AEW versions are being studied as well as tankers and other C-130 roles.

Variants and operators
C-130J: Australia; UK; USA

Payload
Cargo: 17,264 kg (38,061 lb)
Accommodation: 2 pilots; 1 crew; 128 troops; 92 paratroops; 74 stretchers

Lockheed Martin C-141 StarLifter USA

Heavy strategic transport

The StarLifter entered service in 1964 as the USAF's first all jet-powered transport. One problem found with its narrow design was that it was often physically packed to the limits without reaching maximum take-off weight. The fuselage was lengthened but it still cannot carry many of the US Army's armoured vehicles.

Variants and operators
C-141: USAF

Payload
Cargo: 41,222 kg (90,880 lb)
Accommodation: 2 pilots; 3 crew; 154 troops; 123 paratroops; 80 stretchers

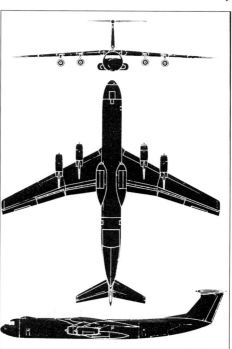

Length: 51.3 m (168 ft 3 in) Wingspan: 48.7 m (159 ft 11 in) Height: 11.9 m (39 ft 3 in)

Features: High/swept wing; four turbofans; narrow fuselage

159

Lockheed Martin P-3 Orion USA

Maritime patrol aircraft

Length: 35.6 m (116 ft 10 in) Wingspan: 30.4 m (99 ft 8 in) Height: 10.2 m (33 ft 8 in)

Developed from the Lockheed Electra airliner, the P-3 first flew in 1958. Several companies are offering mid-life upgrades to keep the Orions flying into the next century. Japan and the USA operate a number of EP-3E Aries electronic intelligence aircraft which can be recognized by their dorsal and ventral fairings for surveillance equipment.

Variants and operators

P-3: Australia; Canada; Chile; Greece; Iran; Japan; South Korea; Netherlands; Norway; Pakistan; Portugal; Spain; Thailand; USN
EP-3E: Japan; USN

Accommodation

2 pilots; 2 crew; 6 mission crew

Armament

Internal bomb bay
Hardpoints: 10 wing
Warload: 9,071 kg (20,000 lb)
Weapons: AIM-9 Sidewinder; AGM-84 Harpoon; torpedoes; mines; depth charges

Features: Low/straight wing; four turboprops; MAD boom in tail

Lockheed Martin P-3 AEW&C USA

Airborne early warning aircraft

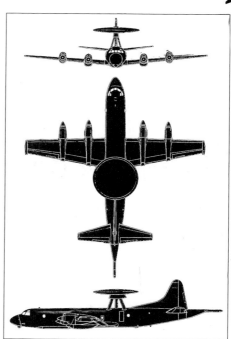

Length: 35.6 m (116 ft 10 in) Wingspan: 30.4 m (99 ft 8 in) Height: 10.2 m (33 ft 8 in)

Developed specially for the US Coast Guard the P-3 AEW&C is used along the South coast of the USA hunting drug smugglers and illegal immigrants. Known as the 'P-3 Dome' to its crews. Lockheed is offering the aircraft for export.

Variants and operators
P-3 AEW&C: USCG; US Customs

Payload
AN/APS-138 airborne radar
Accomodation: unknown number of mission specialists

Features: Low/straight wing; four turboprops; radar rotordome

161

Lockheed Martin MC-130E Combat Talon USA

Special operations aircraft

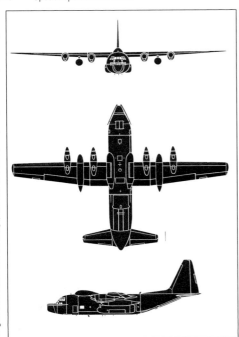

Length: 29.7 m (97 ft 9 in) Wingspan: 40.4 m (132 ft 7 in) Height: 11.6 m (38 ft 3 in)

Combat Talons are equipped with terrain following radar, electronic defensive systems, and an airborne recovery system. Used by USAF special operations squadrons to infiltrate special forces, keep them re-supplied and then extract them. EC-130E Rivet Riders carry psychological warfare equipment capable of broadcasting doctored TV and radio messages, originally only capable of working on US channels it now has a global capability.

Variants and operators
MC-130: USAF EC-130E: USAF

Payload
MC-130: around 40 troops, plus classified special operations equipment
EC-130E: world wide television broadcast facilities
Accomodation: 2 pilots unknown number of mission specialists

Features: High/straight wing; four turboprops; antennas on tailfin

Lockheed Martin S-3 Viking USA

Carrier-borne anti-submarine aircraft

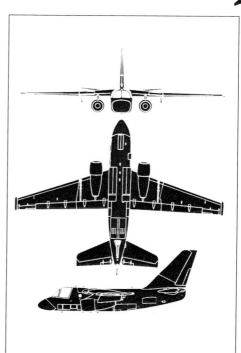

First flown in 1972, the Viking was designed to carry all the equipment found in large land-based maritime patrol aircraft in a small carrier-borne airframe. Since then it has been fitted with electronic warfare equipment, aerial refuelling probes and can now carry the Harpoon anti-ship missile.

Variants and operators
S-3: USN ES-3A: USN

Accomodation
2 pilots; 2 systems operators

Armament
Internal bomb bay
Hardpoints: two wing
Weapons: AGM-84 Harpoon; torpedoes; nuclear/conventional depth charges; bombs; rockets

Features: High/swept wing; twin turbofan; folding tail and wing

Length: 16.3 m (53 ft 4 in) Wingspan: 20.9 m (68 ft 8 in) Height: 6.9 m (22 ft 9 in)

Lockheed Martin U-2/TR-1A USA

High altitude reconnaissance aircraft

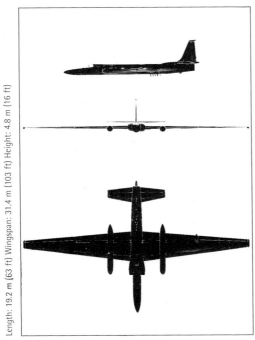

Length: 19.2 m (63 ft) Wingspan: 31.4 m (103 ft) Height: 4.8 m (16 ft)

With the final retirement of the SR-71 Blackbird, the U-2 is the only manned photo/reconnaissance aircraft in the USAF. The USAF is pursuing an all UAV reconnaissance fleet for the next century and the U-2/TR-1 family is slowly being replaced. Some TR-1s carry a large dorsal fairing for extra equipment.

Variants and operators
U-2/TR-1: USAF; NASA

Payload
Optical, electronic and signals intelligence gathering equipment
Accommodation: 1 pilot

Features: Mid/straight sailplane wing; single engine; single seat

Myasischev M-55 Mystic Russia

High altitude research aircraft

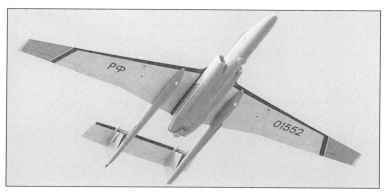

The M-55 set a number of altitude records before production was terminated in 1994. Used for environmental research and surveillance operations, it has an endurance of six and a half hours.

Variants and operators
M-55: Russia

Payload
Optical, infra-red and electronic imaging equipment
Accomodation: 1 pilot

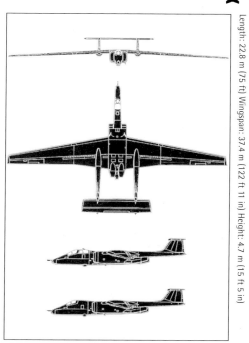

Features: High/swept wing; twin turbofans; twin boom tail

Length: 22.8 m (75 ft) Wingspan: 37.4 m (122 ft 11 in) Height: 4.7 m (15 ft 5 in)

Myasischev VM-T Atlant Russia

Outsized cargo transport

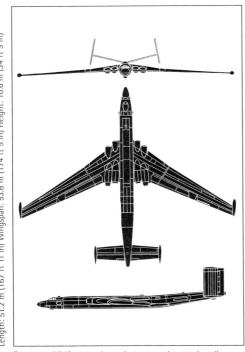

Length: 51.2 m (167 ft 11 in) Wingspan: 53.6 m (174 ft 5 in) Height: 10.6 m (34 ft 9 in)

Features: Mid/swept wing; wingroot engines; twin tails

Developed from the now retired Bison-C bomber, the two Atlants are used to carry outsize loads such as Engeria rocket sections between the manufacturing plants and Baikonur cosmodrome.

Variants and operators
VM-T: Russia

Payload
Piggy back cargo: 50,000 kg (110,320 lb)
Accomodation: 2 pilots; 3 crew

Northrop Grumman E-2C Hawkeye USA

Carrier-borne early warning aircraft

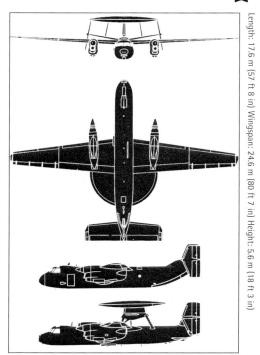

First flown in 1960, the Hawkeye was originally designed for carrier operations, but is operated from land bases by several export customers. France and the US Navy are the only naval operators. The C-2A Greyhound is a modified airframe without the radar, used as a carrier-on board delivery aircraft.

Variants and operators
E-2C: Egypt; France; Israel; Japan; Singapore; Taiwan; USN C-2A: USN

Payload
AN/APS-145 airborne radar
AN/APA-172 control system
Accommodation: 2 pilots; 3 mission crew

Features: High/straight wing; twin turboprops; radar rotordome

Length: 17.6 m (57 ft 8 in) Wingspan: 24.6 m (80 ft 7 in) Height: 5.6 m (18 ft 3 in)

Northrop Grumman E-8 Joint STARS USA

Battlefield surveillance aircraft

Length: 46.6 m (152 ft 11 in) Wingspan: 44.4 m (145 ft 9 in) Height: 12.9 m (42 ft 6 in)

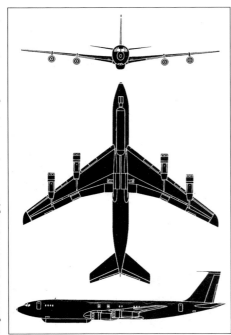

Features: Low/swept wing; four turbofans; ventral canoe

The Joint STARS (Surveillance and Target Attack Radar System) was rushed into service for the 1991 Gulf War and proved to be a battle winning system. Army commanders were able to see directly into Iraqi lines of communication, and direct devastating attacks, while keeping track of their own forces.

Variants and operators
E-8: USAF/US Army

Payload
AN-APY-3 side-looking phased-array radar
JTIDS, advanced comms systems
Accomodation: unknown number of mission
specialists

Northrop Grumman OV-1 Mohawk USA

Battlefield surveillance aircraft

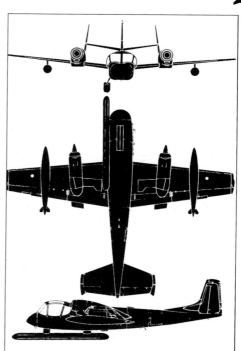

Length: 12.5 m (41 ft) Wingspan: 14.6 m (48 ft) Height: 3.9 m (12 ft 8 in)

Specially designed for the US Army, the OV-1 first flew in 1959. Withdrawn from US service, a number have found their way into the Argentine and South Korean air forces. Argentine aircraft lack the Sideways Looking Radar. It has an armoured cockpit for low level operations.

Variants and operators
OV-1D: Argentina; South Korea

Payload
AN/APS-94D Sideways-looking radar
Optical and infra-red imaging equipment
Accomodation: 2 pilots

Features: Mid/straight wing; twin turboprops; three tailfins

Northrop Grumman S-2 Tracker USA

Carrier-borne anti-submarine aircraft

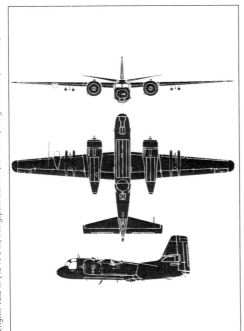

Length: 13.3 m (43 ft 6 in) Wingspan: 22.1 m (72 ft 7 in) Height: 5.1 m (16 ft 7 in)

Features: High/straight wing; twin piston or turboprop engines; searchlight in right wing leading edge

Brazil is the only country to keep a (limited) carrier-borne capability for the S-2, other operators use it from shore bases. Civilian versions are being offered for firefighting. Taiwan and Argentina have upgraded their aircraft with two Garrett turboprops.

Variants and operators
S-2: Argentina; Brazil; South Korea; Peru; Taiwan; Thailand; Turkey; Uruguay

Accommodation
2 pilots; 2 systems operators

Armament
Internal bomb bay
Hardpoints: six wing
Warload: 2,182 kg (4,810 lb)
Weapons: torpedoes; depth charges; bombs; rockets

Piaggio PD.808 Italy

Utility aircraft

The Italian air force operates a number of PD.808s for VIP transport, radar calibration and electronic warfare. ECM versions have dorsal and ventral antennas. First flown in 1964, a civil version was built but was not produced in great numbers.

Variants and operators
PD.808: Italy

Payload
Cargo: 862 kg (1,900 lb)
Accommodation: 2 pilots; 9 passengers

Features: Low/straight wing; twin tail mounted turbofans; wingtip tanks

Length: 12.8 m (42 ft 2 in) Wingspan: 13.2 m (43 ft 3 in) Height: 4.8 m (15 ft 9 in)

Raytheon (Beechcraft) RC-12N Guardrail USA

Electronic intelligence aircraft

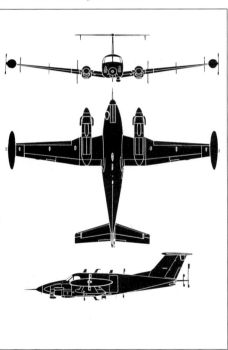

The family of RC-12 aircraft provides real-time targeting data for US field commanders. Capable of identifying radio and radar transmissions and locating their position, Guardrails transmit the data directly to artillery and staff groups for rapid retaliation strikes.

Variants and operators
RC-12: US Army

Payload
Classified range of targeting and signals intelligence equipment
Accommodation: unknown number of mission specialists

Length: 13.3 m (43 ft 9 in) Wingspan: 16.6 m (54 ft 6 in) Height: 4.5 m (15 ft)

Features: Low/straight wing; twin turboprops; T-tail

Saab 340 AEW&C Sweden

Airborne early warning aircraft

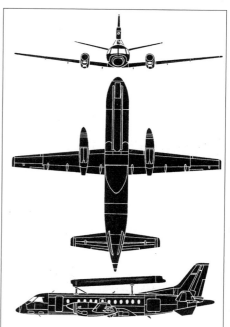

Developed from the Saab 340B airliner, the 340 AEW&C first flew in 1994. The phased array radar enables the crew to identify targets 350km (217 miles) away and direct fighters to intercept. Despite its sideways looking fixing, it does have a full 360 degree coverage, but best performance is 150 degrees either side.

Variants and operators
340AEW&C: Sweden

Payload
PS-890 Erieye sideways-looking radar
Accommodation: 2 pilots; 1 crew; unknown number of mission specialists

Features: Low/straight wing; twin turboprops; dorsal radar housing

ShinMaywa US-1A Japan

Search and rescue amphibian

Length: 33.5 m (109 ft 9 in) Wingspan: 33.1 m (108 ft 9 in) Height: 9.9 m (32 ft 7 in)

Features: High/straight wing; four turboprops; T-tail

First flown in 1974, the PS-1 is capable of long range search and rescue, troop transport, anti-submarine warfare and firefighting. A dipping sonar is carried in the boat hull and is deployed during brief landings on the ocean. The relatively calm waters of the Pacific mean flying boats have remained popular among Pacific nations like Japan, China and Russia.

Variants and operators
US-1A: Japan

Payload
Accommodation: 2 pilots; 2 crew; 20 troops or survivors; 12 stretchers

Transall C-160 France/Germany

Medium tactical transport

Developed jointly between France and Germany as a tactical transport aircraft, the C-160 is used as an aerial refueller with hose and drogue equipment by the French air force. The French air force also has four fitted out as communications relay aircraft to support the French nuclear deterrence.

Variants and operators
C-160: France; Germany; Turkey

Payload
Cargo: 16,000 kg (35,275 lb)
Accommodation: 2 pilots; 1 crew; 93 troops; 68 paratroops; 62 stretchers

Features: High/straight wing; twin turboprop; rear loading ramp

COMBAT TRAINING AIRCRAFT

Aermacchi (SIAI-Marchetti) SF.260 Italy

Primary trainer / ground attack aircraft

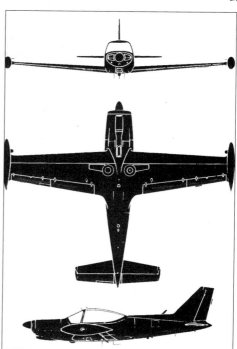

Length: 7.1 m (23 ft 3 in) Wingspan: 8.3 m (27 ft 4 in) Height: 2.4 m (7 ft 11 in)

Built in three main versions, the first SF.260s were powered by a piston engine, later SF.260TPs by a turboprop. The SF.260TP can be recognized by its longer nose and twin exhausts underneath the engine cowling. The Warrior was armed and able to carry out light strike and forward air control missions.

Variants and operators

SF.260: Belgium; Burundi; Italy; Philippines; Singapore; Tunisia; Turkey; Venezuela; Zambia; Zimbabwe **SF.260TP:** Ethiopia; Haiti; Philippines; Sri Lanka; UAE; Zimbabwe
Warrior: Brunei; Burundi; Chad; Ireland; Libya; Singapore; Sri Lanka; Tunisia; Zimbabwe

Accommodation

2 pilots

Armament

Hardpoints: two wing
Warload: 300 kg (661 lb)
Bombs; rockets; machine gun pods

Features: Low/straight wing; side-by-side cockpit; wingtip tanks

177

Aermacchi (Valmet) M-290TP Redigo Italy/Finland

Primary trainer / liaison aircraft

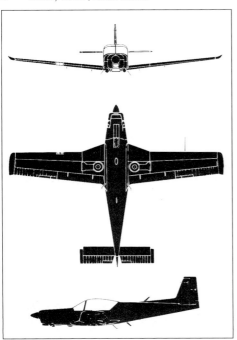

Length: 8.5 m (27 ft 11 in) Wingspan: 10.6 m (34 ft 9 in) Height: 3.2 m (10 ft 6 in)

Features: Low/straight wing; cranked leading edge; side-by-side cockpit

Aermacchi took over production and support of the Redigo in 1997, and is now marketing it with a number of improvements to the engine and aircraft systems. First flown by Valmet of Finland in 1985, production ceased after 31 had been built. A single stretcher or two passengers can be carried in the rear cockpit.

Variants and operators
M-290TP: Eritrea; Finland; Mexico

Accommodation
2 pilots

Armament
Hardpoints: six wing
Warload: 800 kg (1,764 lb)
Bombs; rockets; machine gun pods

AIDC T-CH-1 Chung-Shing Taiwan

Primary trainer / ground attack aircraft

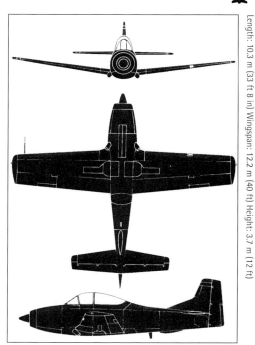

Length: 10.3 m (33 ft 8 in) Wingspan: 12.2 m (40 ft) Height: 3.7 m (12 ft)

Developed from the North American T-28 Trojan, the Chung-Shing was designed to incorporate a wider range of weapons. The Taiwanese Air Force insists that every aircraft have a war role and basic trainers are no exception.

Variants and operators
T-CH-1: Taiwan

Accommodation
2 pilots

Armament
Hardpoints: four wing
Bombs; rockets; machine gun pods

Features: Low/straight wing; single piston engine; tandem cockpits

179

BAe (SA) Bulldog UK

Elementary trainer / ground attack aircraft

Length: 7.1 m (23 ft 3 in) Wingspan: 10.1 m (33 ft) Height: 2.3 m (7 ft 5 in)

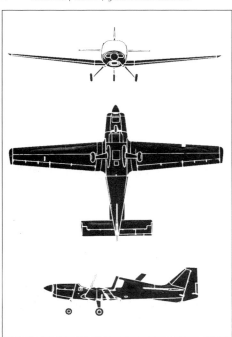

First flown in 1969, the majority of Bulldogs operate in the Royal Air Force elementary flight training programme at the major university air training squadrons. Export versions can be fitted with armament for light ground attack missions. A civil version, the Beagle Pup, is virtually identical.

Variants and operators
Bulldog: Jordan; Lebanon; Kenya; Malaysia; Sweden; UK

Accommodation
2 pilots

Armament
Hardpoints: four wing
Warload: 290 kg (640 lb)
Bombs; rockets; grenade launchers; machine gun pods

Features: Low/straight wing; single piston engine; side-by-side cockpit

Daewoo KTX-1 Woong-Bee South Korea

Primary trainer

Production began in 1998, following a maiden flight in 1991. The South Korean air force has orders for 100 with deliveries beginning in 1999. Very similar to the Tucano, one recognition feature is the cockpit canopy: the Tucano has no central spar.

Variants and operators
Woong-Bee: South Korea

Accommodation
2 pilots

Armament
No armament fitted as standard

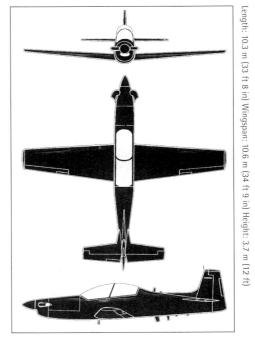

Length: 10.3 m (33 ft 8 in) Wingspan: 10.6 m (34 ft 9 in) Height: 3.7 m (12 ft)

Features: Low/straight wing; single turboprop; tandem cockpit

181

EMBRAER EMB-312 Tucano Brazil

Primary trainer

Length: 9.9 m (32 ft 4 in) Wingspan: 11.1 m (36 ft 6 in) Height: 3.4 m (11 ft 1 in)

Features: Low/straight wing; single turboprop; tandem one piece canopy

Over 650 examples of the Tucano have been built since 1983, and the type has been adopted by 14 air forces. Continued development for future markets has led to the Super Tucano which is mentioned separately. First flown in 1980, the Tucano is licence-built in the UK as the S312, and assembled from kit form in Egypt.

Variants and operators

EMB-312: Argentina; Brazil; Colombia; Egypt; France; Honduras; Iran; Iraq; Kenya; Kuwait; Paraguay; Peru; Venezuela **S312:** UK

Accommodation

2 pilots

Armament

Hardpoints: four wing
Warload: 250 kg (551 lb)
Bombs; rockets; machine gun pods

EMBRAER EMB-312 Super Tucano Brazil

Primary trainer / ground attack aircraft

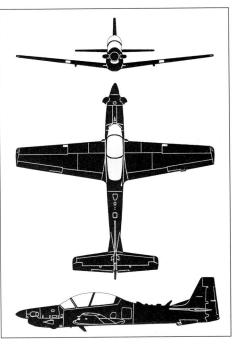

Developed from the Tucano, the Super Tucano has a stretched fuselage to accept a more powerful engine giving increased take-off-weight. An armed version called the ALX has been developed for border patrol missions over the Amazon basin. It will be produced in both single- and twin-seat versions.

Variants and operators
Super Tucano: Brazil   **ALX:** Brazil

Accommodation
2 pilots

Armament
Hardpoints: six wing
Warload: 250 kg (551 lb)
Bombs; rockets; machine gun pods

Features: Low/straight wing; single turboprop; three piece tandem canopy

Length: 11.4 m (37 ft 5 in) Wingspan: 11.1 m (36 ft 6 in) Height: 3.9 m (12 ft 9 in)

183

ENAER T-35 Pilan Chile

Primary trainer

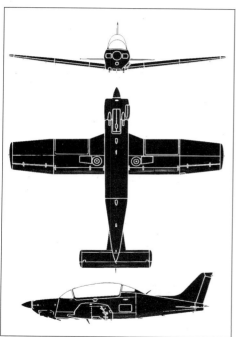

Length: 8 m (26 ft 3 in) Wingspan: 8.8 m (29 ft) Height: 2.6 m (8 ft 8 in)

Originally developed by US company Piper, the Pilan (Devil) first flew in 1981. ENAER began by assembling kits and has now taken over full production, including kits for CASA to assemble for the Spanish Air Force. A turboprop-powered version, the Turbo Pilan, has been flown but no orders have been received.

Variants and operators
T-35: Chile; Guatemala; Panama; Paraguay; Spain

Accommodation
2 pilots

Armament
No armament fitted as standard

Features: Low/straight wing; single piston engine; tandem cockpit

Fuji T-3 Japan

Primary Trainer

The T-3 was developed from the Raytheon (Beechcraft) T-34 Mentor. The family resemblance can be seen in the shape of the wings and tail unit, but the cockpit is an enclosed cabin rather than the Mentor's bubble canopy.

Variants and operators

T-3: Japan

Accommodation

2 pilots

Payload

13.6 kg (30 lb)

Features: Low/straight wing; single piston engine; enclosed tandem cabin

185

Fuji T-5 Japan

Primary trainer

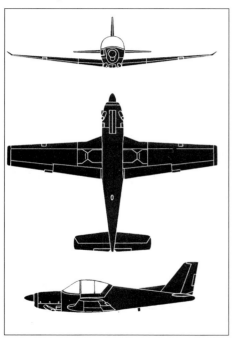

Length: 8.4 m (27 ft 8 in) Wingspan: 10 m (32 ft 11) Height: 2.9 m (9 ft 8 in)

Features: Low/straight wing; single turboprop; side-by-side cockpit

Developed from the piston-engined T-3, the T-5 is powered by an Allison 250-B17D turboprop. The nose has been re-profiled and the cockpit arrangement changed to side-by-side seating. Seats can be fitted in the rear of the cabin to allow for an extra two passengers making it capable of carrying out a liaison role.

Variants and operators
T-5: Japan

Accommodation
2 pilots

Payload
200 kg (441 lb)

HAL HPT-32 Deepak India

Primary trainer

First flown in 1977, production continued until 1987. Used as a basic trainer by both the Indian Air Force and Navy, the Deepak can also be seen carrying target towing equipment and training weapons. A third seat behind the pilots can be used by an observer or passenger in the liaison role.

Variants and operators
HPT-32: India

Accommodation
2 pilots

Armament
Hardpoints: four wing
Warload: 255 kg (562 lb)
Training bombs; rockets; machine gun pods

Features: Low/straight wing; single piston engine; fixed undercarriage

Length: 7.7 m (25 ft 4 in) Wingspan: 9.5 m (31 ft 2 in) Height: 2.9 m (9 ft 7 in)

NAMC CJ-6A China

Primary trainer

Length: 8.4 m (27 ft 9 in) Wingspan: 10.2 m (33 ft 6 in) Height: 3.3 m (10 ft 8 in)

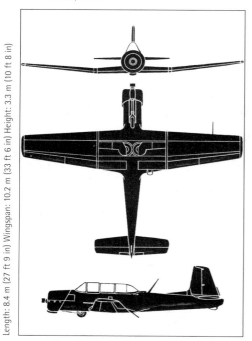

Features: Low/straight wing; single radial engine; tandem cockpit

NAMC was originally set up to licence-build the Yak-18 basic trainer in 1951. The CJ-6 was a development of the Yak-18 and first flew in 1958. Easily identified because of its distinctive radial engine, some of the 1,700 built are finding their way into private hands in the West and can often be seen painted to resemble Japanese World War II bombers.

Variants and operators
CJ-6: Albania; China; North Korea; Zambia
PT-6: Bangladesh

Accommodation
2 pilots

Armament
No armament fitted as standard,

Neiva N261 T-25 Universal Brazil

Primary trainer

Being replaced in Brazilian service by the Tucano, the Universal was built in two versions, an unarmed trainer and armed border patrol aircraft, the AT-25. First flown in 1966 production ceased in 1980, Chile and Paraguay have retired their T-25s, Brazil still operates about 90.

Variants and operators
T-25: Brazil AT-25: Brazil

Accommodation
2 pilots

Armament
Hardpoints: two wing
Machine gun pods

Length: 8.8 m (28 ft 89 in) Wingspan: 11 m (36 ft 1 in) Height: 3 m (9 ft 9 in)

Features: Low/straight wing; single piston engine; side-by-side cockpit

PAC Airtrainer CT4 New Zealand

Primary trainer

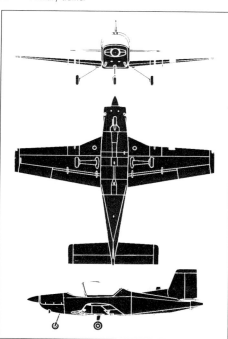

Length: 7 m (23 ft 2 in) Wingspan: 7.9 m (26 ft) Height: 2.6 m (8 ft 6 in)

Features: Low/straight wing; single piston engine; fixed landing gear

The PAC (Pacific Aerospace Corporation) Airtrainer is a military development of the Australian Victa Aircruiser private aircraft. A Thai requirement for a more powerful trainer has spurred development of a turboprop powered version. A version with retractable landing gear CT-4CR is also under development.

Variants and operators
CT-4: Australia; New Zealand; Thailand

Accommodation
2 pilots

Armament
No armament fitted as standard

PAC **Mushshak** Pakistan

Primary trainer / ground attack aircraft

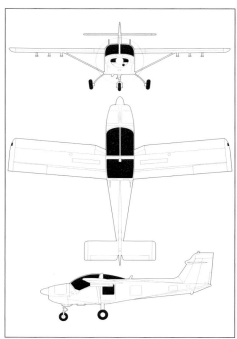

The Mushshak is a licence built version of the Saab Safari. The original safari was first used in the ground attack role by the mercenary air force of Count Carl Gustav von Rosen during the Biafran war of 1969. The Mushshak first flew in 1975 and a re-engined model called Shabaz flew in 1987.

Variants and operators
Mushshak: Iran; Oman; Pakistan; Syria
Supporter: Norway; Denmark; Zambia

Accommodation 2 pilots

Armament
Hardpoints: six wing
Warload; 300 kg (661 lb)
Anti-tank missiles; bombs; rockets; gun pods

Features: High/straight wing; single piston engine; side-by-side cockpit

191

Pilatus PC-7 Switzerland

Primary trainer

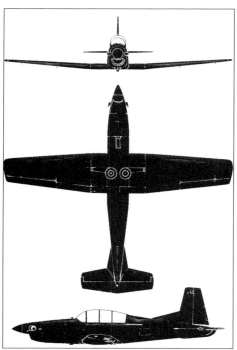

Length: 9.8 m (32 ft 1 in) Wingspan: 10.4 m (34 ft 1 in) Height: 3.2 m (10 ft 6 in)

Features: Low/straight wing; single turboprop; cranked tailfin

First flown in 1978, over 500 examples of the PC-7 had been produced by 1998. A modified version, the Mk II, was developed for South Africa, assembled locally from kits. Although not normally fitted with armament, export versions can carry offensive or training weapons.

Variants and operators
PC-7: Angola; Austria; Bolivia; Bophuthatswana; Botswana; Brunei; Chile; France; Guatemala; Iran; Iraq; Malaysia; Mexico; Myanmar (Burma); Netherlands; South Africa; Surinam; Switzerland; UAE; Uruguay

Accommodation
2 pilots

Armament
Hardpoints: six wing (two wet)
Warload: 1,000 kg (2,205 lb)
Bombs; rockets; cannon pods

Pilatus PC-9 Switzerland

Primary trainer

Developed from the PC-7, the PC-9 can be recognized by its central canopy bar and longer tail fin. Winner of the US Joint Primary Aircraft Training System competition, the PC-9 will be built under licence by Raytheon in the USA under the name T-6A Texan II.

Variants and operators

PC-9: Angola; Australia; Croatia; Cyprus; Iraq; Myanmar (Burma); Saudi Arabia; Switzerland; Thailand; Slovenia **T-6A:** Greece; USAF; USN

Accommodation

2 pilots

Armament

Hardpoints: six wing (two wet)
Warload: 1,000 kg (2,205 lb)
Bombs; rockets cannon pods

Features: Low/straight wing; single turboprop; cranked tailfin

193

PZL Mielec M-26 Iskierka Poland

Primary trainer

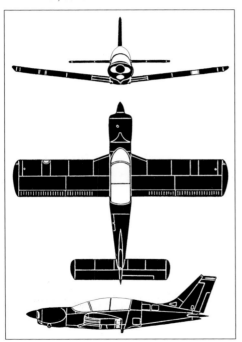

Two versions of the Iskierka have been developed, one fitted with a Polish PZL engine, M-26 00, the other with a Textron Lycoming engine, M-26 01. Orders for the military version have been received from a number of South American countries, with civilian distribution starting in the USA.

Variants and operators
M-26: USA

Accommodation
2 pilots

Armament
Hardpoints: two wing
Warload: 120 kg (265 lb)
Bombs; rockets; machine gun pods

Length: 8.3 m (27 ft 2 in) Wingspan: 8.6 m (28 ft 2 in) Height: 2.9 m (9 ft 8 in)

Features: Low/straight wing; single piston engine; tandem cockpit

PZL Warszawa PZL-130TB Turbo Orlik Poland

Primary trainer

The English translation of Orlik means 'spotted eaglet'. Originally a piston-engined design, all work was halted on the Orlik in 1990 and concentrated on the turboprop powered Turbo Orlik. Service trials with the Polish air force led to modifications including an ejection seat and improved avionics.

Variants and operators
PZL-130TB: Poland

Accommodation
2 pilots

Armament
Hardpoints: six wing (two wet)
Warload: 800 kg (1,764 lb)
Bombs; rockets; machine gun pods

Length: 9 m (29 ft 6 in) Wingspan: 9 m (29 ft 6 in) Height: 3.5 m (11 ft 7 in)

Features: Low/straight wing; swept wingtips; ventral fin

Raytheon (Beech) T-34 Mentor USA

Primary trainer / ground attack aircraft

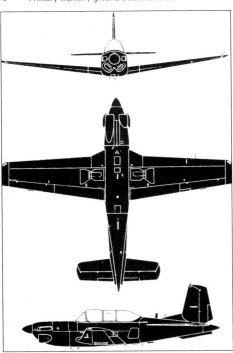

Length: 8.7 m (28 ft 8 in) Wingspan: 10.2 m (33 ft 3 in) Height: 2.9 m (9 ft 7 in)

Features: Low/straight wing; single turboprop; tandem cockpit

Beech re-engined the T-34 in 1972, installing a Pratt & Whitney Canada PT6 turboprop in place of the original piston engine. The new aircraft was designated T-34C Turbo Mentor and finished production in 1990. The armed T-34C-1 can carry out forward air control and counter insurgency operations.

Variants and operators

T-34: Argentina; Colombia; Dominican Republic; Indonesia; El Salvador; Uruguay;

T-34C: Algeria; Argentina; Ecuador; Gabon; Indonesia; Morrocco; Peru; Taiwan; Uruguay; USA

Accommodation

2 pilots

Armament

Hardpoints: four wing
Warload: 544 kg (1,200 lb)
AGM-22; bombs; rockets; machine gun pods

RFB **Fantrainer** Germany

Primary trainer

Despite looking like a jet, the Fantrainer is powered by an Allison turboshaft driving a ducted fan in the circular mid section. This arrangement makes the Fantrainer a simple design to operate and instruct on, while its flight characteristics mimic those of fast jets, enabling students to move directly onto operational aircraft.

Variants and operators
Fantrainer 400/800: Thailand

Accommodation
2 pilots

Armament
No armament fitted as standard

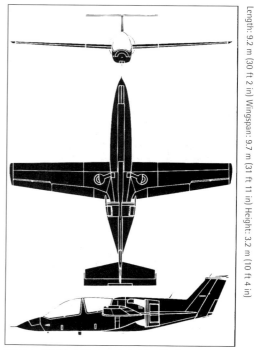

Length: 9.2 m (30 ft 2 in) Wingspan: 9.7 m (31 ft 11 in) Height: 3.2 m (10 ft 4 in)

Features: Mid/straight wing; ducted fan; T-tail

197

Slingsby T67/T-3A Firefly UK

Elementary trainer

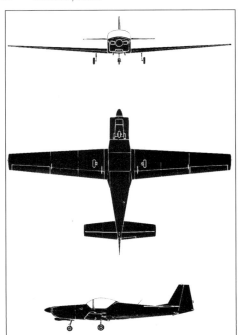

Length: 7.3 m (24 ft) Wingspan: 10.6 m (34 ft 9 in) Height: 2.4 m (7 ft 9 in)

Features: Low/straight wing; single piston engine; side-by-side cockpit

The original Firefly was designed for the commercial training market, and was bought by a number of airlines and training facilities. Military versions were then developed for elementary flight training. USAF aircraft will be built by Northrop Grumman.

Variants and operators

T67: Belize; Canada; Netherlands; Norway; Switzerland; Turkey; UK
T-3A: USAF

Accommodation

2 pilots

Armament

No armament can be carried

Socata TB 30 Epsilon France

Primary trainer \ ground attack aircraft

The Epsilon was designed to create a more cost effective training process for the French Air Force. First flown in 1979, it has been exported in armed and unarmed training configurations. The Togolese Air Force operate theirs in a counter-insurgency role. French and Portuguese aircraft are unarmed.

Variants and operators
TB 30: France; Portugal; Togo

Accommodation
2 pilots

Armament
Hardpoints: four wing
Warload: 300 kg (661 lb)
Bombs; rockets; machine gun pods

Length: 7.6 m (24 ft 10 in) Wingspan: 7.9 m (25 ft 11 in) Height: 2.7 m (8 ft 8 in)

Features: Low/straight wing; single turboprop; tandem cockpit

UTVA-75 Federal Republic of Yugoslavia

Primary trainer

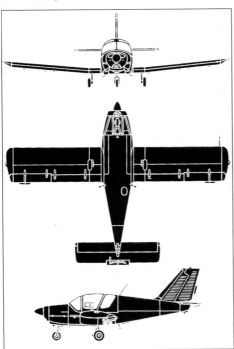

Length: 7.1 m (23 ft 4 in) Wingspan: 9.7 m (31 ft 11 in) Height: 3.2 m (10 ft 4 in)

Features: Low/straight wing; single piston engine; swept tail fin

Designed to meet a Former Yugoslav government requirement for a four-seat utility/training aircraft. Slovenia and Croatia both inherited some of the 150 aircraft produced. Croatia and Bosnia also took possession of some UTVA 65 agricultural aircraft and used them as improvized bombers.

Variants and operators

UTVA-75: Croatia; Republika Srbska; Slovenia; Yugoslavia

Accommodation

2 pilots

Armament

Hardpoints: two wing
Warload: 200 kg (440 lb)
Bombs; rockets; machine gun pods

CIVIL JET AIRLINERS

Airbus A300 France/Germany/Spain/UK

Medium-haul airliner

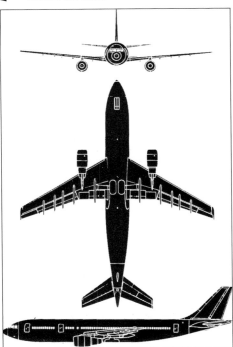

Length: 54.1 m (177 ft 11 in) Wingspan: 44.8 m (147 ft 1 in) Height: 16.6 m (54 ft 6 in)

Features: Low/swept wing; twin underwing turbofans; widebody

First flown in 1972, the A300 was the first aircraft built by the multi-national Airbus consortium. An improved version flew in 1985 with wingtip fences and avionic improvements and remains in production. The A300 also formed the structural basis of the SATIC Super Transporter (p. 294).

Variants and operators

A300: Air France; Air India; Air Inter Europe; Air Liberte; Air Scandic; Alitalia; American; Channel Express; China Airlines; China Eastern; China Northern; China Northwest; Egyptair; Emirates; Faucatt Peru; Finnair; Garuda Indonesia; Iberia; Indian Airlines; Iran Air; Japan Air Systems; Korean Air Lines; Kuwait Airways; Lufthansa; Malaysia Airlines; Monarch; Olympic; Pakistan International; Philippine Air Lines; Permair; Qatar; Saudia; South African; Thai Airways international; Tunisair; VASP

Payload

Passengers: 330
Cargo: 39,885 kg (87,931 lb)
Range: 7,505 km (4,664 m)

Airbus A310 France/Germany/Spain/UK

Medium-haul airliner

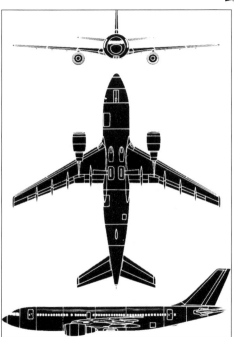

Length: 46.6 m (153 ft 1 in) Wingspan: 43.9 m (144 ft) Height: 15.8 m (51 ft 10 in)

Shorter than the A300 from which it was developed, the A310 was the first airliner to be operated by Fly-by-Wire when it first flew in 1982. An extended range version the A310-300 has small delta winglets and is also operated by the armed forces of Canada, France and Germany.

Variants and operators

A310: Aeroflot; Aerolineas; Air Afrique; Air Algerie; Air France; Air Jamaica; Air Liberte; Air Niugini; Armenian; Austrian; Biman; China Northwest; CSA; Cyprus; Emirates; Hapag-Lloyd; KLM; Kuwait; Lufthansa; MIAT; Nigeria; Pakistan International; Royal; Royal Jordanian; Sabena; Singapore; Swissair; TAP; Tarom; Thai International; Turkish; VASP; Vietnam.

Payload

Passengers: 280
Cargo: 32,860 kg (72,443 lb)
Range: 6,667 km (3,600 nm)

Features: Low/swept wing; two underwing turbofans; shortened fuselage

203

Airbus A320 France/Germany/Spain/UK

Short-haul airliner

Length: 37.6 m (123 ft 3 in) Wingspan: 33.9 m (111 ft 3 in) Height: 11.8 m (38 ft 9 in)

This family of short haul airliners consists of the standard 37.6 m long A320 (top) a shortened version the A319 (33.8 m) and a stretched version the A321 (44.5 m) (bottom). First flown in 1987 the A319 has the longest range of any airliner in its class, and has been offered as a large corporate transport with a transatlantic range.

Features: Low/swept wing; twin underwing turbofans; narrow fuselage

Variants and operators A319/320/321:
ACES; Adria; Aero Lloyd; Air 2000; Air Canada; Air France; Air Inter Europe; Air Jamaica; Air Macao; Air Malta; Air Nippon; Airlanka; Airtours; Airworld; Alitalia; All Nippon; America West; Ansett; Asiana; Austrian; Balkan Bulgarian; British Airways; Caledonian; Canada 3000; Canadian; China Southern; Condor; Croatia; Cyprus; Cyprus Turkish; Egyptair; Eurowings; GB; Gulf; Air; Iberia; Kuwait; Kyrgyzstan; Lan Chile; Lufthansa; Mexicana; Middle East; Monarch; Northwest; Philippine Air Lines; Permair; Royal Jordanian; Sichuan; South African; Swissair; TACA; TAM Brazil; TAP; Transair; Transasia; Tunisair; United; US; Vietnam; Virgin

Payload Passengers: 179
Cargo: 19,220 kg (42,372 lb)
Range: 4,970 km (2,650 nm)

Airbus A330 France/Germany/Spain/UK

Medium-haul airliner

Developed alongside the four engined A340, the A330 was designed to carry more passengers over shorter distances than the A340 while sharing similar components and production line. First flown in 1992, the A330 entered service in 1994.

Variants and operators

A330: Aer Lingus; Asiania; Austrian; Cathay Pacific; Emirates; Garuda Indonesia; Gulf Air; Korean Air Lines; LTU; Malaysia Airlines; Monarch; Northwest; Philippine Air Lines; Sabena; Swissair; Thai International; Trans World; Transasia; US

Payload

Passengers: 440
Cargo: 46,715 kg (102,958 lb)
Range: 8334 km (4500 nm)

Length: 63.6 m (208 ft 10 in) Wingspan: 60.3 m (197 ft 2 in) Height: 16.2 m (52 ft 11 in)

Features: Low/swept wing; twin underwing turbofans; narrow fuselage

205

Airbus A340 France/Germany/Spain/UK

Long-haul airliner

Length: 59.4 m (194 ft 10 in) Wingspan: 60.3 m (197 ft 10 in) Height: 16.7 m (54 ft 11 in)

Features: Low/swept wing; four underwing turbofans; narrow fuselage

Along with the A330 the A340 was the first airliner to be designed entirely with computer-aided design. First flown in 1991 Airbus is continuing to develop a number of extended range and higher capacity aircraft based on the A340. A unique plastic coating was fitted to a Cathay Pacific aircraft to reduce drag and increase range.

Variants and operators

A340: Aerolineas Argentinas; Air Canada; Air China; Air France; Air Mauritius; Airlanka; Air Nippon; Air Tahiti; Austrian; Cathay Pacific; China Eastern; China Southwest; Egyptair; Emirates; EVA; Gulf Air; Iberia; Kuwait; Lufthansa; Philippine Air Lines; Sabena; Singapore; Turkish; Virgin

Payload

Passengers: 335
Cargo: 45,915 kg (101,915 lb)
Range: 13,343 km (7,450 nm)

Aerospatiale/BAe Concorde France/UK

Supersonic airliner

The only supersonic airliner in operation, the Concorde is the only aircraft to regularly fly above the speed of sound. Concorde was first flown in 1969 and has a top speed of 2,174 km/h (1,345 mph) or Mach 2.04. Upgrade programmes are in place to keep them flying until 2014, by which time the US hopes to have supersonic airliners in service.

Variants and operators
Concorde: Air France; British Airways

Payload
Passengers: 128
Cargo: 12,700 kg (28,000 lb)
Range: 6,580 km (3,550 nm)

Features: Tailless delta; four underwing turbojets; narrow fuselage

Length: 62.1 m (203 ft 9 in) Wingspan: 25.5 m (83 ft 10 in) Height: 11.4 m (37 ft 5 in)

207

Avro Avroliner (BAe 146) UK

Short-haul commuter

Features: High/swept wing; four underwing turbofans; T-tail

Length: 26.6 m (93 ft 11 in) Wingspan: 26.2 m (86 ft) Height: 8.6 m (28 ft 3 in)

Successor to the BAe 146, the RJ Avroliner retains much of the 146s structure, but has new engines and is made by a new manufacturing company. The RJ comes in three variants: the short fuselage RJ70 (bottom); mid length fuselage RJ85 (top) and stretched RJ100 (picture).

Variants and operators

Avroliner/146: Aer Lingus; Air Atlantic 1995; Air Baltic; Air Botswana; Air China; Air Foyle; Air Jet; Air Malta; Air Nova; Air UK; Air Wisconsin; Air Zimbabwe; Ansett Australia; Ansett New Zealand; Atlantic South East; Australian Airlink; Aviasca; Azzurra; Cityflyer Express; China Eastern; China Northwest; Crossair; Contiflug; Dan Air; Debonair; Delta Air Transport; Druk Air; Eurowings; Jersey European; Lanchilie; Loganair; Lufthansa; Manx; Meridiana; Mesaba; Northwest; Pelita; Safair; SAL Air; SAM; Qantas; Thai International; TNT; Turkish; US; Uzbekistan; WestAir

Payload

Passengers: 70
Cargo: 10,070 kg (22,000 lb)
Range: 1,600 km (2,963 nm)

BAe (BAC) One-Eleven UK

Short-haul airliner

Length: 28.5 m (93 ft 6 in) Wingspan: 28.5 m (93 ft 6 in) Height: 7.4 m (24 ft 6 in)

Development began in 1961, several versions being built and licence production in Romania being carried out by Romaero. The only noticeable difference between all the different versions is the stretched fuselage of the One-Eleven-500 (bottom).

Variants and operators
One-Eleven: Ledeco; Maersk; Pelita; Tarom

Payload
Passengers: 119
Cargo: 9,647 kg (21,268 lb)
Range: 3,700 km (1,997 nm)

Features: Low/swept wing; two tail turbofans; T-tail

209

Boeing 707 USA

Long-haul airliner

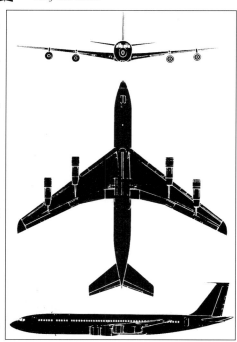

Length: 46.6 m (152 ft 11 in) Wingspan: 44.4 m (145 ft 9 in) Height: 12.9 m (42 ft 5 in)

Features: Low/swept wing; four underwing turbojets; narrow fuselage

First flown in 1954, the last commercial delivery took place in 1982 after more than 1,000 had been produced. Many civilian 707s have found their ways into air forces around the world, some being refitted as aerial tankers in South Africa and Israel.

Variants and operators

707: (military) Argentina; Australia; Benin; Canada; Colombia; Egypt; Germany; India; Indonesia; Iran; Israel; Italy; Liberia; Morocco; NATO; Pakistan; Paraguay; Peru; Qatar; Romania; Saudi Arabia; South Africa; Spain; Togo; UAE; Venezuela; Zaire (civil) Aerovias; Air Afrique; Air Zimbabwe; Azza Air Transport; Iran Air; Kuwait; Lan Chile; Middle East; Pakistan International; Primeras; Royal Air Maroc; Royal Jordanian; Saudia; SkyAir Largo; Tarom; Trans Arabian; TransBrazil; Vietnam

Payload

Passengers: 219
Cargo: 40,324 kg (88,900 lb)
Range: 9,265 km (5,000 nm)

Boeing 717 USA

Short-haul airliner

Boeing has relaunched the McDonnell Douglas MD-95 under its own designation, Boeing 717. The latest development of the DC-9/MD-80 family. Boeing intends to build three versions: the standard 717-200 as described below, an 80 seat version the 717-100 and the 717-300 with 120 seats. The 717 is virtually identical to the MD-95 which can be distinguished from earlier MD-80s by its larger engine nacelles to accommodate the BR175 turbofans.

Variants and operators

717 (as MD-80/90): Aero Lloyd; Aerolineas; Aeromexico; Aeropostal; Aerovias; Air Aruba; Air Liberte; AirTran; Alaska; Alitalia; American; AOM; Austrian; Aviaco; China Eastern; China Northern; Continental; Crossair; Cyprus Turkish; Delta; Eva; Far Eastern; Finnair; Iberia; Japan Air Systems; Korean Air Lines; Northwest; SAS; Saudia; Trans World; US

Payload

Passengers: 102
Cargo: 12,220 kg (26,940 lb)
Range: 3,593 km (1,940 nm)

Length: 34.4 m (112 ft 8 in) Wingspan: 28.5 m (93 ft 5 in) Height: 8.9 m (29 ft 1 in)

Features: Low/swept wing; twin tail turbofans; T-tail

211

Boeing 727 USA

Short-haul airliner

Length: 46.7 m (153 ft 2 in) Wingspan: 32.9 m (108 ft) Height: 10.4 m (34 ft)

Features: Low/swept wing; three tail turbofans; T-tail

Boeing rolled out the 727 in 1962 as a short-haul complement to their 707. The two aircraft share many parts, the fuselage being almost identical. The obvious difference was the change to rear mounted engines and a totally new tail assembly.

Variants and operators

727: ACES; Aerolineas; Aeroperu; Aerovias; Air Algerie; Air Jamaica; American; Ansett; Ariania; Continental; Cyprus Turkish; Delta; Faucatt Peru; Iberia; Iran Air; Iraqi; JAT; Mexicana; Mongolian; Northwest; Palestinian Airlines; Planet; Royal Air Maroc; Royal Nepal; Ryan; Skyservice; Sunworld International; Trans World; United; Varig

Payload

Passengers: 189
Cargo: 28,622 kg (63,102 lb)
Range: 2,370 km (4,392 nm)

Boeing 737-100/200 USA

Short-haul airliner

The original 737 was first flown in 1967, starting a production run that has now included over 2,000 aircraft making it the best selling airliner in the world. Early 737s can be recognized by the long/thin engines under the wing.

Variants and operators

737-100/200: Aerolineas; Air Afrique; Air Algerie; Air Europa; Air Foyle; Air France; Air Gabon; Air Liberte; Air Madagascar; Air Namibia; Air New Zealand; Air Nippon; Air Tanzania; AirTran; Air Zimbabwe; Alaska; All Nippon; America West; Bouraq; Braathens; British Airways; Canadian; Continental; Delta; Egyptair; El Al; Ethiopian; Euralair; Far Eastern; Faucatt Peru; GB; Iran Air; Iraqi; Jugoslovenski; Kenya; Ledeco; Lan Chile; Lithuanian; Lufthansa; Malev; Nigeria; Olympic; :PLUNA; Primeras; Royal Air Maroc; Ryan; Ryanair; Sabena; Saudia; South African; TAP; Transaero; Transavia; Tunisair; Ukraine; United; US; Varig; VASP; West Jet; Winair

Payload

Passengers: 130
Cargo: 15,860 kg (34,966 lb)
Range: 4,179 km (2,255 nm)

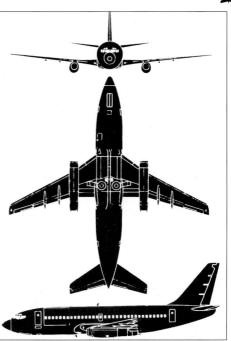

Features: Low/swept wing; two underwing turbofans; narrow engine nacelles

Length: 29.5 m (96 ft 11 in) Wingspan: 28.3 m (93 ft) Height: 11.3 m (37 ft)

Boeing 737-300/400/500 USA

Short-haul airliner

USA

Features: Low/straight wing; two large underwing turbofans; cranked tailfin

Length: 33.4 m (109 ft 7 in) Wingspan: 28.8 m (94 ft 9 in) Height: 11.1 m (36 ft 6 in)

214

The 737-300 was the first major re-design of the Boeing's best selling airliner. The wings were improved with an extended leading edge, and the fuselage extended forward. But the most obvious difference was the deeper engine nacelles for the new CFM-56 turbofans.

Variants and operators

737-300/400/500: Aer Lingus; Air Belgium; Air Berlin; Air Caledonie; Air China; Air Europa; Air Foyle; Air France; Air Madagascar; Air Malawi; Air New Zealand; Air Nippon; Air Pacific; Alaska; America West; Ansett; Asiana; Balkan; Braathens; British Airways; British Midland; China Airlines; China Hainan; China Southern; China Southwest; Color Air; Condor; Continental; CSA; Delta; Deutsche; EasyJet; Egyptair; Estonian; Euralair; Garuda Indonesia; GB; Hapag-Lloyd; Icelandair; Japan Airlines; JAT; Kenya; KLM; Ledeco; Lauda; Lot; Lufthansa; Malaysia; Malev; Monarch; Olympic; Pakistan International; Philippine Air Lines; Qantas; Royal Air Maroc; Ryan; Sabena; SAS; Southwest; TAP; Tarom; TAT; Thai International; Transaero; Transavia; TransBrazil; Tunisair; Turkish; Turkmenistan; Ukraine; United; US; Varig; VASP; Vietnam; Virgin Express; Western Pacific

Payload

Passengers: 149
Cargo: 9,072 kg (20,000 lb)
Range: 5,278 km (2,850 nm)

Boeing 737-600/700/800 USA

Short-haul airliner

The latest in a line of improvements for the 737, Boeing asked 30 major airlines to help define how they could improve the aircraft. Greater range and speed were prime requests along with lower noise and emissions. Range increases give the latest 737s a true transatlantic range for the first time.

Variants and operators

737-600/700/800: Air Berlin; Air Europa; Air Pacific; American; Angel; Ansett; Aviation Methods; Bavaria; Braathens; China Airlines; Continental; GATX; General Electric; GE Capital; Germania; Hapag-Lloyd; International Lease Finance; Jet; Lauda; Lot; Maersk; Royal Air Maroc; Sabre; SAS; Southwest; Tombo Aviation Services; THY; Transavia; TUI; Virgin Express

Payload

Passengers: 189 max
Cargo: 9,072 kg (20,00 lb)
Range: 5,981 (3,230 nm)

Length: 33.6 m (110 ft 4 in) Wingspan: 34.3 m (112 ft 7 in) Height: 12.5 m (41 ft 2 in)

Features: Low/straight wing; two underwing turbofans; short or long fuselage

215

Boeing 747 USA

Long-haul airliner

Length: 70.7 m (321 ft 10 in) Wingspan: 59.6 m (195 ft 8 in) Height: 19.3 m (63 ft 5 in)

Features: Low/swept wing; four underwing turbofans; two decks

The original widebody airliner over 1,100 747s have been produced since the prototype first flew in 1969. A longer range version, the 747SP (picture), was created by shortening the fuselage to decrease weight and increasing fuel storage. Freighter versions have an upward swinging nose door.

Variants and operators

747: Aerolineas; Aerovias; Air China; Air France; Air Gabon; Air Hongkong; Air India; Air Madagascar; Air Namibia; Air New Zealand; Air Pacific; Alitalia; Alliance Air; All Nippon; Ansett; Asiana; Atlas Air; British Airways; Canadian; Cathay Pacific; China Airlines; Continental; Egyptair; El Al; Eva; Garuda Indonesia; Iberia; Iran Air; Iraqi; Japan Air Systems; Japan Airlines; Japan Asia; KLM; Korean; Kuwait; Lufthansa; Malaysia; Martinair; Middle East; Northwest; Olympic; Pakistan International; Philippine Air Lines; Qantas; Qatar; Royal Air Maroc; Sabena; SAS; Saudia; Singapore; South African; Swissair; Thai International; Tower Air; Trans World; United; Virgin

Payload

Passengers: 452
Cargo: 102,058 kg (225,000 lb)
Range: 14,630 km (7,900 nm)

Boeing 747-400 USA

Long-haul airliner

Announced in 1985, the 747-400 has increased payload and range. First flown in 1988 the 747-400 can be recognized by its longer upper deck and winglets. Improved avionics enabled the flight crew to be reduced from three to two.

Variants and operators

747-400: Air Canada; Air China; Air France; Air India; Air New Zealand; All Nippon; Asiana; British Airways; Canadian; Cathay Pacific; China Airlines; El Al; Eva; Garuda Indonesia; Japan Air Systems; Japan Airlines; KLM; Korean; Kuwait; Lufthansa; Malaysia; Northwest; Philippine Air Lines; Qantas; Royal Air Maroc; Saudia; Singapore; South African; Thai International; United; Virgin

Payload

Passengers: 421
Cargo: 113,000 kg (249,122 lb)
Range: 13,390 km (7,230 nm)

Length: 70.6 m (231 ft 10 in) Wingspan: 64.4 m (211 ft 5 in) Height: 19.4 m (63 ft 8 in)

Features: Low/swept wing; winglets; top deck extends to mid fuselage

Boeing 757 USA

Medium-haul airliner

Features: Low/swept wing; twin underwing turbofans; narrow fuselage

Designed as the first part of Boeing's new technology airliner fleet, the 757 was to replace the 707. Greater reliability and improved power to weight ratios enabled the four engines of the 707 to be replaced with two on the 757. The 757 was the first Boeing to be offered with Rolls Royce engines.

Variants and operators

757: Aeromexico; Aeroperu; Aerovias; Air 2000; Air Belgium; Air Europa; Airtours; America West; American; Britannia; British Airways; Caledonian; China Southern; China Southwest; Condor; Continental; Delta; Ethiopian; Far Eastern; Finnair; Gulf Air; Iberia; Icelandair; Iraqi; Ledeco; Lauda; LTU; Mexicana; Monarch; Northwest; Royal Air Maroc; Royal Brunei; Royal Nepal; Trans World; Transaero; Transavia; Transbrazil; United; US

Payload

Passengers: 239
Cargo: 32,754 kg (72,210 lb)
Range: 7,408 km (4,000 nm)

Boeing 767 USA

Long-haul airliner

The 767 is now being offered as a replacement airframe for the USAF C-135 fleet. Aerial tankers, electronic reconnaissance and Joint STARS versions are being considered and an AWACS version has already entered service with the Japanese Air Self Defence Force (p. 131).

Variants and operators

767: Aeroflot; Aeromexico; Aerovias; Air Algerie; Air Canada; Air China; Air Europe; Air France; Air Gabon; Air Madagascar; Air New Zealand; Air Pacific; Air Seychelles; Air Zimbabwe; Airborne Express; Airtours; Alitalia; All Nippon; American; Asiana; Balkan; Britannia; British Airways; Canadian; China Southern; Condor; Continental; Delta; Egyptair; El Al; Ethiopian; Eva; Gulf Air; Japan Airlines; KLM; Lanchilie; Lauda; Lot; LTU; Malev; Martinair; Monarch; Qantas; Royal Brunei; SAS; Skymark; South African; Swiss World; Trans World; Transbrazil; Ukraine; United; US; Varig; Vietnam

Payload
Passengers: 242
Cargo: 16,574 kg (36,540 lb)
Range: 12,603 km (6,805 nm)

Length: 48.5 m (159 ft 2 in) Wingspan: 47.6 m (156 ft 1 in) Height: 15.8 m (52 ft)

Features: Low/swept wing; twin underwing turbofans; wide body

219

Boeing 777 USA

Long-haul airliner

Length: 63.7 m (209 ft 1 in) Wingspan: 60.9 m (199 ft 11 in) Height: 18.5 m (60 ft 9 in)

Features: Low/swept wing; twin underwing turbofans; wide body

The largest twin-engined airliner in the world the 777 first flew in 1994. The outer sections of the wings can fold upwards like carrier aircraft to enable the 777 to safely negotiate smaller airports. The 777 also boasts Boeing's first fly-by-wire system.

Variants and operators

777: Aeroflot; Air France; All Nippon; Asiana; British Airways; Cathay Pacific; China Southern; Continental; Egyptair; Emirates; Garuda Indonesia; Japan Airlines; Korean Air Lines; Kuwait; Lauda; Malaysia; Saudia; South African; Thai International; TransBrazil; United; Virgin; Varig

Payload

Passengers: 440
Cargo: 54,660 kg (120,500 lb)
Range: 13,667 km (7,880 nm)

Boeing (McDonnell Douglas) DC-8 USA

Long-haul airliner

Length: 45.9 m (150 ft 6 in) Wingspan: 43.4 m (142 ft 5 in) Height: 12.9 m (42 ft 4 in)

The DC-8 family of airliners were designed around standard wing and fuselage sections, and identical auxiliary systems. To increase range or payload the fuselage was stretched by adding extra sections, a process copied by many other manufacturers. The ultra long-range Super 61 was over 9 m longer than the original. The picture shows a US Navy E-6, based on the DC-8.

Variants and operators
DC-8: Air India; Airborne Express; Lan Chile; Saudia

Payload
Passengers: 179
Cargo: 15,585 kg (34,360 lb)
Range: 7,710 km (4,159 nm)

Features: Low/swept wing; four underwing turbojets; auxiliary chin intakes

Boeing (McDonnell Douglas) DC-9 USA

Short-haul airliner

Length: 36.4 m (199 ft 3 in) Wingspan: 28.5 m (93 ft 5 in) Height: 8.4 m (27 ft 6 in)

Features: Low/swept wing; twin tail turbofans; T-tail

Development began in 1962, as a short haul counterpart to the DC-8. Like its larger stablemate the DC-9 was designed to accept fuselage plugs to increase capacity and range. The top silhouette shows the original DC-9 series 10, the bottom silhouette the longest version, DC-9 Series 50.

Variants and operators

DC-9: Adria; Aero California; Aeromexico; Aeropostal; Air Canada; Airborne Express; AirTran; Alitalia; Allegiant Air; Continental; Finnair; Hawaiian; Iberia; Japan Air Systems; JAT; Merpati; Northwest; Ryan; Trans World

Payload

Passengers: 115
Cargo: 14,118 kg (31,125 lb)
Range: 3,095 km (1,670 nm)

Boeing (McDonnell Douglas) DC-10 USA

Medium-haul airliner

The DC-10 was designed to offer a widebody/high capacity airliner for medium distance routes. First flown in 1970 it shares a striking resemblance to the Lockheed Martin Tristar which was designed for the same requirement. The third engine in the tail is mounted away from the fuselage, the Tristar's is buried in the tail.

Variants and operators

DC-10: Air Liberte; Air Afrique; American; AOM; British Airways; Caledonian; Challenge Air Cargo; Condor; Continental; Cubana; Garuda Indonesia; Hawaiian; Iberia; Japan Airlines; Japan Asia; Jugoslovenski; Malaysia; Mexicana; Monarch; Nigeria; Northwest; Philippine Air Lines; Permair; Primeras; Thai International; Transaero; Transair International; United; Varig; World

Payload

Passengers: 380
Cargo: 48,330 kg (106,550 lb)
Range: 7,413 km (4,000 nm)

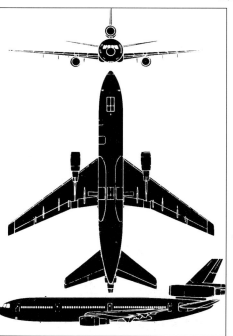

Length: 55.5 m (182 ft 1 in) Wingspan: 50.4 m (165 ft 4 in) Height: 17.7 m (58 ft 1 in)

Features: Low/swept wing; two underwing and one tail turbofans; widebody

223

Boeing (McDonnell Douglas) MD-11 USA

Long-haul airliner

Length: 61.2 m (200 ft) Wingspan: 51.7 m (169 ft 10 in) Height: 17.6 m (57 ft 9 in)

Features: Low/swept wing; two underwing one tail turbofans; winglets

A development of the DC-10 the MD-11 was unveiled in 1985, with first deliveries beginning in 1990. Engine and aerodynamic improvements increased the range with further improvements planned. One major difference between the two is the addition of winglets.

Variants and operators

MD-11: Alitalia; American; China Airlines; China City Bird; Eastern; Delta; Eva; FedEx; Finnair; Garuda Indonesia; Japan Airlines; KLM; Korean Air Lines; LTU; Malaysia; Martinair; Saudia; Swissair; Thai International; Varig; VASP; World

Payload

Passengers: 405
Cargo: 51,058 kg (112,564 lb)
Range: 12,569 km (6,787 nm)

224

Canadair Regional Jet Canada

Short-haul commuter

Canadair's regional jet was developed from the successful Challenger corporate jet, carrying more passengers over shorter ranges. First flown in 1991 over 500 have been ordered. A corporate shuttle version carries fewer passengers in executive commuter service.

Variants and operators

Regional Jet: Adria; Air Canada; Air Littoral; Air Nostrum; Atlantic Southeast; ASA; Brit Air; Comair; LAC; Kendall; Lauda; Lufthansa; Mesa; Midway; Saega; Skywest; Southern winds; TAG; Tyrolean; Xerox

Payload

Passengers: 50
Cargo: 3,728 kg (8,220 lb)
Range: 1,815 km (980 nm)

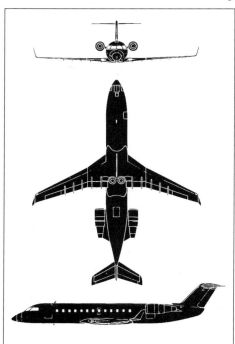

Length: 26.7 m (87 ft 10 in) Wingspan: 21.2 m (69 ft 7 in) Height: 6.2 m (20 ft 5 in)

Features: Low/swept wing; twin tail turbofans; T-tail

225

EMBRAER EMB-145 Brazil

Short-haul commuter

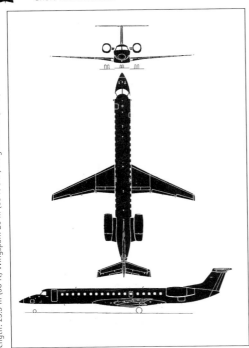

Length: 29.9 m (98 ft) Wingspan: 20 m (65 ft 9 in) Height: 6.7 m (22 ft)

Features: Low/swept wing; twin tail turbofans; T-tail

Brazil's first jet airliner, it is aimed at the corporate and military markets. EMBRAER are already developing a version equipped with the Swedish Erieye sideways looking radar, (see photo above) and also believe a low-cost tanker can be built. First flown in 1995 the EMB-145 has already secured 190 orders.

Variants and operators

EMB-145: American Eagle; British Midlands; Regional Airlines France; Continental Express; Manx; National Jet Services; Portugalia; Skyways; TransBrazil; Trans States

Payload

Passengers: 50
Cargo: 5,515 kg (12,158 lb)
Range: 2,574 km (1,390 nm)

Fokker F28 Fellowship Netherlands

Short-haul commuter

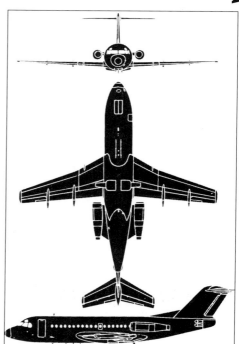

Fokker built the F28 in collaboration with MBB of Germany and Shorts of the UK. First flown in 1967 it was Fokker's first jet design. Several variants have been produced including stretched and shortened fuselages and cargo aircraft.

Variants and operators

F28: Aeroperu; Air Gabon; Air Niugini; Biman; Canadian Regional; Delta Air Transport; Merpati; Pelita; SAS; US

Payload

Passengers: 65 max
Cargo: 10,478 kg (23,100 lb)
Range: 3,169 km (1,710 nm)

Features: Low/swept wing; twin tail turbofans; T-tail

227

Fokker 100/70 Netherlands

Short-haul commuter

Length: 35.5 m (116 ft 6 in) Wingspan: 28.1 m (92 ft 1 in) Height: 8.5 m (27 ft 10 in)

Features: Low/swept wing; twin tail turbofans; T-tail

The 100 replaced the F28 on the production line in 1988, being a stretched and improved version of the final F28 Series 4000. The engine nacelles are larger and the wingspan increased. Over 290 had been ordered by 1998.

Variants and operators

100/70: Air Europe; Air Gabon; Air Inter Europe; Air Ivorie; Air Littoral; American; Aviasca; Bangkok; Braathens; British Midland; China Eastern; Formosa; Garuda Indonesia; Inter-Canadian; Iran Air; KLM; Korean Air; Merpati; Mexicana; Midway; Palair; Pelita; Portugalia; Royal Swazi; Sempati; Swissair; TABA; TAM; TAT; Tyrolean; US

Payload

Passengers: 79
Cargo: 11,108 kg (24,486 lb)
Range: 2,389 km (1,290 nm)

Ilyushin Il-62M Classic Russia

Long-haul airliner

The Il-62 began operating on Aeroflot's long distance routes in 1974 three years after it first appeared at the Paris Air Show. From 1985 a series of improvements were fitted to the Il-62 aimed at reducing noise and pollution emissions to keep up with Western standards.

Variants and operators

Il-62: Aeroflot; Air India; Cubana; Tarom

Payload

Passengers: 178
Cargo: 23,000 kg (50,700 lb)
Range: 9,200 km (4,963 nm)

Length: 53.2 m (174 ft 3 in) Wingspan: 43.2 m (141 ft 9 in) Height: 12.3 m (40 ft 6 in)

Features: Low/swept wing; four tail turbofans; T-tail

Ilyushin Il-86 Russia

Medium-haul airliner

Length: 59.4 m (195 ft 8 in) Wingspan: 48.1 m (157 ft 8 in) Height: 15.8 m (51 ft 10 in)

Ilyushin's first widebody design the Il-86 first flew in 1976. Forms the basis of the Il-87 airborne command post. It can be recognized by a large dorsal canoe and two underwing pods holding auxiliary generators (p. 154).

Variants and operators
Il-86: Aeroflot; Armenian; China Northern

Payload
Passengers: 350
Cargo: 42,000 kg (92,600 lb)
Range: 4,600 km (2,480 nm)

Features: Low/swept wing; four underwing turbofans; widebody

Ilyushin Il-96 Russia

Long-haul airliner

To overcome the inadequacies of the Il-86's main engines, Ilyushin began designing the Il-96 around four much improved Aviadvigatel PS-90A turbofans. The Il-96 retains a similar silhouette to the Il-86, the main changes were in the engines and manufacturing process, Il-96s however have winglets and a longer fuselage.

Variants and operators

Il-96: Aeroflot; Domodedvo

Payload

Passengers: 234
Cargo: 40,000 kg (88,185 lb)
Range: 11,000 km (5,940 nm)

Length: 55.4 m (181 ft 7 in) Wingspan: 57.7 m (189 ft 2 in) Height: 17.6 m (57 ft 7 in)

Features: Low/swept wing; four underwing turbofans; winglets

Lockheed Martin L1011 Tristar USA

Long-haul airliner

Length: 54.2 m (177 ft 8 in) Wingspan: 47.3 m (155 ft 4 in) Height: 16.8 m (55 ft 4 in)

Features: Low/swept wing; two underwing one tail turbofans; widebody

Lockheed, now Lockheed Martin, designed the Tristar for the same requirements as the DC-10. The two aircraft first flew within months of each other in 1970 and are very similar in appearance. The Tristar's third engine is buried in the fuselage tail whereas the DC-10's stands ⅓ way up the tailfin. Marshall Aerospace have refitted six Tristars as tanker/transports for the RAF.

Variants and operators

L-1011: (military) Jordan; Saudi Arabia; UK (civil) Air Canada; Air India; Airlanka; Caledonian; Faucatt Peru; Royal; Royal Jordanian; Saudia; TAP; Trans World

Payload

Passengers: 400
Cargo: 40,345 kg (88,946 lb)
Range: 8,400 km (4,533 nm)

Tupolev Tu-134 Crusty Russia

Short-haul commuter

Russian designers kept installing glazed noses on their bombers long after they had gone out of fashion in the West. However the Tu-134's glazed nose is unique among airliners. Its purpose is unclear as modern avionics make it unnecessary to carry a navigator, the only person who could make use of it. On some aircraft it has been replaced.

Variants and operators

Tu-134: (military) Angola; Armenia; Bulgaria; Czech Republic; Kazakhstan; Poland; Russia; Ukraine (civil) Aeroflot; Balkan; Estonian; Malev; Vietnam

Payload

Passengers: 72
Cargo: 7,700 kg (16,975 lb)
Range: 3,070 km (1,655 nm)

Features: Low/swept wing; twin tail turbofans; glazed nose

Length: 35 m (114 ft 10 in) Wingspan: 29 m (95 ft 1 in) Height: 9 m (29 ft 7 in)

Tupolev Tu-154 Careless Russia

Medium-haul airliner

Length: 47.9 m (157 ft 1 in) Wingspan: 37.5 m (123 ft 2 in) Height: 11.4 m (37 ft 4 in)

Features: Low/swept wing; three tail turbofans; T-tail

An experimental Tu-154 has been fitted with a cryogenic fuel system using natural gas for fuel. Designated the Tu-156, Tupolev hope to have it flying before the end of the century. The original Tu-154 first flew in 1973, and was replaced in production by the modified Tu-154B in 1977.

Variants and operators

Tu-154: (military) Belarus; Czech Republic; Germany; Kazakhstan; Kolavia; Jana-Arka; North Korea; Poland; Russia; Slovakia; Ukraine (civil) Aeroflot; Ariana; Balkan; China Northwest; China Southwest; CSA; Cubana; Iran Air; Lao; Malev; Tarom; Turkmenistan; Vnukovo

Payload

Passengers: 167
Cargo: 20,000 kg (44,090 lb)
Range: 5,280 km (2,850 nm)

Tupolev Tu-204 Russia

Medium-haul airliner

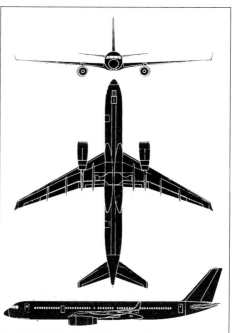

Very similar in appearance to the Boeing 757, the Tu-204 is produced in three main variants: the basic 204 for medium haul routes; the combination passenger/cargo 214; and the shortened 224 for commuter links. Tupolev also hopes to find military applications to replace Il-18 May anti-submarine aircraft.

Variants and operators

Tu-204: Aeroflot; Air Cairo; Transaero; Vnukovo

Payload

Passengers: 214
Cargo: 21,000 kg (46,269 lb)
Range: 6,330 km (3,415 nm)

Features: Low/swept wing; twin underwing turbofans; winglets

Length: 46 m (150 ft 11 in) Wingspan: 42 m (137 ft 9 in) Height: 13.9 m (45 ft 7 in)

235

Yakovlev Yak-40 Codling Russia

Short-haul commuter

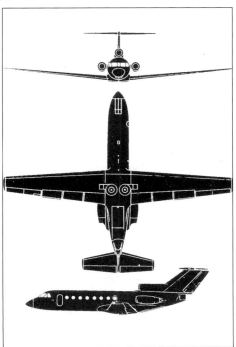

Length: 20.4 m (66 ft 9 in) Wingspan: 25 m (82 ft) Height: 17 m (55 ft 9 in)

Features: Low/straight wing; three tail turbofans; T-tail

236

Designed to replace the Russian-built DC-3 in Aeroflot service it can be operated from very rough airfields and even grass strips. The most widely used airliner inside the former Soviet Union, they carried 8 million passengers 108 million miles in their first six years of operation.

Variants and operators
Yak-40: Aeroflot; Ariana; Cubana; Estonian; Vietnam; Volga-Dnepr

Payload
Passengers: 32
Cargo: 1,360 kg (3,000 lb)
Range: 2,000 km (1,080 nm)

Yakovlev Yak-42 Clobber Russian

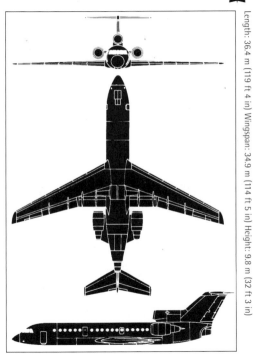

Short-haul airliner

Entering service in 1980 five years after it first flew, the Yak-42 was designed to replace the Tu-134 on short internal routes. Still in production, Yakovlev continues to improve it with western avionics and a stretched fuselage. Its rugged design enables it to operate from semi-permanent airstrips under a wide range of conditions.

Variants and operators

Yak-42: China; Cuba; Kazakhstan; Lithuania; Russia; Turkmenistan; Ukraine

Payload

Passengers: 120
Cargo: 13,000 kg (28,660 lb)
Range: 2,000 km (1,080 nm)

Features: Low/swept wing; three tail turbofans; T-tail

Length: 36.4 m (119 ft 4 in) Wingspan: 34.9 m (114 ft 5 in) Height: 9.8 m (32 ft 3 in)

CIVIL TURBOPROP AIRLINERS

Airtech/CASA CN-235 Indonesia/Spain

Medium-haul commuter

The civil version of the Indonesian-Spanish CN-235 has not sold as well as the military version described separately. In its commuter role the rear loading ramp is retained but the cargo area behind is separated from the passenger cabin. It also retains the military version's short/rough field capability.

Variants and operators

CN-235: Austral; Binter; Binter Mediterraneo; Korean Air; Mandala; Merpati

Payload

Passengers: 44
Cargo: 4,000 kg (8,818 lb)
Range: 3,908 km (2,110 nm) max

Length: 21.4 m (70 ft 2 in) Wingspan: 25.8 m (84 ft 8 in) Height: 8.2 m (26 ft 10 in)

Features: High/straight wing; twin turboprops; high tail assembly

239

Antonov An-38 Ukraine

Short-haul commuter

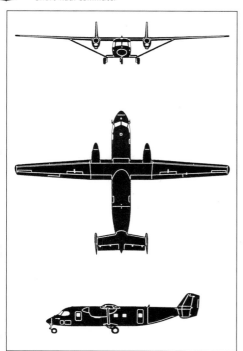

Length: 15.5 m (51 ft) Wingspan: 22 m (72 ft 4 in) Height: 4.3 m (14 ft 1 in)

Features: High/straight wing; twin turboprops; twin tails

Developed from the earlier An-28, Antonov stretched the fuselage and replaced the radial engines with Garrett Turboprops. Production of the An-38 began in 1997, following its first flight in 1994. Several versions are being offered including commuter, cargo; medical evacuation; ice and maritime patrol; aerial photography/survey and geophysical prospecting aircraft. Poland licence builds them under the designation M-28.

Variants and operators
An-28: Poland; Russia; Ukraine **An-38:** Russia;
Ukraine **M-28:** Poland

Payload
Passengers: 26
Cargo: 3,200 kg (7,055 lb)
Range: 1,600 km (863 nm)

ATR 42/72 France/Italy

Medium-haul airliner

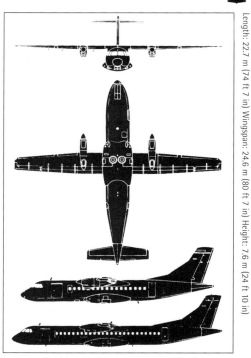

Aerospatiale and Aeritalia (now Alenia) announced the formation of the Avions de Transport Regional (ATR) group in 1980, to jointly develop regional airliners. Their first aircraft the ATR 42 flew in 1984, a military cargo version the ATR 52 is under development. A stretched version, the ATR 72 is 27.2 m (89 ft 1 in) long and can carry 74 passengers.

Variants and operators

ATR 42/72: ACES; Aeromar; Air Caledonie; Air Dolomiti; Air France; Air Littoral; Air Malawi; Air Mauritius; Air New Zealand; Air Nostrum; Air Tahiti; Alitalia; AMR Eagle; Atlantic Southeast; Bangkok Air; Brit Air; Canadian Regional; CIC; Cityflyer; Continental Express; CSA; Eurowings; Finnair; JAT; Lao; Lot; Olympic; Oman Air; TACA; TAT; Thai; Trans States; Vietnam

Payload

Passengers: 50
Cargo: 4,910 kg (10,824 lb)
Range: 4,482 km (2,420 nm)

Length: 22.7 m (74 ft 7 in) Wingspan: 24.6 m (80 ft 7 in) Height: 7.6 m (24 ft 10 in)

Features: High/straight wing; twin turboprop; T-tail

241

BAe (HS) 748 UK

Short-haul airliner

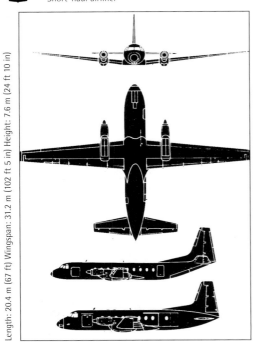

Length: 20.4 m (67 ft) Wingspan: 31.2 m (102 ft 5 in) Height: 7.6 m (24 ft 10 in)

Features: Low/straight wing; twin turboprops; stepped engine nacelle

The 748 first flew as an Avro design in 1960. It has since flown under the Hawker Siddeley and BAe name. Civil operators are now few although the type remains popular with military operators, especially India who operate over 50.

Variants and operators

748: (civil) Air Creebec; Air Madagascar; Bouraq Indonesia; Liat; Royal Nepal; Makung (military) Australia; Brazil; Burkina Faso; Colombia; Ecuador; India; South Korea; Madagascar; Nepal; Thailand; Zambia

Payload

Passengers: 58
Cargo: 5,136 kg (11,323 lb)
Range: 2,892 km (1,590 nm)

BAe ATP UK

Short-haul airliner

Designed as a replacement for the BAe (HS) 748 the Advanced TurboProp (ATP) shares the same fuselage as the 748 with an improved wing and swept tail. The ATP's main engines drive six blade propellers making it the quietest aircraft in its class.

Variants and operators

ATP: Air Europa Express; Air Wisconsin; Biman; British Midland; British World; Canarias Regional; LAR Portugal; Loganair; Manx; Merpati; Sun Air; THT

Payload

Passengers: 68
Cargo: 7,167 kg (15,800 lb)
Range: 4,296 km (2,230 nm)

Length: 26 m (85 ft 4 in) Wingspan: 30.6 m (100 ft 6 in) Height: 7.6 m (24 ft 11 in)

Features: Low/straight wing; twin turboprops; cranked tailfin

243

BAe Jetstream 41 UK

Short-haul commuter

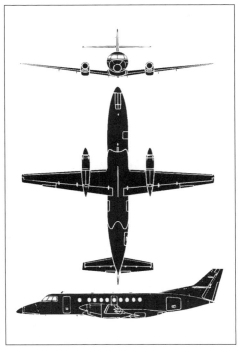

Length: 19.2 m (63 ft 2 in) Wingspan: 18.3 m (60 ft) Height: 5.7 m (18 ft 10 in)

Features: Low/straight wing; twin turboprop; mid-mounted tail

Based on the successful Jetstream 31 corporate transport, the Jetstream 41's fuselage is 5 m (16 ft) longer, increasing passenger capacity and range. The wingspan was increased and the engines now drive a five blade contrarotating propellers.

Variants and operators

Jetstream 41: Air Atlantic; Air Normandie; AlliedSignal; American Eagle; Atlantic coast; Flight West; Highland Air; Impulse Transportation; KwaZulu-Natal; Loganair; Manx; SA Airlink; Seoul Air; Sun-Air; Royal Thai Army; Trans States Airlines

Payload

Passengers: 29
Cargo: 3,628 kg (8,000 lb)
Range: 1,433 km (774 nm)

Beriev Be-32 Cuff Russia

Short-haul STOL commuter

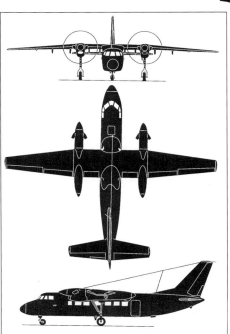

Beriev began work on a short-haul commuter in 1967. Then named the Be-30 the aircraft was cancelled when Aeroflot ordered large numbers of Let-410s. The programme was re-started in 1993 when hard currency shortages stopped the purchase of the Czech aircraft. Production is to be carried out by IAR in Romania.

Variants and operators
Production underway, launch customer Moscow Airways

Payload
Passengers: 17
Cargo: 1,900 kg (4,190 lb)
Range: 1,750 km (944 nm)

Features: High/straight wing; twin turboprops; anhedral wing

Length: 15.7 m (51 ft 6 in) Wingspan: 17 m (55 ft 9 in) Height: 5.5 m (18 ft 1 in)

245

Convair CV 440 Metropolitan USA

Regional Airliner

Length: 24.1 m (79 ft 2 in) Wing Span: 32.1 m (105 ft 4 in) Height: 8.6 m (28 ft 2 in)

Features: Low/straight wing; twin radial engines or turboprops; tapered leading edge

The Metropolitan was developed from the earlier 340 Liner, incorporating soundproofing for the passenger cabin and increased speed. Several version were produced including the 540/580/600/640 series with two Rolls-Royce Dart Rda. 10 turboprops, which increased range and maximum take-off weight.

Variants and operators

Metropolitan: AeroCaribe; Air Niagara Express; Avensa; Canair Cargo; European Air Transport; Air Venezuela; Four Star Air Cargo; Jetall; Kelowna Flightcraft; Kitty Hawk Air Cargo; Provincial; Sierra Pacific; Zantop

Payload

Passengers: 52
Cargo: 7,000 kg (16,000 lb)
Range: 3,225 km (1,740 nm)

De Havilland DHC Dash 7 Canada

Medium-haul STOL airliner

The Dash 7 first flew in 1975 and 113 were built. The Canadian department of the Environment operates a single Dash 7 fitted with an observation cabin on top of the fuselage, sideways looking radar and laser survey equipment. It is used to survey ice floes near drilling rigs and shipping lanes.

Variants and main operators

Dash 7: Adria; Air Niugini; Arkia; Bradley Air; BA; Continental Express; Farwest; Groenlandsfly; Paradise Island; Pelita; Piedmont; Ross; Tyrolean

Payload

Passengers: 50
Cargo: 5,130 kg (11,310 lb)
Range: 2,168 km (1,170 nm)

Length: 24.6 m (80 ft 7 in) Wingspan: 28.3 m (93 ft) Height: 8 m (26 ft 2 in)

Features: High/straight wing; four turboprops; T-tail

De Havilland Canada DHC-8 Dash 8 Canada

Short-haul commuter

Length: 22.3 m (73 ft) Wingspan: 25.9 m (85 ft) Height: 7.5 m (24 ft 7 in)

First flown in 1983 the Dash 8 was designed to fill the gap between the 50 seat Dash 7 and 20 seat DHC-6 Twin Otter. Designed for maximum efficiency with minimum noise pollution the Dash 8 series 300 was stretched by 3.4 m (11 ft 3 in) to increase passenger load to 56.

Variants and main operators

Dash 8: Air Atlantic; Air Creebec; Air Maldives; Air Namibia; Air Nova; Air Ontario; AIRBC; AIRES; Allegheny; ALM Antiliean; Aloha Islandair; Amakusa; Ansett; Augsberg; Bahamasair; BA; Canadian Regional; CCAIR; Eastern Australia; ERA; Flight West; Great China; Hamburg; Horizon Air; Intercontinental; Liat; Mesa Air; Mesaba; Piedmont; SA Express; Schreiner; Surinam; Tyrolean; Wideroe

Payload

Passengers: 37
Cargo: 4,134 kg (9,144 lb)
Range: 1,518 km (820 nm)

Features: High/straight wing; twin turboprops; T-tail

248

Dornier Do. 228 Germany

Short-haul commuter

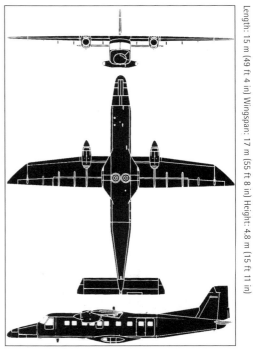

The Dornier 228 first flew in 1981, and was designed to carry out a wide range of duties. Military versions are described separately in this book. The Dornier 228-100 has the standard 15 m (49 ft 4 in) long fuselage while the stretched 228-200 is longer by 1.5 m (4 ft 9 in). Civil specialist versions include pollution surveillance and geophysical survey. India licence builds the aircraft as it is no longer produced in Germany.

Variants and operators

Dornier 228: Air Caledonie; Air Jamaica; Air Malawi; Air Maldives; Air Marshall Islands; Druk Air; Flexair; Formosa; Highland Air; Jagson; Olympic; SA Airlink; Sata; Silkair; Societe Nouvelle; Suckling; Tahiti Conquest; Taiwan

Payload

Passengers: 20
Cargo: 2,127 kg (4,689 lb)
Range: 1,343 km (724 nm)

Features: High/straight wing; twin turboprops; swept wingtips

249

Dornier Do. 328 Germany

Short-haul commuter

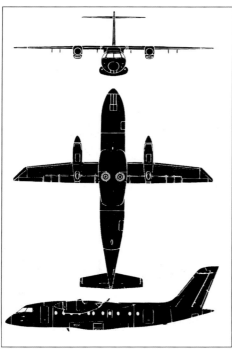

Length: 21.3 m (69 ft 9 in) Wingspan: 21 m (68 ft 10 in) Height: 7.3 m (23 ft 9 in)

Features: High/straight wing; swept wingtips; T-tail

250

Dornier first flew the 328 in 1991, and are already studying radical developments. A turbofan powered version, the 328JET flew in January 1998, retaining the fuselage and wing of the original. A hydrogen powered version is also under consideration with two large underwing tanks.

Variants and operators

Dornier 328: Afrimex Aviation; Air Alps; Air Engiadina; Air Salzburg; Air Stord; Air Ukraine; Archana; Arcus Air; Corning Glass; Federico II; Formosa Airlines; Horizon Air; Lone Star; Minerva; Mountain Air Express; PB Air; Proteus; Air France; Air Inter; PSA; US Air Express; Satena; Suckling; Air UK; Thuringia; Tyrolean Jet Service; Western Pacific

328JET: Aspern Air; Midwest Express; Modern Air; Proteus

Payload

Passengers: 33
Cargo: 3,450 kg (7,605 lb)
Range: 1,556 km (840 nm)

Douglas DC-6 USA

Long-haul cargoliner

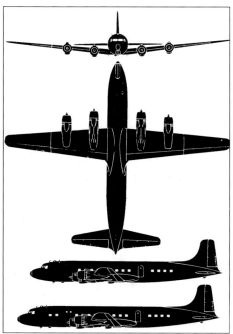

The elderly DC-6 is still in use as a cargo aircraft in North and South America. First flown in 1946, 176 aircraft were built including C-118 Liftmasters for the US Air Force. The stretched DC-7 replaced in production, of which 336 were built. DC-7s can be recognized by the longer fuselage and straight centre wing section.

Variants and operators
DC-6: Dominica de Aviacon; Filair; Northern Air Cargo; Trans-Air-Link

Payload
Passengers: 76
Cargo: 12,247 kg (27,000 lb)
Range: 6,112 km (3,300 nm)

Features: Low/straight wing; four radial engines; dihedral wing

Length: 30.7 m (100 ft 7 in) Wingspan: 13.6 m (117 ft 6 in) Height: 8.7 m (28 ft 5 in)

251

EMBRAER EMB-110 Bandeirante Brazil

Short-haul commuter

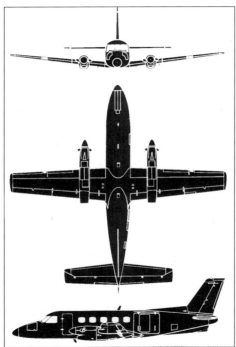

Length: 14.6 m (47 ft 10 in) Wingspan: 15.3 m (50 ft 3 in) Height: 4.9 m (16 ft 1 in)

Features: Low/straight wing; twin turboprops; ventral tail fin

500 Bandeirantes have been sold to operators in 80 countries since the Brazilian air force took delivery of the first in 1973. The Brazilian Air Force operate a large number of EMB-110s in transport, search and rescue, aerial survey, electronic training and Navaid calibration variants. A maritime patrol version was produced with a longer nose section containing a search radar, and underwing hardpoints, designated EMB-111.

Variants and operators

EMB-110: Aeroperlas; Air Burkina; Air Creebec; Air Fiji; Air Vanuatu; AIRES; Brasil Central; Eagle; Flight West; MUK; Nordeste; Sun-Air; TABA

Payload

Passengers: 21
Cargo: 1,712 kg (3,774 lb)
Range: 2,000 km (1,080 nm)

EMBRAER EMB-120 Brasilia Brazil

Medium-haul commuter

First flown in 1983 two retrofit kits have become available for the Brasilia, the EMB-120ER with increased range and payload and the EMB-120RT short take-off version powered by Pratt & Whittney PW118 engines. All production models are now finished to EMB-120ER standard. A cargo version is also available with a payload of 3,403 kg (7,500 lb)

Variants and operators

EMB-120: Air Aruba; Air Exel; Air Littoral; Air Midwest; Air Normandie; ASA; Bop Air; Britt; Comair; Delta Air Transport; DLT; Ematec; Flight West; Great Lakes; Interbrasil; Luxair; Mesa; Midway; Nordeste; Norsk Air; Ontario Express; Pantanal; Passarredo; Penta; Rio-Sul; Sky West; Star; Texas Air; Total; UTC, WestAir

Payload

Passengers: 30
Cargo: 2,950 kg (6,504 lb)
Range: 3,185 km (1,720 nm)

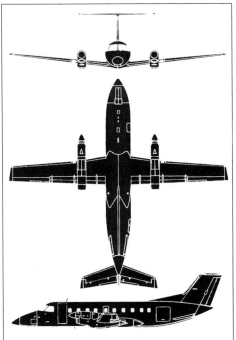

Features: Low/straight wing; twin turboprops; T-tail

Length: 20 m (65 ft 7 in) Wingspan: 19.8 m (64 ft 10 in) Height: 6.4 m (20 ft 10 in)

Fairchild Metro USA

Medium-haul commuter

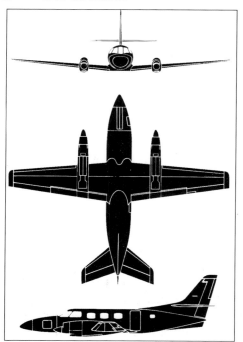

Length: 18 m (59 ft 4 in) Wingspan: 17.4 m (57 ft) Height: 5 m (16 ft 8 in)

Features: Low/straight wing; twin turboprops; mid-mounted swept tail

Over 1,000 Metros have been produced since 1966, with deliveries to civil and military operators. The Merlin is an executive transport version with seating for 14, the Expediter is a parcel delivery aircraft. Special mission variants have been tested by the USAF and include AEW, surveillance and ELINT models.

Variants and operators

Metro/Merlin/Metroliner: Aerosur; Air Atlantique; Comair; Empire; European Air Transport; Hazelton; Horizon; Jetall; Lone Star; Mesaba; Provincial; Skywest

Payload

Passengers: 30
Cargo: 2,268 kg (5,000 lb)
Range: 2,065 km (1,115 nm)

Fokker F27 Friendship Netherlands

Short-haul airliner

First flown in 1955, deliveries began in 1958 and continued until the larger Fokker 50 replaced it in production in 1986. Of the 786 built, Fairchild produced 205 in the USA as the FH-227, minor changes were made to the US-built version (bottom silhouette), the forward cargo door was reduced in size to allow for more passengers.

Variants and operators

F-27: Air Algerie; Air Comores; Air Ivorie; Air Sinai; Airkenya; Brasil Central; Channel Express; Comair; Cubana; East-West; Egyptair; Empire; Expresso Aero; Farner Air; FedEx; Iran Asseman; Jersey European; Lesotho; Libyan Arab; Lignes; Lloyd; Merpati; Myanma; Pakistan International; Ratioflug; Sempati; TAAG; **FH-227:** Aero Cozumel; Aerocaribe; AIRES; CATA; Iran Asseman; Empire; TABA

Payload Passengers: 60
Cargo: 5,896 kg (13,000 lb)
Range: 1,741 km (935 nm)

Features: High/straight wing; twin turboprops; cranked tailfin

Length: 23.6 m (77 ft 3 in) Wingspan: 29 m (95 ft 1 in) Height: 8.6 m (28 ft 2 in)

255

Fokker 50 Netherlands

Medium-haul airliner

Length: 25.3 m (82 ft 10 in) Wingspan: 29 m (95 ft 1 in) Height: 8.3 m (27 ft 3 in)

Features: High/straight wing; twin turboprops; longer fuselage

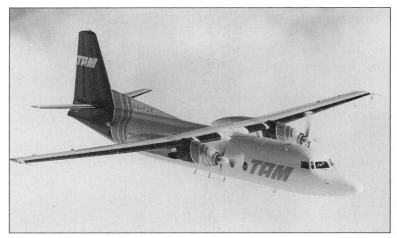

A follow-on development of the F27 the first F50 prototypes flew in 1985 using existing fuselages wedded to a new wing and engine assembly. Production versions made great use of composite materials and advance manufacturing techniques. The passenger door was relocated to the front, the fuselage stretched and more windows installed.

Variants and operators

F50: Aer Lingus; Aerovias; Air Nostrum; Air Zimbabwe; Contact; Ethiopian; Formosa; Icelandair; Kenya; KLM Cityhopper; Luxair; Malaysia; Nordeste; Palestine; Philippine; TAM; VLM

Payload

Passengers: 58
Cargo: 6,846 kg (15,093 lb)
Range: 2,252 km (1,216 nm)

Ilyushin Il-18 Coot Russia

Long-haul airliner

The Il-18 prototype first flew in 1957 under the name Moskva (Moscow). Production began in 1959 with deliveries beginning later that year. The Il-18 formed the basis of the Il-20 reconnaissance and Il-38 May maritime patrol aircraft. Cargo variants were produced for Aeroflot, and an atmospheric research aircraft the Il-18D Cyclone.

Variants and operators

Il-18: Aeroflot; Balkan Bulgarian; Romavia; TAROM; Vietnam

Payload

Passengers: 110
Cargo: 13,500 kg (29,750 lb)
Range: 6,500 km (3,508 nm)

Length: 35.9 m (117 ft 9 in) Wingspan: 37.4 m (122 ft 8 in) Height: 10.2 m (33 ft 4 in)

Features: Low/straight wing; four turboprops; deeper inner engine nacelles

257

Ilyushin Il-114 Russia

Medium-haul airliner

Length: 26.9 m (88 ft 2 in) Wingspan: 30 m (98 ft 5 in) Height: 9.3 m (30 ft 7 in)

Features: Low/straight wing; twin turboprops; low-mounted tail plane

Designed to replace the An-24 as the standard feederliner for internal Russian airways. The Il-114 has had a troubled development with government funding being removed after the crash of the second prototype. Uzbekistan Airlines had two before they were grounded due to a lack of adequate overhaul facilities. Ilyushin is now receiving export interest, Iran has discussed setting up a licence-build production line but no orders have yet been announced.

Variants and operators

Il-114: Balkan Bulgarian; Uzbekistan - awaiting firm orders

Payload

Passengers: 75
Cargo: 6,500 kg (14,330 lb)
Range: 4,800 km (2,490 nm)

IPTN N-250 Indonesia

Short-haul airliner

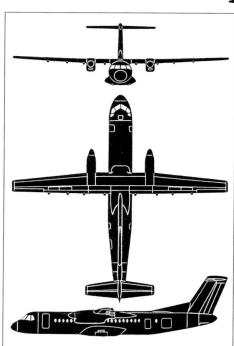

Indonesia's first indigenous transport aircraft, the N-250 first flew in 1995. Production may be started in USA and Germany if orders reach 18 a year. The three versions available include the short fuselage N-250-50, mid length N-250-100 and stretched N-270. IPTN also plan to develop an AEW version fitted with the Erieye or Argus radar system.

Variants and operators

N-250: Garuda; Sempati - awaiting firm orders

Payload

Passengers: 62
Cargo: 6,000 kg (13,227 lb)
Range: 1,481 km (800 nm)

Features: High/straight wing; twin turboprops; T-tail

259

LET L-410 Turbolet Czech Republic

Short-haul commuter

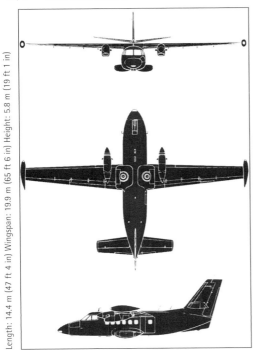

Length: 14.4 m (47 ft 4 in) Wingspan: 19.9 m (65 ft 6 in) Height: 5.8 m (19 ft 1 in)

Features: High/straight wing; twin turboprops; wingtip tanks

The L-410 was chosen as the standard aircraft to replace Li-2 (DC-3) airliners in the former eastern bloc in 1970. By 1997 1,050 had been built and were operating in 40 countries. A stretched version the L-430 is under development and internal configurations can include commuter, executive, air ambulance and paratroop transport.

Variants and operators

L-410: Argentina; Belarus; Bolivia; Brazil; Bulgaria; Caribbean; Chile; Colombia; Congo; Costa Rica; Czech Rep: Denmark; Djibouti; Dominican Rep; Egypt; Estonia; Finland; Gabon; Germany; Guinea; Hungary; India; Kazakstan; Kenya; Latvia; Libya; Lithuania; Mali; Philippines; Poland; Russia; Slovak Rep; Slovenia; Somalia; South Africa; Sudan; Tunisia; Uganda; Ukraine; UK; USA; Zaire

Payload

Passengers: 19
Cargo: 1,615 kg (3,560 lb)
Range: 1,380 km (744 nm)

LET L-610 Czech Republic

Medium-range commuter

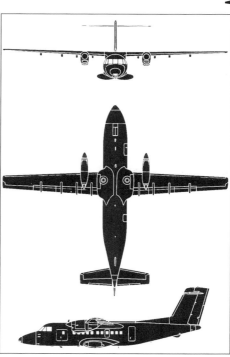

Length: 21.7 m (71 ft 3 in) Wingspan: 25.6 m (84 ft) Height: 8.2 m (26 ft 10 in)

Developed as a follow-on to the L-410 the L-610 first flew in 1992. Financial problems in former eastern bloc nations led to the type failing to get the large orders hoped for. Let are now trying to export it to the West and the prototypes are currently undergoing US certification. Of similar design to the L-410 it has a T-tail and lacks the wingtip tanks.

Variants and operators
L-610: CSA - awaiting firm orders

Payload
Passengers: 40
Cargo: 4,200 kg (9,259 lb)
Range: 2,370 km (1,280 nm)

Features: High/straight wing; twin turboprops; T-tail

Lockheed L-188 Electra USA

Medium-haul airliner

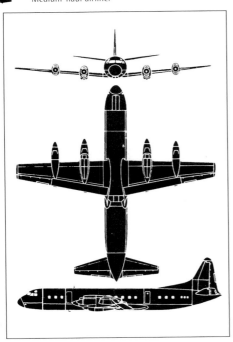

Length: 31.8 m (104 ft 6 in) Wingspan: 30.2 m (99 ft) Height: 9.8 m (32 ft 1 in)

Features: Low/straight wing; four turboprops; dihedral tailplane

The first Electras were ordered straight from the drawing board before the first prototype flew in 1957. Designed as insurance against the failure of then-revolutionary turbojet airliners only 175 Electras were built, many remaining in service. The airframe was used to develop the P-3 Orion anti-submarine patrol aircraft.

Variants and operators

L-188: Air Atlantique; Channel Express; Filair; Fred Olsen; Hunting Cargo; Mandala; Reeve Alleutian; Zantop

Payload

Passengers: 85
Cargo: 9,815 kg (21,638 lb)
Range: 4,458 km (2,407 nm)

Raytheon (Beechcraft) 1900 USA

Medium-haul commuter

Length: 17.6 m (57 ft 10 in) Wingspan: 17.7 m (57 ft 11 in) Height: 4.7 m (15 ft 6 in)

First flown in 1982 the 1900 has been produced in both commuter and executive versions. The USAF and Egyptian air force operate them in a transport role the Egyptians also using them for maritime patrol and ELINT work.

Variants and operators

BE-1900: Air Alliance; Air Creebec; Air Express; Air MidWest; Air Namibia; Continental Express; Danish Air; Liberty; Mesa; MidWest

Payload

Passengers: 19
Cargo: 907 kg (2,000 lb)
Range: 2,778 km (1,500 nm)

Features: Low/straight wing; twin turboprops; T-tail with winglets

Saab 340B Sweden

Short-haul commuter

Length: 19.7 m (64 ft 8 in) Wingspan: 21.4 m (70 ft 4 in) Height: 6.9 m (22 ft 10 in)

Features: Low/straight wing; twin turboprops; dihedral tailplane

Originally a joint Saab-Fairchild project, Saab took full responsibility in 1985 with the aircraft making its first flight 1983. The initial version was improved to keep up with customer demands, the 340B was developed for hot and high climates and the 340BPlus incorporated many of the improvements of the Saab 2000. Combi passenger/cargo version and search and rescue versions are also available

Variants and operators

Saab 340B: Aigle Azur; Air Baltic; Air Nelson; Air Osrava; AMP; AMR Eagle; Andesmar; Brit Air; Business Air; Business Express; Calm Air; Chautauqua; Chicago Express; Colgan; Comair; Crossair; Deutsche BA; Finnaviation; FMV; Formosa; Golden Air; Goodyear; Grossman; Hazelton; Japan Air Commuter; Japan Maritime Safety Agency (search and rescue); Kendell; KLM Cityhopper; LAPA; Mellon Bank; Mesaba; NWAL; Raslan; Regional; regional Lineas Aereas; Shandong; Skyways; Slovak; TAN; TAPSA; Tatra

Payload

Passengers: 37
Cargo: 3,880 kg (8,554 lb)
Range: 1,732 km (935 nm)

Saab 2000 Sweden

Medium-haul airliner

More than a stretched version of the Saab 340 with which it shares common parts, the Saab 2000 was designed using CAD/CAM technology and a new technology wing enables the aircraft to attain jet like speed with turboprop efficiency. It may become the standard airframe for the Swedish AEW requirement, which currently uses the Saab 340.

Variants and operators

Saab 2000: Air Marshall Islands; Crossair; Regional Airlines; Skyways; SAS; Deutsche BA; Lithuanian; GM World Travel

Payload

Passengers: 50
Cargo: 5,900 kg (13,007 lb)
Range: 2,639 km (1,425 nm)

Length: 27 m (88 ft 8 in) Wingspan: 24.8 m (81 ft 2 in) Height: 7.7 m (25 ft 4 in)

Features: Low/straight wing; twin turboprops; dihedral tailplane

265

Shorts 330 UK

Medium-haul commuter

Length: 17.7 m (58 ft) Wingspan: 22.8 m (74 ft 10 in) Height: 5 m (16 ft 5 in)

Features: High/straight wing; twin turboprops; twin tail

Derived from the smaller Skyvan the Shorts 330 first flew in 1974. The standard passenger version has been followed by the 330-UTT utility transport and Sherpa cargo aircraft. Both have strengthened fuselage floors and a rear loading ramp. US Air National Guard and USAF operate cargo versions designated C-23 for short/small cargo missions.

Variants and operators
S.330: MUK; Olympic Aviation; Sunflower **C-23:** USAF

Payload
Passengers: 30
Cargo: 3,302 kg (7,280 lb)
Range: 1,912 km (1,031 nm)

Shorts 360 Sherpa UK

Short-haul commuter

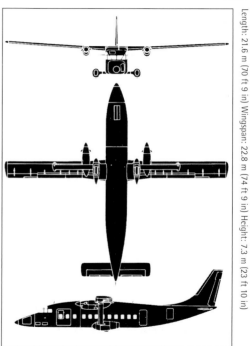

Length: 21.6 m (70 ft 9 in) Wingspan: 22.8 m (74 ft 9 in) Height: 7.3 m (23 ft 10 in)

The re-design of the Shorts 330 led to a re-modeled single tailfin and improved engines. The Shorts 360 first flew in this form in 1981. The latest version, 360-300, features synchrophasing propellers, cambered wing struts and low-drag engine nacelles to improve speed and range.

Variants and operators

Shorts 360: Aeroperlas; Air Atlantique; Air Kenya; AMR Eagle; Aurigny; Bahamasair; Canadian Regional; CCair; Gill; Jersey European; La Costera; Liberty; Loganair; Manx; MUK; Philippine; Sunstate; U-Land

Payload

Passengers: 36
Cargo: 3,765 kg (8,300 lb)
Range: 1,178 km (636 nm)

Features: High/straight wing; twin turboprops; wing bracing struts

267

CIVIL UTILITY AIRCRAFT

Aeroprogress T-101 Grach Russia

Utility aircraft

Aeroprogress was founded in 1990 to design and build utility aircraft. The T-101 was their first design to fly, in 1994. Designed as a replacement for the An-2 Colt series of aircraft, the T-101SKh is remarkable in having the same wing as the others but its is attached to the lower fuselage and the bracing struts inverted. This enables it to operate chemical spray jets like other agricultural aircraft.

Variants and operators

T-101P: firefighter on non-amphibious floats
T-101L: ski landing gear **T-101SKh:** agricultural version with low wing **T-101S:** military version with two wing hardpoints **T-101V:** floatplane

Payload

Passengers: 11
Cargo: 3,086 kg (1,400 lb)
Range: 1,270 km (685 nm)

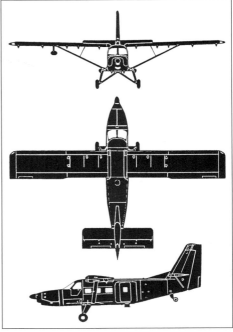

Features: High/straight wing; single turboprop; fixed strut landing gear

Length: 15.1 m (49 ft 5 in) Wingspan: 18.2 m (59 ft 8 in) Height: 4.9 m (15 ft 11 in)

AeroRIC Dingo Russia

Air cushioned utility aircraft

Length: 12.9 m (42 ft 5 in) Wingspan: 14.6 m (46 ft 9 in) Height: 3.4 m (11 ft 2 in)

Features: Low/straight wing; twin boom tail; air cushion landing gear

The Dingo combines a conventional twin boom pusher structure with a unique air cushion landing gear system. An air cushion is formed under the wings and central fuselage and contained using the two float like bladders. Capable of operation from snow, water, ice and normal airfields it can also clear objects 30 cm (1 ft) high and ditches up to 1 m (3 ft 3 in) allowing for operation from very rough sites and tundra type wastes.

Variants and operators
Production of the first 15 is just beginning

Payload
Passengers: 9
Cargo: 850 kg (1,874 lb)
Range: 1,500 km (810 nm)

ASTA (GAF) Nomad Australia

STOL utility aircraft

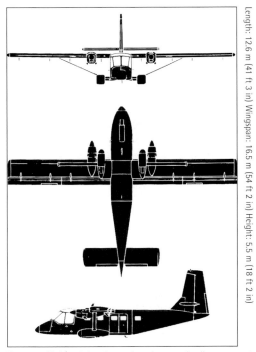

Length: 12.6 m (41 ft 3 in) Wingspan: 16.5 m (54 ft 2 in) Height: 5.5 m (18 ft 2 in)

First flown in 1971 the Nomad was designed as a feederliner and transport for operations in the Australian outback. Its rugged design has made it adaptable to many bush-type operations and military service. Australia's famed Flying Doctor service operate the Medicmaster air ambulance, Thailand, Indonesia and Australian coast guard operate the maritime patrol versions.

Variants and operators

N22B: short fuselage civil transport
Medicmaster: air ambulance **Surveymaster:**
geological and geophysical research platform
Floatmaster: amphibious version equipped with
floats **N24A:** stretched fuselage civil transport
Searchmaster: maritime patrol

Payload

Passengers: 12
Cargo: 784 kg (1,784 lb)
Range: 1,352 km (730 nm)

Features: High/straight wing; twin turboprops; landing gear spats

271

Antonov An-2 Colt Ukraine

Utility biplane

Length: 12.9 m (42 ft 6 in) Wingspan: 18.2 m (59 ft 8 in) Height: 4.2 m (13 ft 9 in)

Features: Straight/biplane; single rotary or turboprop engine; fixed landing gear

More than 5,000 An-2s were built in Ukraine following its first flight in 1947. Production moved to Poland in 1960 where a further 11,730 were built. Limited production continues in Poland and China. An upgraded version has been fitted with a Glushenkov turboprop in Ukraine and is known as the An-3 (picture).

Variants and operators

An-2A: Metrological research aircraft **An-2L:** firefighter **An-2M:** agricultural crop sprayer **An-2V:** floatplane **An-2S:** air ambulance **Y-5B:** Chinese agricultural aircraft **Y-5N:** Chinese transport version

Payload

Passengers: 12
Cargo: 1,500 kg (3,300 lb)
Range: 905 km (488 nm)

Antonov An-14 Clod Ukraine

STOL utility aircraft

Despite flying in 1958 it was not until 1965 that the An-14 entered serial production. Major re-design work was carried out on the wing and tail assembly, clamshell doors were installed in the tail to assist loading. Called Pchelka (little bee) in Russian service, the An-14 was also built in small numbers in China.

Variants and operators

An-14: agricultural sprayer; cloud seeder; transport; executive transport

Payload

Passengers: 8
Cargo: 720 kg (1,590 lb)
Range: 680 km (366 nm)

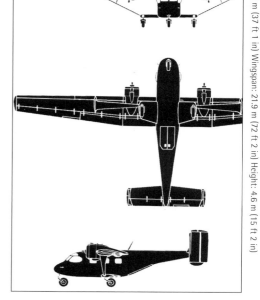

Features: High/straight wing; twin piston engines; twin tails

Length: 11.3 m (37 ft 1 in) Wingspan: 21.9 m (72 ft 2 in) Height: 4.6 m (15 ft 2 in)

273

Antonov An-30 Clank Ukraine

Aerial survey aircraft

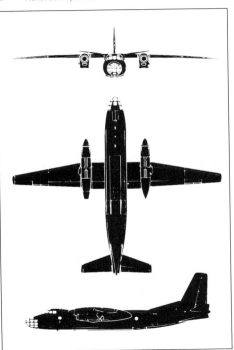

Length: 24.3 m (79 ft 7 in) Wingspan: 29.2 m (95 ft 9 in) Height: 8.3 m (27 ft 3 in)

Features: High/straight wing; twin turboprops; glazed nose

A specially designed An-26, the Clank was primarily used for photographic surveillance. Since then it has found a number of specialist roles, the most bizarre being an aerial rainmaker. Containers of frozen carbon dioxide are ejected in flight to create artificial rainclouds.

Variants and operators

An-30: Afghanistan; Bulgaria; China; Cuba; Czech Republic; Kazakhstan; Romania; Russia; Vietnam

Payload

Crew: 7
Equipment: 5,500 kg (12,125 lb)
Range: 2,630 km (1,420 nm)

Canadair CL-415 Canada

Utility amphibian

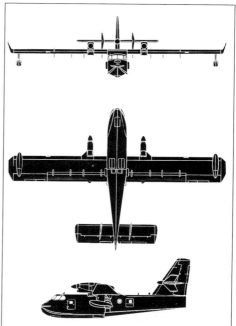

Length: 19.8 m (65 ft) Wingspan: 28.6 m (93 ft 11 in) Height: 8.9 m (29 ft 5 in)

The original Canadiar CL-215 was powered by a pair of radial piston engines, in 1991 it was decided to fit all production aircraft with turboprops and refit older CL-215s with the new engine. New built aircraft were designated CL-415, re-engined aircraft as CL-215T. A purpose built aerial firefighter the CL-415 can deliver 6,140 litters (1,622 US gallons) in one pass, or more than 50,000 litters (14,303 US gallons) in three hours.

Variants and operators

CL-215: two radial piston engines **CL-415:** standard firefighter, in service in Canada, Croatia, Greece, France and Italy **CL-415M:** under development for maritime patrol and special missions

Payload

Passengers: 30 max
Cargo: 6,123 kg (13,500 lb)
Range: 2,426 km (1,310 nm)

Features: High/straight wing; high-mounted twin turboprops; amphibian hull

275

Cessna 208 Caravan 1 USA

Utility transport

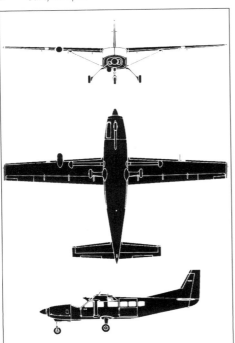

Length: 11.5 m (37 ft 7 in) Wingspan: 15.8 m (52 ft 1 in) Height: 3.6 m (11 ft 8 in)

Features: High/straight wing; single turboprop; ventral pannier

Commissioned by Federal Express the Caravan was designed to carry small packages and mail from widely dispersed post offices in the USA. Over 844 have now been built and operate in 52 countries. Since it first flew in 1984, the Caravan has been modified to carry greater loads, while a new quick change interior means it can carry up to 14 passengers in place of the mail.

Variants and operators

208: standard mail carrier with underfuselage pannier **208B**: stretched fuselage version with no cabin windows **208Floatplane**: fitted with amphibious floats

Payload

Passengers: 7-14
Cargo: 1,587 kg (3,500 lb)
Range: 2009 km (1,085 nm)

De Havilland Canada DHC-2 Beaver Canada

Utility STOL aircraft

Most of the 1,692 Beavers produced were delivered to the US Army and USAF, where it was designated U-6A. First flown in 1947 it is no longer in service with the US armed forces. However many ex-military examples have found their way into civil hands. The Turbo Beaver has a much longer, pointed nose with a PT-6A turboprop.

Variants and operators
DHC-2: standard piston engined STOL transport
DHC-2 Mk1: Beaver amphibious floatplane
DHC-2 Turbo Beaver: upgraded with a single turboprop

Payload
Passengers: 7
Cargo:
Range: 1,252 km (676 nm)

Features: High/straight wing; single radial piston engine, curved tailfin

277

De Havilland Canada DHC-6 Twin Otter Canada

Utility STOL aircraft

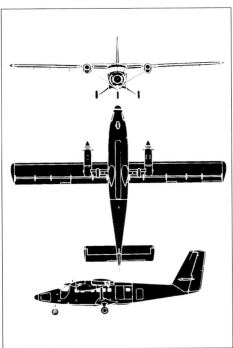

Length: 15.8 m (51 ft 9 in) Wingspan: 19.8 m (65 ft 6 in) Height: 5.9 m (19 ft 6 in)

Designed for bush operations the Twin Otter first flew in 1965. Delivered to the US and Canadian Armed Forces the Twin Otter remains in service in the airforces of Argentina, Chile, Haiti, Norway and Paraguay. The floatplane version has a smaller nose section and ventral fins under the tail. Some 844 were produced in both military and civil versions and many are still operated in 80 countries.

Variants and operators

DHC-6 series 100: original transport version
DHC-6 series 200/300: fitted with more powerful engines **DHC-6 Floatplane:** amphibious transport **DHC-6M:** military versions including transport, counter insurgency and maritime reconnaissance.

Payload

Passengers: 20
Cargo: 1,941 kg (4,280 lb)
Range: 1,704 km (920 nm)

Features: High/straight wing; twin turboprops; fixed landing gear

Dornier Do.28D Skyservant Germany

Utility STOL aircraft

The Skyservant's distinctive engine arrangement makes it simple to identify; both engines are fixed by small wings to the lower fuselage, the landing gear is then fixed to the engine nacelles. This leaves the leading edge of the wing unbroken from root to wingtip and improves efficiency, which helped set a number of records within its class. The Turbo Skyservant is powered by two PT-6A turboprops and has longer engine nacelles.

Variants and operators

Do.28: El Salvador; Germany; Greece; Kenya; Malawi; Morocco; Niger; Thailand; Turkey **Do.28 Turbo Skyservant:** Cameroon; Nigeria

Payload

Passengers: 13
Cargo: 1,273 kg (2,806 lb)
Range: 1,050 km (566 nm)

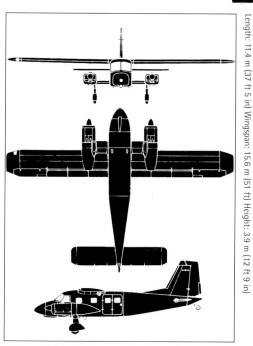

Length: 11.4 m (37 ft 5 in) Wingspan: 15.6 m (51 ft) Height: 3.9 m (12 ft 9 in)

Features: High/straight wing; twin piston engines; engines fixed to landing gear

279

Galivan 358 Colombia

Utility aircraft

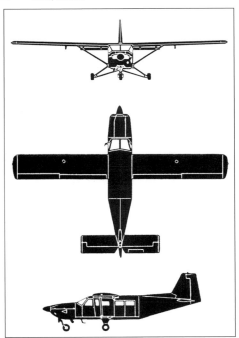

Length: 9.5 m (31 ft 3 in) Wingspan: 12.8 m (42 ft) Height: 3.7 m (12 ft 3 in)

Features: High/straight wing; single piston engine; large square windows

Colombia's first indigenous design, the Galivan project started in 1987 and the final version was flying by 1990. The Colombian Air Force is expected to be the launch customer, and is negotiating for 10. Convertible to passenger, cargo or ambulance the Galivan looks similar to the Cessna Caravan or larger Piper aircraft. The large square windows, and square cross section fuselage set it apart.

Variants and operators
Production planned at four per month

Payload
Passengers: 8
Cargo: 716 kg (1,580 lb)
Range: 1,750 km (945 nm)

Grob G-250 Strato Germany

High altitude surveillance and research aircraft

Developed by a consortium of companies to meet a German Luftwaffe requirement, the Strato first flew under the name Egrett in 1987. The Luftwaffe cancelled its order in 1994 and Grob is now looking at civilian environment agencies and export orders.

Variants and operators

G-250: standard production version

Payload

12 payload bays in fuselage for a wide range of communications, optical and research equipment

Features: Mid/straight wing; one turboprop; high altitude wing form

Length: 12 m (39 ft 4 in) Wingspan: 33 m (108 ft 3 in)
Height: 5.7 m (18 ft 7 in)

HAMC Y-12 China

Utility STOL aircraft

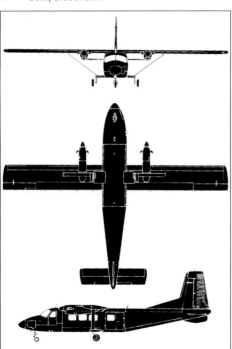

Length: 14.9 m (48 ft 9 in) Wingspan: 17.2 m (56 ft 6 in) Height: 5.7 m (18 ft 7 in)

Features: High/straight wing; twin turboprops; ventral fin

The original Y-12 (I) has been replaced in production by the improved Y-12 (II) which has higher rated engines and a smaller ventral fin. The latest version, Y-12 (III) has a higher all-up weight, western avionics and modifications to the wingtips and landing gear. Future developments include a stretched fuselage and one with a pressurized cabin.

Variants and operators

Y-12: Cambodia; China General Aviation; China Southwest; Flying Dragon; Guizhou; Zongfei; Eritrea; Fiji Air; Iran Air; Lao Aviation; Berjaya Air Charter; Mauritania; Mongolian; Nepal; Pakistan; Peru; Island Holding; Sri Lanka; Tanzania; Zambia; Zimbabwe

Payload

Passengers: 17
Cargo: 1,700 kg (3,748 lb)
Range: 1,340 km (723 nm)

Helio AU-24A Stallion USA

Light utility STOL aircraft

First flown in 1964 the Stallion was used extensively in South East Asia by the USAF and paramilitary units. Most aircraft ended up in the Lao and Cambodian air force's. Helio tried to put it back in production in the mid 80s but could find no launch customers.

Variants and operators
AU-24A: military version H-600B: civil version

Payload
Passengers: 10
Cargo: 644 kg (1,420 lb)
Range: 1,755 km (1,090 nm)

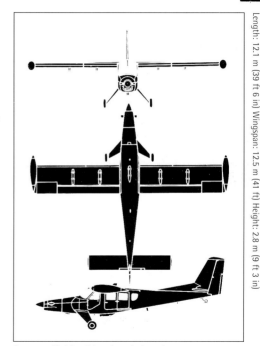

Length: 12.1 m (39 ft 6 in) Wingspan: 12.5 m (41 ft) Height: 2.8 m (9 ft 3 in)

Features: High/straight wing; single turboprop; swept fixed landing gear

283

Helio Super Courier USA

Light utility STOL aircraft

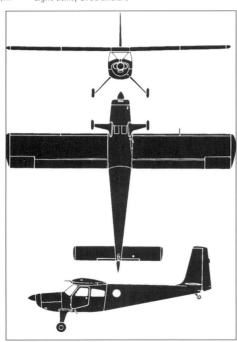

Length: 9.4 m (31 ft) Wingspan: 11.9 m (39 ft) Height: 2.7 m (8 ft 10 in)

Features: High/straight wing; single piston engine; fixed landing gear

The Super Courier pioneered Helio's STOL wing embodying slotted trailing edge slats over three quarters of the length of the wing. This wing gave it unparalleled characteristics when it first flew in 1958. Reputedly a very difficult aircraft to master, later versions included tricycle landing gear, a turboprop and floats.

Variants and operators

Super Courier: standard civil version **U-10:** USAF designation **Trigear:** with tricycle landing gear

Payload

Passengers: 6
Cargo: 454 kg (1000 lb)
Range: 2,220 km (1,198 nm)

Mitsubishi Mu-2 Japan

Utility STOL aircraft

The last Mu-2 was built in 1987 after 755 had been produced. The Mu-2 has been fitted with a number of engines, the major variants include a search and rescue aircraft with a thimble radar in the nose and a stretched version with a 2.8 m (9 ft 1 in) fuselage extension.

Variants and operators

Mu-2: standard production version **Mu-2J/N/K/P:** up-engined version **Mu-2L/M:** stretched versions

Payload

Passengers: 8
Cargo: 170 kg (374 lb)
Range: 2,700 km (1,460 nm)

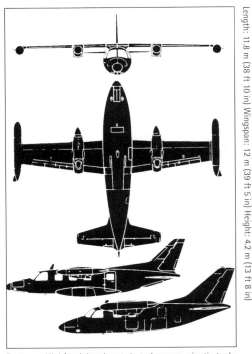

Length: 11.8 m (38 ft 10 in) Wingspan: 12 m (39 ft 5 in) Height: 4.2 m (13 ft 8 in)

Features: High/straight wing; twin turboprops; wingtip tanks

Myasishchev M-101T Russia

Light utility aircraft

Length: 9.9 m (32 ft 5 in) Wingspan: 13 m (42 ft 8 in) Height: 3.7 m (12 ft 2 in)

Features: Low/straight wing; single turboprop; long nose section

First displayed at the Moscow Air Show in 1990, the first prototype flew in 1995. A number of different engines were used before production began in 1997. Production aircraft use a Walter turboprop. Westernized versions will be fitted with a Pratt & Whittney turboprop, improved avionics and a Hartzell propeller.

Variants and operators

M-101T: standard production model with Russian engine and avionics M-101PW: Westernized version

Payload

Passengers: 2 pilots; 4 passengers
Cargo: 540 kg (1,190 lb)
Range: 2,500 km (1,349 nm)

Partenavia P.68 Victor Italy/India

Light utility aircraft

Production began in 1978 in Italy but was moved to India in 1994 after 400 had been built. TAAL of India has three main versions in production aside from the basic P.68C transport, a turbocharged version for better hot and high performance is available designated P.68TC. The P.68 Observer is used by specialist government surveillance units such as border and coastal patrol. It can be recognized by its transparent nose section.

Variants and operators
P.68: standard production version **P.68**
Observer: with fully glazed nose **P.68 Pulsar:** with retractable landing gear

Payload
Passengers: 6
Cargo: 181 kg (399 lb)
Range: 2,241 km (1,210 nm)

Features: High/straight wing; twin piston engines; fixed landing gear with spats

Length: 9.5 m (31 ft 4 in) Wingspan: 12 m (39 ft 4 in) Height: 3.4 m (11 ft 1 in)

287

Pilatus PC-6 Turbo Porter Switzerland

Utility STOL aircraft

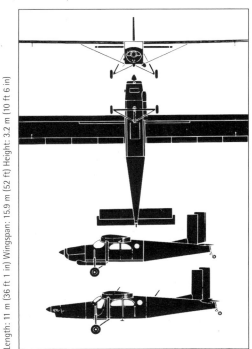

Length: 11 m (36 ft 1 in) Wingspan: 15.9 m (52 ft) Height: 3.2 m (10 ft 6 in)

Features: High/straight wing; single turboprop; square tailfin

Pilatus designed the Porter to operate in restricted areas such as the Alps and glaciers. It is capable of operating from strips as short as 360 ft, and with its engine in full reverse can come to a halt in under 70 ft. To allow safe operation within the confines of mountainous regions it can climb at 45 degrees at 1,700 ft per second. The upper silhouette shows the shorter nose section of the original piston engined Porter.

Variants and operators

PC-6: initial piston engined version **PC-6 Turbo Porter:** standard production version **AU-23A:** armed version

Payload

Passengers: 11
Cargo: 1,130 kg (2,491 lb)
Range: 1,612 km (870 nm)

Pilatus PC-12 Switzerland

Short-range executive turboprop

Length: 14.4 m (47 ft 2 in) Wingspan: 19.1 m (52 ft 9 in) Height: 4.3 m (13 ft 11 in)

First flown in 1993 the PC-12 is a multi-role aircraft capable of being fitted out for light cargo personnel transport or executive transport. The PC-12 Eagle carries a ventral reconnaissance pod for surveillance missions and border patrol. Under development is a turbofan powered version with two overwing Williams FJ44s.

Variants and operators

PC-12: standard civil combi version **Executive:** six seat executive transport **Cargo:** all cargo version **Eagle:** surveillance platform

Payload

Passengers: 9
Cargo: 1,197 kg (2,639 lb)
Range: 2,963 km (1,600 nm)

Features: Low/straight wing; single turboprop; T-tail

Pilatus Britten Norman Islander UK

Utility transport

Length: 10.8 m (35 ft 7 in) Wingspan: 14.9 m (49 ft) Height: 4.2 m (13 ft 8 in)

Features: High/straight wing; twin piston engines; landing gear fixed to engines

The Islander was designed around an inexpensive airframe with low running costs to link outlying communities such as islands to the mainland by air. Romania and the Philippines produced the Islander under licence. Military versions are called Defender and can carry out a variety of missions, some have been equipped to carry AEW and stand-off battlefield surveillance radars, and can carry stores on four wing hardpoints.

Variants and operators

BN-2: standard civil version **BN-2 Defender:** armed version with two wing hardpoints **BN-2T:** with Allison turboprops

Payload

Passengers: 10
Cargo: 692 kg (1,526 lb)
Range: 2,252 km (1,216 nm)

Pilatus Britten Norman Trislander UK

Utility transport

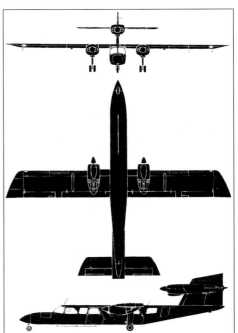

Length: 15 m (49 ft 3 in) Wingspan: 16.2 m (53 ft) Height: 4.3 m (14 ft 2 in)

The Trislander is undergoing something of a renaissance, the first to be delivered for 18 years was handed over to Aurigny Air Services in 1996. A number of uncompleted airframes are in storage in Florida and Guernsey and these are once again being offered for sale. The third engine gives the Trislander greater range and payload capability.

Variants and operators
Trislander: standard production version

Payload
Passengers: 18
Cargo: n/a
Range: 1,610 km (868 nm)

Features: High/straight wing; two wing, one tail piston engines; long nose

PZL-Warszawa PZL-105L Flaming Poland

Light utility aircraft

Length: 8.6 m (28 ft 5 in) Wingspan: 12.9 m (42 ft 6 in) Height: 2.8 m (9 ft 5 in)

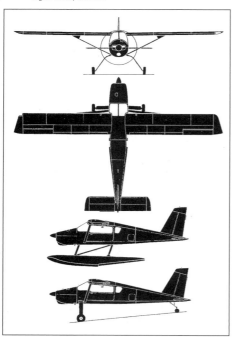

The Flaming (Flamingo) first flew in 1989. Suitable for general cargo and passenger transport the Flaming is also being used for glider towing, parachute training, air ambulance, survey, floatplane and agricultural spraying. Two engine types are on offer, a flat-six Textron unit and a Polish radial engine.

Variants and operators

PZL-105L: standard production version PZL-105M: re-engined version

Payload

Passengers: 6
Cargo: 450 kg (992 lb)
Range: 981 km (529 nm)

Features: High/straight wing; single piston engine; swept wingtips

Reims F406 Caravan II France

Utility aircraft

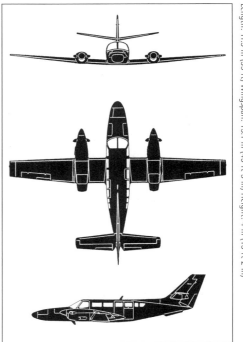

Length: 11.9 m (39 ft) Wingspan: 15.1 m (49 ft 5 in) Height: 4 m (13 ft 2 in)

First flight took place in 1983, and a number of variants have been developed since. The standard Caravan II for passenger and cargo transport. The cargo version can carry a ventral pod. A maritime patrol version has a ventral radar while the Vigilant can be fitted with FLIR and search and rescue communications systems. The Surmar can be fitted with four wing hardpoints.

Variants and operators

Caravan II: standard production version
Vigilant: surveillance version **Polmar II:** radar equipped maritime patrol **Surmar:** radar equipped with two wing hardpoints

Payload

Passengers: 12
Cargo: 1,563 kg (3,446 lb)
Range: 2,135 km (1,153 nm)

Features: Low/straight wing; twin piston engines; swept tailfin

SATIC A300-600T Beluga France

Outsized transporter

Length: 56.2 m (184 ft 10 in) Wingspan: 44.8 m (147 ft) Height: 17.3 m (57 ft 3 in)

Features: Low/swept wing; twin turbofan; outsized cargo cabin

Airbus Industrie has a requirement for four Belugas to transport sub-assemblies between the group's manufacturing plants. Airbus is now hiring out its aircraft to other companies requiring the same bulk cargo requirements. SATIC believe there is a major market for such outsized load carriers as more aircraft are built by widespread multi-national groups.

Variants and operators

A300-600T: standard production version

Payload

Passengers: four flight crew
Cargo: 45,500 kg (100,310 lb)
Range: 1,666 km (900 nm)

Socata TBM 700 France

Utility aircraft

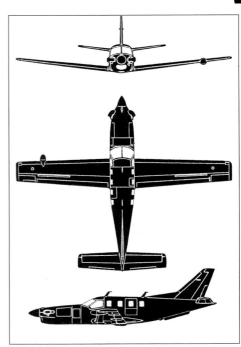

Socata describe the TBM 700 as a multi-role aircraft capable of carrying out medevac; target towing; ECM; freight cargo; maritime patrol; law enforcement; navaid calibration and aerial photography. The aircraft first flew in 1988 and over 95 have been delivered since production began in 1990.

Variants and operators

TBM 700: standard production version **TBM 700C:** cargo version **TBM 700S:** stretched version

Payload

Passengers: 7
Cargo: 150 kg (330 lb)
Range: 2,870 km (1,550 nm)

Features: Low/straight wing; single turboprop; dihedral wing and tailplane

295

Shorts Skyvan UK

Utility transport

Length: 12.2 m (40 ft 1 in) Wingspan: 19.8 m (64 ft 11 in) Height: 4.6 m (15 ft 1 in)

Features: High/straight wing; twin turboprops; box section fuselage

Design started as a private venture in 1959 with the first prototype flying in 1963. The Skyvan was the first type to be certified in the UK as a true STOL aircraft. The larger Shorts 330 and 360 were developments of the Skyvan sharing the same fuselage and wing design on a larger scale.

Variants and operators

Skyvan: standard production version
3M: military version

Payload

Passengers: 19
Cargo: 2,086 kg (4,600 lb)
Range: 1,115 km (600 nm)

Technovia SM-92 Finist Russia

Utility STOL aircraft

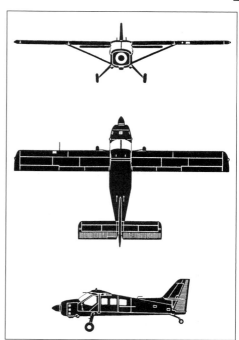

First flown in 1993 the Finist is named after the mythical bird that was transformed into a prince. An armed version for border patrol was developed alongside the civil utility aircraft. Production will be carried out in Romania and may also be started in Canada. Canadian versions may be fitted with the PT-6A turboprop.

Variants and operators
SM-92: standard production version
SM-92P: armed version for border patrol

Payload
Passengers: 7
Cargo: 600 kg (1,323 lb)
Range: 1,380 km (745 nm)

Features: High/straight wing; single radial engine; single-strut landing gear

297

UTVA 66 Yugoslavia

Light utility aircraft

Length: 8.4 m (27 ft 6 in) Wingspan: 11.4 m (37 ft 5 in) Height: 3.2 m (10 ft 6 in)

Development of the 66 began in 1967, the basic utility version can be used for glider towing and can transport four people in the liaison role. An air ambulance version can accommodate two stretcher patients and an attendant, while the 66H has been fitted with floats. In service with the armed forces of Republika Srpska and Federal Yugoslavia.

Variants and operators

UTVA 66: standard production version UTVA-66H: floatplane

Payload

Cargo: 400 kg (881 lb)
Three passengers; two stretchers

Features: High/straight wing; single piston engine; fixed landing gear

PRIVATE EXECUTIVE AIRCRAFT

AASI Jetcruzer 500 USA

Light executive aircraft

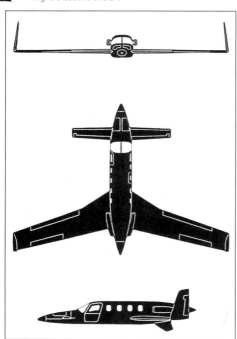

Length: 8.6 m (28 ft 2 in) Wingspan: 12.8 m (42 ft 2 in) Height: 3.2 m (10 ft 5 in)

Features: Integral swept wing with forward canards; single pusher turboprop; wingtip tailfins

The Jetcruzer first flew in 1992 and had secured around 80 orders by the time production began in 1998. The standard aircraft can be fitted out in either corporate, executive, air ambulance or transport configurations. Military versions on offer include an unmanned version to make it one of the largest UAVs available for reconnaissance missions.

Variants and operators

Jetcruzer 500: standard civil version Jetcruzer ML-1: unmanned military reconnaissance vehicle Jetcruzer ML-2: manned liaison/observation.

Payload

Passengers: 6
Cargo space: 0.71 m3 (22.25 cu ft)
Range: 2,926 km (1,580 nm)

Aerospatiale SN 601 Corvette France

Short-range executive jet

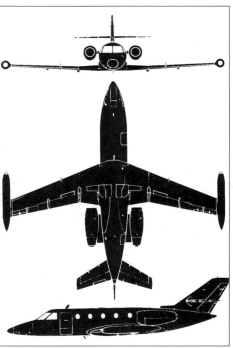

First flown in 1972, production of the 40th and final aircraft was in 1978. In addition to its executive transport role it was designed to carry out other jobs such as air ambulance, light freighter, trainer and radar calibration. Can be fitted with wingtip tanks for extended range.

Variants and operators

SN 601: sole version built between 1972 and 1978

Payload

Passengers: 14
Cargo: 1,000 kg (2,205 lb)
Range: 2,555 km (1,380 nm)

Length: 13.8 m (45 ft 4 in) Wingspan: 12.8 m (42 ft 2 in) Height: 4.2 m (13 ft 10 in)

Features: Low/swept wing; twin tail turbofans; wingtip tanks

BAe Jetstream 31 UK

Short-range executive turboprop

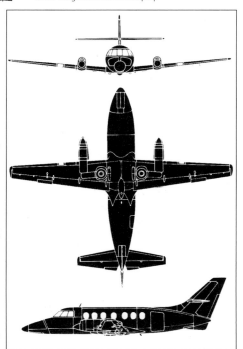

Length: 14.4 m (47 ft 1 in) Wingspan: 15.8 m (52 ft) Height: 5.4 m (17 ft 8 in)

Features: Low/straight wing; twin turboprops; mid-mounted tail

Designed by Handley Page and Scottish Aviation the original Jetstream first flew in 1967. BAe developed the original aircraft into the Jetstream 31 in 1980, changing the engines and tailoring it for the commuter and light business market. Almost 400 have been produced by BAe with fewer than 30 original Jetstream 1 and 2s remaining.

Variants and operators

Jetstream 1 / 2: Original version with Astazou engines in narrow nacelles. **Jetstream 31:** Garrett engined with intakes above propeller. **Jetstream 31EZ and T Mk.1/2/3:** aircrew trainer with ventral or nose thimble radar.

Payload

Passengers: 10
Cargo: 1,805 kg (3,980 lb)
Range: 1,111 km (643 nm)

Bombardier BD-700 Global Express Canada

Long-range executive jet

Launched in 1991 the first Global Express flew in 1996. Designed to achieve the longest possible range at high speed, Bombardier hope to grab the lion's share of the expected 500-800 new orders for long-range business jets over the next 15 years. Outfitted aircraft cost around $34 million each.

Variants and operators

BD-700: standard corporate jet **Special Missions:** Raytheon E-systems developed version for the UK's Airborne Stand-off Radar (ASTOR) requirement.

Payload

Passengers: 19
Cargo: 3,265 kg (7,200 lb)
Range: 10,158 km (5,485 nm)

Features: Low/swept wing; twin tail turbofans; T-tail

303

Canadair Challenger Canada

Medium-range executive jet

Length: 20.8 m (68 ft 5 in) Wingspan: 19.6 m (64 ft 4 in) Height: 6.3 m (20 ft 8 in)

Features: Low/swept wing; twin tail turbofans; T-tail

The Challenger began life in 1978 and formed the basis of the Canadair Regional Jet and Bombardier Global Express. A total of 367 have been produced and are operated in both the executive and regional transport role. The Canadian armed forces operate a number for coastal patrol and light transport. Costs around $20 million.

Variants and operators

Challenger 600: standard civil version, production complete **601-1A:** re-engined with CF34 engines **601-3A:** with glass cockpit and digital flight management system **601-3R:** extended range version with longer tailcone housing extra fuel tank **604:** latest long range version

Payload

Passengers: 19
Cargo: 2,377 kg (5,240 lb)
Range: 6,685 km (3,585 nm)

Cessna 525 Citationjet USA

Short-range executive jet

The smallest of the Citation family the Citationjet can be recognized by its T-tail. First flown in 1991 deliveries began in 1993 and over 200 have been produced. Cessna believes there is a market for 1,000 Citationjets which cost approximately $3.1 million apiece.

Variants and operators
Citationjet: no major variants under development

Payload
Passengers: 6
Cargo: 327 kg (721 lb)
Range: 2,750 km (1,485 nm)

Length: 12.9 m (42 ft 7 in) Wingspan: 14.3 m (46 ft 9 in) Height: 4.2 m (13 ft 8 in)

Features: Low straight wing; twin tail turbofans; T-tail

Cessna 550 Citation II USA

Medium-range executive jet

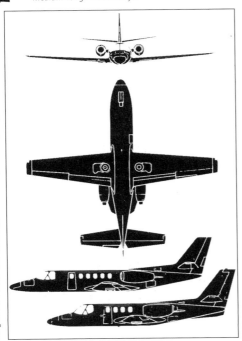

Length: 14.4 m (47 ft 2 in) Wingspan: 15.9 m (52 ft 2 in) Height: 4.6 m (15 ft)

Features: Low/straight wing; twin tail turbofans; mid-mounted tail

Cessna began production of the Citation I in 1971 and from that developed the Citation II in 1977. The Citation II used the engines, wing and fuselage of the original aircraft but was stretched with the addition of an extra fuselage section. 733 aircraft have been built at a cost of around $4.4 million each.

Variants and operators

501 Citation I: (bottom side view) earlier version
550 Citation II: stretched fuselage (top side view) **550 Citation Bravo:** advanced technology engines and digital flight controls.

Payload

Passengers: 10
Cargo: 1,406 kg (3,100 lb)
Range: 3,260 km (1,760 nm)

Cessna 650 Citation III USA

Long-range executive jet

A departure from the basic Citation line the Citation III was Cessna's first swept wing design. First flown in 1979, a simplified/low cost version the 650 Citation VI was rolled out in 1991. The two aircraft are very similar in external appearance, major changes being the replacement of the Garrett engines for AlliedSignal TFE731 turbofans, bringing the price down to around $8.1 million.

Variants and operators
Citation III: standard civil version **Citation VI:** re-engined low/cost version **Citation VII:** re-engined more powerful version of the VI

Payload
Passengers: 9
Cargo: 1,583 kg (3,489 lb)
Range: 4,348 km (2,346 nm)

Features: Low/swept wing; twin tail turbofans; T-tail

Cessna 560 Citation V USA

Medium-range executive jet

Length: 14.9 m (48 ft 10 in) Wingspan: 15.9 m (53 ft 2 in) Height: 4.6 m (15 ft)

Features: Low/straight wing; swept leading-edge roots; twin tail turbofans

Development of the standard Citation began in 1983 with the Citation S/II; changes were made to the wing and aerodynamic improvements led to decreased drag with no loss of short field performance. The Citation V was a further development flying for the first time in 1987. Stretched by 0.5 m it has a seventh cabin window.

Variants and operators

Citation S/II: improved Citation II **Citation V:** stretched S/II **T-47A:** US Navy aircrew trainer

Payload

Passengers: 10
Cargo: 2,132 kg (4,700 lb)
Range: 3,558 km (1,920 nm)

Cessna 750 Citation X USA

High-speed long-range executive jet

First flown in 1994 the Citation X is a much improved version of the Citation III family. A re-designed wing and tailplane coupled to more powerful Allison engines give much higher operating speeds and a transatlantic range.

Variants and operators
Citation X: standard civil version, no major variants in development

Payload
Passengers: 12
Cargo: 3,000 kg (6,000 lb)
Range: 6,019 km (3,250 nm)

Features: Low/swept wing; twin tail turbofans; sharp swept T-tail

Length: 22 m (72 ft 2 in) Wingspan: 19.5 m (63 ft 11 in) Height: 5.8 m (18 ft 11 in)

Dassault Falcon 50 France

Long-range executive jet

Length: 18.5 m (60 ft 9 in) Wingspan: 18.9 m (61 ft 10 in) Height: 6.9 m (22 ft 10 in)

Features: Low/swept wing; three tail turbofans; mid-mounted tail plane

At $16 million a copy the Falcon 50 is one of the more expensive executive jets but for your money you get the benefits of a third engine. The safety factor of the extra engine enables the Falcon to carry out long-haul flights across deserts and oceans within public transport regulations.

Variants and operators

Falcon 50: standard civil version (as described) **Air ambulance:** operated by the Italian air force for medevac duties **Falcon 50EX:** extended range version with more efficient engines **Falcon 50 Surmar:** maritime patrol version for French Navy with larger radar and air dropable liferafts.

Payload

Passengers: 9
Cargo: 2,170 kg (4,784 lb)
Range: 6,482 km (3,500 nm)

Dassault Falcon 100 France

Short-range executive jet

First flown in 1970 as the Falcon 10, the 100 has a higher take-off weight and fourth cabin window on the starboard side. Essentially a scaled down Falcon 20/200 (see next entry), the best recognition guide is the number of cabin windows 10/100 has 3 the 20/200 has 5.

Variants and operators

Falcon 10: initial version (picture) **Falcon 100:** improved version with fourth starboard window **Falcon 10MER:** naval aircrew trainer

Payload

Passengers: 8
Cargo: 1,305 kg (2,875 lb)
Range: 2,900 km (1,595 nm)

Length: 13.8 m (45 ft 5 in) Wingspan: 13.1 m (42 ft 11 in) Height: 4.6 m (15 ft 1 in)

Features: Low/swept wing; twin tail turbofans; mid-mounted tailplane

Dassault Falcon 200 France

Medium-range executive jet

Length: 17.2 m (56 ft 3 in) Wingspan: 16.3 m (53 ft 6 in) Height: 5.3 m (17 ft 5 in)

Features: Low/swept wing; twin tail turbofans; mid-mounted tailplane

First flown in 1963 as the Falcon 20 with the Falcon 200 entering production in 1980. A very popular platform for Coast Guard and military surveillance, examples can be found carrying out target towing, aircrew training, electronic warfare and air ambulance.

Variants and operators

Falcon 20: initial production version **Falcon 200**: later production model **HU-25A Guardian**: search and rescue/offshore surveillance version **HU-25C**: anti-smuggling variant with APG-66 radar

Payload

Passengers: 12
Cargo: 1,265 kg (2,790 lb)
Range: 4,650 km (2,510 nm)

Dassault Falcon 900 France

Long-range executive jet

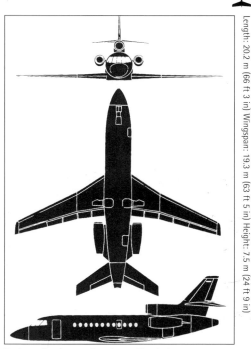

One of the most expensive executive transports at around $27.9 million each, the Falcon 900 is also one of the fastest. A development of the Falcon 50 line, the 900 can be recognized by its longer/wider fuselage and its numerous cabin windows.

Variants and operators

Falcon 900: standard civil version **Falcon 900B:** for operation from unpaved runways **Falcon 900EX:** extended range version **MSA:** maritime surveillance version for Japan

Payload

Passengers: 19
Cargo: 1,385 kg (3,053 lb)
Range: 7,229 km (3,900 nm)

Features: Low/swept wing; three tail turbofans; mid-mounted tailplane

EMBRAER EMB-121 Xingu Brazil

Short-range executive turboprop

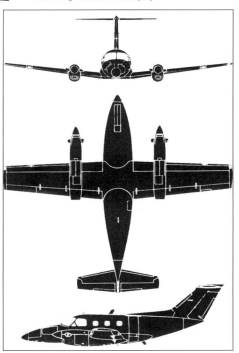

Length: 12.2 m (40 ft 2 in) Wingspan: 14.1 m (46 ft 1 in) Height: 4.8 m (15 ft 10 in)

Features: Low/straight wing; twin turboprops; T-tail

First flown in 1976, 105 Xingus were built before production ended in 1987. Similar in design to the much larger Brasilia, the Xingu has a very wide fuselage for its size. Operated by the Brazilian and French armed forces in a light transport role.

Variants and operators

EMB-121A: standard civil version EMB-121A1: re-engined version, has two small strakes on tailcone

Payload

Passengers: 9
Cargo: 860 kg (1,896 lb)
Range: 2,352 km (1,270 nm)

Gulfstream II/III USA

long-range executive jet

A total of 462 Gulfstream II and IIIs were built between 1966 and 1986, including a number of specialist aircraft for the US Armed forces. The SRA-1 special missions aircraft can be recognized by its long ventral canoe, housing SLAR and electronic surveillance systems.

Variants and operators

Gulfstream II: original production version with no winglets **Gulfstream III:** later version with winglets **SRA-1:** US special missions aircraft **C-20:** USAF VIP transport

Payload

Passengers: 19
Cargo: 726 kg (1,600 lb)
Range: 7,598 km (4,100 nm)

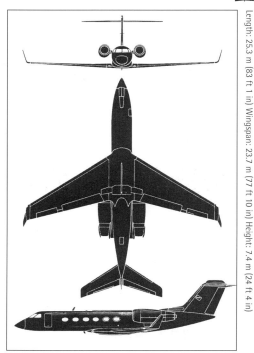

Features: Low/swept wing; twin tail turbofans; T-tail

Length: 25.3 m (83 ft 1 in) Wingspan: 23.7 m (77 ft 10 in) Height: 7.4 m (24 ft 4 in)

Gulfstream IV/V USA

Long-range executive jet

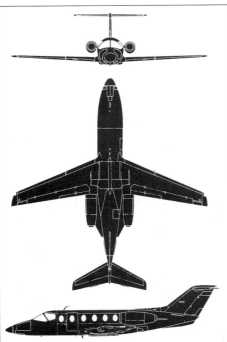

Length: 29.4 m (96 ft 5 in) Wingspan: 28.5 m (93 ft 6 in) Height: 7.9 m (25 ft 10 in)

Features: Low/swept wing; twin tail turbofans; T-tail

Work began on an improved version of the Gulfstream III in 1983. The wing was refined and Rolls-Royce Tay engines installed. The Gulfstream V was stretched by 2.1 m (7 ft) but had no extra windows. The Gulfstream IV has set 11 world records for its class, including time/distance and speed, and at $30 million a copy are one of the most expensive private jets.

Variants and operators

Gulfstream IV: improved Gulfstream III with larger engine nacelles and six windows
Gulfstream V: stretched version **SRA-4**: special requirements aircraft **C-20F/G/H**: US Armed forces high priority transport **U-4**: Japanese multi-mission aircraft

Payload

Passengers: 19
Cargo: 2,948 kg (6,500 lb)
Range: 12,038 km (6,500 nm)

IAI 1123 Westwind Israel

Medium-range executive jet

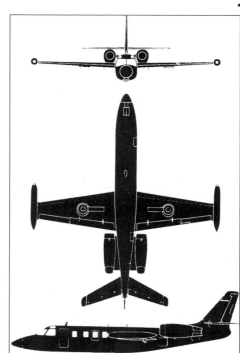

The Westwind began life as the Rockwell Jet Commander in 1963, production was moved to Israel in 1968. The Sea Scan was developed for maritime patrol duties and has an enlarged nose containing search radar. Several Sea Scans are operated by the Australian customs.

Variants and operators

Westwind: initial production version **Westwind 1:** improved version from 1978 onwards **Westwind 2:** developed for hot and high conditions, fitted with winglets **Sea Scan:** maritime patrol version with nose radar

Payload

Passengers: 10
Cargo: 1,496 kg (3,300 lb)
Range: 4,490 km (2,420 nm)

Features: Mid/straight wing; twin tail turbofans; wingtip pods

317

IAI 1125 Astra Israel

Long-range executive transport

Length: 16.9 m (55 ft 7 in) Wingspan: 16 m (52 ft 8 in) Height: 5.5 m (18 ft 2 in)

Features: Low/swept narrow wing; twin tail turbofans; mid-mounted tailplane

Developed from the Rockwell Aero Commander the Astra has carried a number of names in the past including Commodore Jet, Westwind and Westwind 2; its present name came into use on its re-launch in 1979. IAI has launched a re-designed version called Galaxy.

Variants and operators

Astra: initial production version **Astra SP:** refinements for high-altitude performance **Astra SPX:** fitted with winglets and thrust reversers.

Payload

Passengers: 6
Cargo: 1,259 kg (2,775 lb)
Range: 5,211 km (2,814 nm)

Learjet 23-29 USA

Short-range executive jet

The first of almost 1,700 Learjets flew in 1963. Since then the original Learjet 23 has been developed into a number of variants. With a strong family resemblance throughout the class the best way to tell the difference is by counting windows on each side (see below)

Variants and operators

Learjet 23: 1 window **Learjet 24:** 2 windows
Learjet 25: 5 windows **Learjet 28:** 4 windows
Learjet 29: 3 windows

Payload

Passengers: 6
Cargo: 1,755 kg (3,870 lb)
Range: 2,728 km (1,472 nm)

Length: 13.2 m (43 ft 3 in) Wingspan: 10.8 m (35 ft 7 in) Height: 3.7 m (12 ft 3 in)

Features: Low/straight wing; twin tail turbofans; swept T-tail

Learjet 35/36 USA

Medium-range executive jet

Length: 14.8 m (48 ft 8 in) Wingspan: 12 m (39 ft 6 in) Height: 3.7 m (12 ft 3 in)

Features: Low/straight wing; twin tail turbofans; swept T-tail

The basic Learjet was re-designed in 1973 with increased range and stretched fuselage. Although very similar to earlier versions the 35 and 36 have larger engine nacelles and greater wingspan. Many military versions have been built for maritime patrol, electronic warfare, reconnaissance and transport duties.

Variants and operators

Learjet 31: 35 fuselage with 55 wing **Learjet 35:** standard version with 5 windows **Learjet 36:** extended range version **EC-35:** EW trainer **PC-35:** maritime patrol with ventral radar **RC-35:** with ventral reconnaissance pack **U-36/36:** utility version, Japanese aircraft have ventral radar

Payload

Passengers: 8
Cargo: 1,534 kg (3,381 lb)
Range: 4,067 km (2,196 nm)

Learjet 45 USA

Medium-range executive jet

Designed to offer the handling of earlier Learjets with improved efficiency and greater room inside. First flown in 1995, 125 have already been ordered at $6.1 million each. A new wing designed in conjunction with NASA has helped reduce drag and improve efficiency together with digital technology flight systems.

Variants and operators

Learjet 45: initial production version

Payload

Passengers: 10
Cargo: 2,650 kg (1,202 lb)
Range: 3,813 km (2,059 nm)

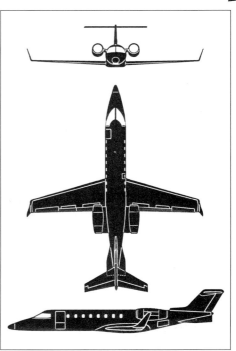

Features: Low/straight wing; twin tail turbofans; swept T-tail

Length: 17.6 m (58 ft) Wingspan: 14.5 m (47 ft 9 in) Height: 4.3 m (14 ft)

Learjet 55/60 USA

Long-range executive jet

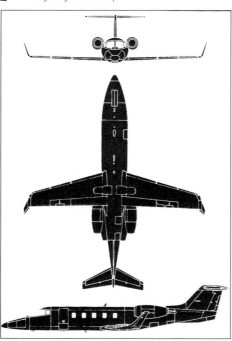

Length: 17.9 m (58 ft 8 in) Wingspan: 13.3 m (43 ft 9 in) Height: 4.5 m (14 ft 8 in)

Features: Low/straight wing; twin tail turbofans; widebody fuselage

A wide body development of the basic Learjet design, the 55 was the first to use the more efficient winglets which have been retrofitted to most other designs. The 55 was replaced in production by the improved 60 in 1990, both are the largest aircraft of the Learjet family.

Variants and operators

Learjet 55: initial production version **Learjet 60:** re-engined with greater internal space

Payload

Passengers: 9
Cargo: 2,650 kg (1,202 lb)
Range: 4,441 km (2,398 nm)

Lockheed Martin Jetstar II USA

Long-range executive jet

Having first flown in 1957, the Jetstar was put back into production in 1975 as the Jetstar II featuring modern avionics and engines. Increased range and lower operating noise levels resulted from the changes which are also available as re-fit packages for older Jetstars.

Variants and operators

Jetstar: initial production version **Jetstar II:** modernized version

Payload

Passengers: 10
Cargo: 1,280 kg (2,822 lb)
Range: 5,132 km (2,770 nm)

Length: 18.4 m (60 ft 5 in) Wingspan: 16.6 m (54 ft 5 in) Height: 6.2 m (20 ft 5 in)

Features: Low/swept wing; four tail turbofans; large wing fairings

323

MBB HFB 320 Hansa Germany

Short-range executive jet

Length: 16.6 m (54 ft 6 in) Wingspan: 14.5 m (47 ft 6 in) Height: 4.9 m (16 ft 2 in)

Features: Mid/forward swept wing; twin tail turbofans; swept T-tail

The Hansa's unique forward swept wing makes it an easy if rare aircraft to spot. First flown in 1964 only 50 were built. Most are used as feederliners with high-density seating for 15.

Variants and operators
HFB 320 Hansa: standard civil version

Payload
Passengers: 11
Cargo: 1,600 kg (3,520 lb)
Range: 2,420 km (1,304 nm)

Piaggio P.180 Avanti Italy

Short-range executive jet

The unique layout of the Avanti is as functional as it is elegant; by placing the wings so far back the cabin is unobstructed by wing roots giving maximum possible internal space. The pusher engines reduce cabin noise. As the foreplane and tail plane also create lift it could be described as a triplane design.

Variants and operators

P.180 Avanti: standard civil version

Payload

Passengers: 9
Cargo: 907 kg (2000 lb)
Range: 2,594 km (1,400 nm)

Length: 14.4 m (47 ft 3 in) Wingspan: 14 m (46 ft) Height: 3.9 m (12 ft 11 in)

Features: Mid/straight wing; twin pusher turboprops; nose foreplane

Piper PA-31-350 Chieftain USA

Short-range executive aircraft

Length: 10.5 m (34 ft 7 in) Wingspan: 12.4 m (40 ft 8 in) Height: 3.9 m (13 ft)

Features: Low/straight wing; twin piston engines; large square windows

Developed from the Piper Navajo light transport the Chieftain has a longer fuselage and is strengthened to facilitate the carriage of light cargo pallets. Used widely as an executive taxi it can also be fitted out with 10 seats for high density feederliner duties.

Variants and operators

Chieftain: standard executive taxi **Commuter:** high density feederliner **PA-31P:** pressurized version with smaller windows.

Payload

Passengers: 6
Cargo: 159 kg (350 lb)
Range: 1,640 km (885 nm)

Raytheon (Beechcraft) 400A Beechjet USA

Medium-range executive jet

Raytheon acquired the rights to the Mitsubishi Diamond II in 1985, they renamed it the Beechjet after making improvements to the avionic and engine systems. Used by the USAF for multi-engine pilot training as the T-1A Jayhawk.

Variants and operators

400A Beechjet: standard executive transport
400T Beechjet: fitted with thrust reversers and long-range navigation systems for JASDF **T-1A Jayhawk:** USAF pilot trainer

Payload

Passengers: 8
Cargo: 1,406 kg (3,100 lb)
Range: 3,519 km (1,900 nm)

Length: 14.7 m (48 ft 5 in) Wingspan: 13.3 m (43 ft 6 in) Height: 4.2 m (13 ft 11 in)

Features: Low swept wing; twin tail turbofans; T-tail

Raytheon (Beechcraft) King Air USA

Medium-range executive transport

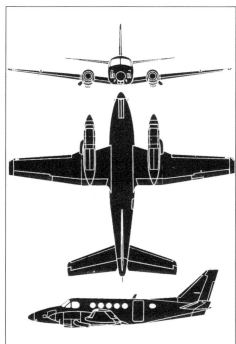

Length: 13.3 m (43 ft 9 in) Wingspan: 16.6 m (54 ft 6 in) Height: 4.6 m (15 ft)

Features: Low/straight wing; twin turboprops; swept wing roots

Design work began in 1970 as the Super King Air. The basic airframe has been tailored for a wide range of missions including cargo, commuter and executive for the civil market. The airframe forms the basis of the RC-12 Guardrail SIGINT aircraft, the maritime patrol version is also used for maritime pollution surveillance.

Variants and operators

Super King Air 200C: cargo **200T:** with wingtip tanks **300:** with advanced avionics **1300:** Commuter **King Air:** with 3 side windows **C90B:** advanced King Air

Payload

Passengers: 8
Cargo: 680 kg (1,500 lb)
Range: 3,656 km (1,974 nm)

Raytheon (Beechcraft) Starship 1 USA

Short-range executive turboprop

An unmistakable design featuring pusher engines mounted on the trailing edge of a crescent wing with tail fins mounted at the wingtips. The foreplanes move from a forward swept position for landing and take-off to a swept position for flight.

Variants and operators
Starship 1: standard eight seat version **Starship 2000A:** long range six seat version

Payload
Passengers: 8
Cargo: 1,125 kg (2,480 lb)
Range: 2,919 km (1,576 nm)

Features: Intregal/swept wing; twin pusher turboprops; wingtip tails; foreplane

Length: 14 m (46 ft 1 in) Wingspan: 16.6 m (54 ft 4 in) Height: 3.9 m (12 ft 11 in)

Raytheon (BAe) 125 UK

Medium-range executive jet

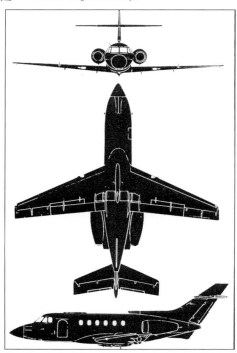

Length: 15.4 m (50 ft 6 in) Wingspan: 14.3 m (47 ft) Height: 5.3 m (17 ft 3 in)

Features: Low/swept wing; twin tail turbofans; high tail

Developed as a private venture by De Haviland the 125 first flew in 1962. Since then the 125 has carried the name Hawker Siddeley and BAe following mergers in the UK aviation industry. Raytheon bought BAe Corporate Jets in 1993 and have marketed the 125 under their name since.

Variants and operators

125 series 1 – 3: initial production series **125 series 400:** improved version with redesigned cockpit appearance **125 series 600:** larger version developed for the US market (as described) **Dominie:** RAF trainer version

Payload

Passengers: 8
Cargo: 907 kg (2,000 lb)
Range: 3,057 km (1,650 nm)

Raytheon (BAe) Hawker 800 UK/USA

Long-range executive jet

Length: 15.6 m (51 ft 2 in) Wingspan: 15.7 m (51 ft 4 in) Height: 5.4 m (17 ft 7 in)

The prototype 125 series 800 first flew in 1983. Renamed Hawker 800 following the Raytheon take over in 1993. Improvements over earlier models include curved windscreen, new engines, greater wingspan, refined aerodynamics and increased internal space.

Variants and operators

800: standard production version **800XP:** extended performance version with Allied Signal engines **C-29A:** USAF transport **U-125:** Japanese search and rescue aircraft

Payload

Passengers: 14
Cargo: 907 kg (2,000 lb)
Range: 5,232 km (2,825 nm)

Features: Low/swept wing; twin tail turbofans; curved windscreen

331

Raytheon (BAe) Hawker 1000 UK/USA

Long-range executive jet

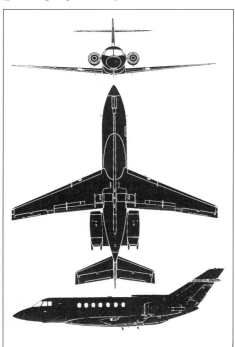

Length: 16.4 m (53 ft 10 in) Wingspan: 15.7 m (51 ft 4 in) Height: 5.2 m (17 ft 1 in)

Features: Low/swept wing; twin tail turbofans; high tail

BAe began developing the 125 in 1988 to incorporate substantial structural and systems changes to meet intercontinental specifications. Produced by Raytheon under the name Hawker 1000. Fuselage plugs forward of the wings created a larger cabin and increased fuel. Only 52 were built before production ended in 1997.

Variants and operators

Hawker 1000: standard production version

Payload

Passengers: 8
Cargo: 1,043 kg (2,300 lb)
Range: 6,204 km (3,350 nm)

Rockwell Sabreliner USA

Medium-range executive jet

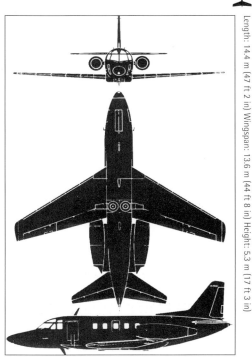

Originally designed to meet a USAF requirement for a utility aircraft/trainer Rockwell built the Sabreliner as a private venture in 1958. Commercial aircraft eventually out sold military versions to the extent that a specialist company, Sabreliner Corp, was formed to develop and support the type in service. The last aircraft was built in 1979.

Variants and operators

T-39: USAF aircrew trainer **CT-39:** utility transport **Sabreliner 60:** initial civil version **Sabreliner 65:** re-engined version with larger nacelles **Sabreliner 75:** with increased cabin space **Sabreliner 75A/80:** standard 75 re-engined and modernized

Payload

Passengers: 10
Cargo: 2,494 kg (5,500 lb)
Range: 3,173 km (1,712 nm)

Features: Low/swept wing; twin tail turbofans; low tail

333

Starcraft SK-700 USA

Medium-range executive aircraft

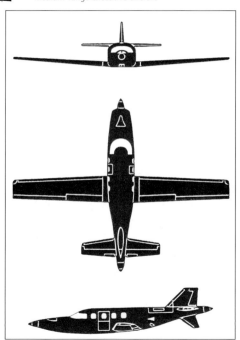

Length: 10.9 m (36 ft) Wingspan: 12.9 m (42 ft 3 in) Height: 4.3 m (14 ft 1 in)

Features: Low/straight wing; fore and aft piston engines; ventral fin

A low-cost executive aircraft concept, the SK-700 first flew in 1994. Three major versions are planned including a single engined light aircraft with fixed landing gear and a stretched 12-seater (see variants). Its unique tractor and pusher configuration maximizes the effect of its twin piston engines giving it a maximum speed of over 400 mph.

Variants and operators

SK-700: standard production version (as described) SK-700SE: singled engined fixed landing gear SK-1100: stretched 12-seat version

Payload

Passengers: 7
Cargo: 658 kg (1,450 lb)
Range: n/a

Swearingen SJ30 USA

Medium-range executive jet

This attractive executive jet has had a troubled history. Developed by Gulfstream as the SA-30 Fanjet Gulfstream pulled out of its development in 1989. The Jaffe group stepped in and under the designation Swearingen/Jaffe SJ30 it flew for the first time in 1991. The aircraft is now to be produced by a joint Taiwanese/US company Sino Swearingen with first deliveries beginning in 1998.

Variants and operators
SJ-30: initial prototype **SJ30-2:** stretched production version

Payload
Passengers: 7
Cargo: 1,270 kg (2,800 lb)
Range: 3,204 km (1,730 nm)

Features: Low/swept wing; twin tail turbofans; sharply swept T-tail

335

Visionaire VA-10 Vantage USA

Short-range executive jet

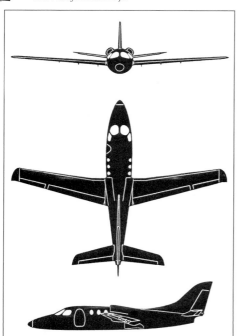

Length: 12.4 m (40 ft 9 in) Wingspan: 14.5 m (47 ft 6 in) Height: xxxx

Features: Mid/forward swept wing; single turbofan; shoulder intakes

The Vantage is the only all-composite executive aircraft in the world, and first flew in 1996. The Vantage is a low-cost aircraft at $1.6 million a copy with operating cost of $416 per hour. The slightly swept forward wing minimizes drag and allows the main spar to pass behind the cabin.

Variants and operators

VA-10: Standard production version

Payload

Passengers: 4
Cargo: 1,000 lb (2,205 kg)
Range: 1,777 km (960 nm)

PRIVATE LIGHT AIRCRAFT

Aero Boero 115 Argentina

Light utility aircraft

Length: 7.1 m (23 ft 2 in) Wingspan: 10.8 m (35 ft 4 in) Height: 2.1 m (6 ft 8 in)

Features: High/straight wing; single piston engine; square cut tail

A rugged design, the Aero Boero 115 has found many roles from elementary trainer to agricultural sprayer. Very similar in design to the Piper Super Cub, the Argentine aircraft has a square cut tail assembly. Landing gear spats are optional and not fitted to later aircraft

Variants and operators
AB 95: initial production version with spats AB 115: elementary trainer (as described) AB 180: Glider tug and agricultural aircraft

Payload
Passengers: three
Cargo: 100 kg (225 lb)
Range: 1,239 km (664 nm)

AviaBellanca **Skyrocket** USA

Light sports aircraft

First flown in 1974, the Skyrocket holds five world time-speed records for its class. Construction was planned to be quick and uncomplicated; initial versions had glass fibre skin over aluminum honeycomb core, later versions have carbonfibre over nomex structure.

Variants and operators
Skyrocket II: initial production version
Skyrocket III: later production version

Payload
Passengers: 6
Cargo: 91 kg (200 lb)
Range: 2,937 km (1,586 nm)

Features: Low/straight wing; single piston engine; retractable landing gear

339

AviaBellanca Viking USA

Light sports aircraft

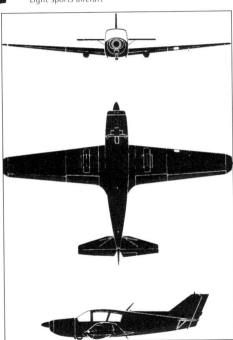

Features: Low/straight wing; single piston engine; underwing fairings for landing gear

Length: 8 m (26 ft 4 in) Wingspan: 10.4 m (34 ft 2 in) Height: 2.2 m (7 ft 4 in)

Over 1,500 Vikings were built before production ceased in 1980. Three major versions have been developed from the initial 260C, changes being confined to the engines and propellers (see variants). The landing gear retracts into two very obvious underwing fairings.

Variants and operators

Viking 300: standard production model **Super Viking 300A:** with 300 hp continental engine
Turbo Viking 300A: with twin turbochargers

Payload

Passengers: 4
Cargo: 84 kg (186 lb)
Range: 1,722 km (929 nm)

Cessna 152 Aerobat USA

Light sports aircraft

Very similar to its larger stablemate the 172 Skyhawk, the Aerobat was based on earlier tail sitting versions of the Model 120/140. Production ended in 1977 after 24,000 had been built, many by Reims in France. Landing gear spats are optional.

Variants and operators
150: initial production version **150F:** improved version with swept tail **152:** re-engined version (as described) strengthened for aerobatics

Payload
Passengers: 2
Cargo: 54 kg (120 lb)
Range: 1,158 km (625 nm)

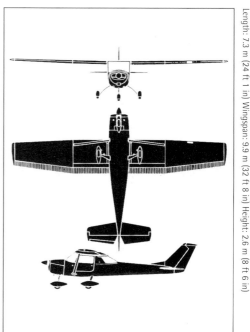

Length: 7.3 m (24 ft 1 in) Wingspan: 9.9 m (32 ft 8 in) Height: 2.6 m (8 ft 6 in)

Features: High/braced straight wing; single piston engine; tricycle landing gear

341

Cessna 172 Skyhawk USA

Light sports aircraft

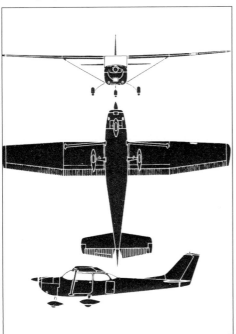

Length: 8.2 m (26 ft 11 in) Wingspan: 10.9 m (35 ft 10 in) Height: 2.7 m (8 ft 9 in)

Features: High/braced straight wing; single piston engine; four side windows

The world's most popular light aircraft, some 35,545 aircraft have been built and production continues, including over 2,000 by Reims in France. To tell it apart from its smaller cousin the 152 Aerobat, look at the number of windows; the Skyhawk's cabin has four on each side and seating for two extra passengers.

Variants and operators

172: standard production model **F172:** Reims-built aircraft **T-41:** military designation

Payload

Passengers: 4
Cargo: 54 kg (120 lb)
Range: 1,620 km (875 nm)

Cessna 180 Skywagon USA

Light sports aircraft

First flown in 1952, over 6,000 were built before production ceased in 1981. The 185 was developed to carry a number of external modifications including floats, skis and a ventral cargo bay (bottom side view).

Variants and operators

180: standard production model **180 Skywagon II:** with long range fuel tanks and improved avionics **185:** utility version **U–17:** military designation

Payload

Passengers: 6
Cargo: 181 kg (400 lb)
Range: 1,872 km (1,010 nm)

Features: High/braced straight wing; single piston engine; tail wheel

Length: 7.8 m (25 ft 7 in) Wingspan: 10.9 m (35 ft 10 in) Height: 2.4 m (7 ft 9 in)

343

Cessna 210 Centurion USA

Light sports aircraft

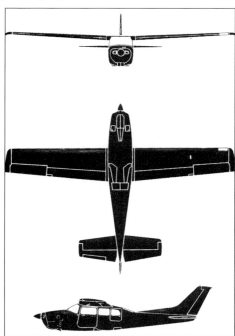

Length: 8.6 m (28 ft 2 in) Wingspan: 12.4 m (38 ft 10 in) Height: 2.9 m (9 ft 8 in)

Features: High/straight wing; single piston engine; retractable landing gear

First flown in 1957, the Centurion was Cessna's first light aircraft to feature retractable landing gear. A pressurised version can be recognized by its four smaller, rounder windows. The Turbo Centurion is fitted with a single turbocharger and lacks the wing bracing struts.

Variants and operators

Centurion: standard production version **Turbo Centurion:** turbocharged engine no wing struts
Pressurised Centurion: with pressurised cabin and smaller windows

Payload

Passengers: 6
Cargo: 109 kg (240 lb)
Range: 1,872 km (1,010 nm)

Cessna T303 Crusader USA

Light transport aircraft

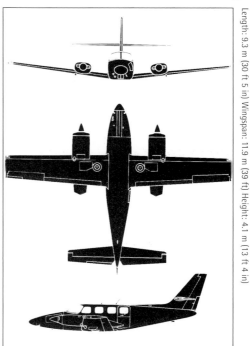

First flown in 1978, production ceased in 1987 after 297 had been built. The built-in air-stair can be replaced by an upwards hinged cargo door for the loading of small pallets and stretchers. The two turbocharged engines power contra-rotating propellers.

Variants and operators

T303: standard production version

Payload

Passengers: 6
Cargo: 267 kg (590 lb)
Range: 1,889 km (1,020 nm)

Features: Low/straight wing; twin piston engines; high tail

Cessna 310 USA

Light transport aircraft

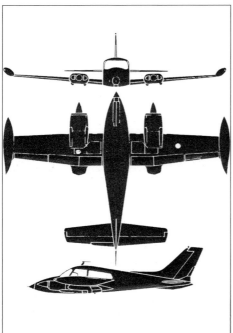

Length: 9.7 m (13 ft 11 in) Wingspan: 11.2 m (36 ft 11 in) Height: 3.3 m (10 ft 8 in)

Features: Low/straight wing; twin piston engines; wingtip pods

First flown in 1953, the turbocharged T310 version was introduced in 1968. Over 5,000 were built, earlier models having an unswept tailfin.

Variants and operators

303: initial production version **T303:** turbocharged version

Payload

Passengers: 5
Cargo: 430 kg (950 lb)
Range: 2,668 km (1,440 nm)

Cessna 340A USA

Light transport aircraft

Developed from the 310, the 340 has a pressurised cabin and more internal space. Designed for the executive commuter market the aircraft can be recognised by its round windows and greater fuselage cross section.

Variants and operators

340A: standard production version

Payload

Passengers: 6
Cargo: 422 kg (930 lb)
Range: 2,552 km (1,377 nm)

Features: Low/straight wing; twin piston engines; circular windows

Length: 10.5 m (34 ft 4 in) Wingspan: 11.6 m (38 ft 1 in) Height: 3.8 m (12 ft 7 in)

Cessna 401/402/421 Golden Eagle USA

Light transport aircraft

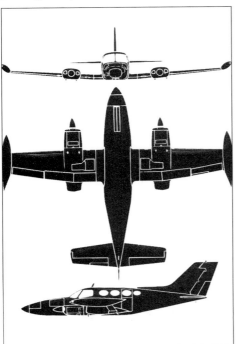

Length: 11 m (36 ft 1 in) Wingspan: 12.1 m (39 ft 10 in) Height: 3.6 m (11 ft 8 in)

Features: Low/straight wing; twin piston engines; low tail

This family of aircraft were designed for the feederliner market, capable of being converted from passenger transport to cargo quickly. The 402 can be recognized by its square windows while the 401 and 421 have four round windows.

Variants and operators

401: standard production version **402:** high density feederliner **421:** executive businessliner

Payload

Passengers: 6
Cargo: 606 kg (1,340 lb)
Range: 2,280 km (1,231 nm)

Cessna Cardinal RGII USA

Lights sports aircraft

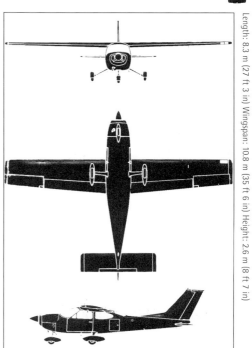

The Cardinal can be recognised by its lack of wing bracing struts. Similar in appearance to the Centurion the Cardinal only has seating for four and lacks the Centurion's extra cabin window. The Cardinal RG has retractable landing gear (picture).

Variants and operators
Cardinal: standard production version **Cardinal RG:** with retractable landing gear

Payload
Passengers: 4
Cargo: 54 kg (120 lb)
Range: 1,657 km (895 nm)

Features: High/straight wing; retractable landing gear on some; two side windows

Length: 8.3 m (27 ft 3 in) Wingspan: 10.8 m (35 ft 6 in) Height: 2.6 m (8 ft 7 in)

349

Cessna Stationair 6 USA

Light transport aircraft

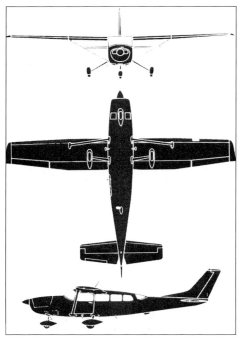

Length: 8.6 m (28 ft 3 in) Wingspan: 10.9 m (35 ft 10 in) Height: 2.8 m (9 ft 3 in)

Features: High/braced straight wing; single piston engine; long cabin

Designed for the easy loading of small pallets and cargo, the Stationair can be configured for all-cargo duties, with one pilot, or all passenger. The 7 and 8 designation refer to the number of passengers they can carry.

Variants and operators
Stationair 6: standard production version
Stationair 7-8: larger versions seating 7 and 8 passengers respectively

Payload
Passengers: 8
Cargo: 422 kg (930 lb)
Range: 1,666 km (900 nm)

Cessna Titan USA

Light transport aircraft

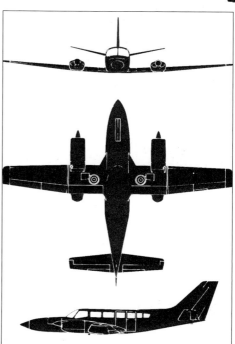

First flown in 1975 the Titan was originally called the Model 404. Capable of operating from small strips, it is used primarily in the feederliner role. Similar to the 402 with its square windows, the Titan has a longer fuselage and carries an extra 2 passengers.

Variants and operators

404 Titan: standard production version 402C: long wingspan and tip tanks

Payload

Passengers: 8
Cargo: 680 kg (1,500 lb)
Range: 3,350 km (1,809 nm)

Length: 12 m (39 ft 6 in) Wingspan: 14.1 m (46 ft 4 in) Height: 4 m (13 ft 3 in)

Features: Low/straight wing; twin piston engines; square windows

Cirrus Design SR-20 USA

Light sports aircraft

Length: 7.6 m (25 ft) Wingspan: 10.6 m (35 ft) Height: 2.8 m (9 ft 2 in)

Features: Low/straight wing; single piston engine; wheel spats

First flown in 1985, the SR-20 entered production in 1997. Cirrus intend to build a family of aircraft around the basic SR-20 airframe including a two seat trainer. The SR-20 is the first aircraft to be fitted with a ballistic safety parachute as standard, enabling recovery of the entire aircraft in the event of engine failure.

Variants and operators

SR-20: standard production version **SRX:** designed for fleet operations

Payload

Passengers: 4
Cargo: 163 kg (360 lb)
Range: 1,481 km (800 nm)

EAM Eagle X-TS Australia/Malaysia

Light sports aircraft

A modern biplane design made entirely from composite materials. The first aircraft were designed and built in Australia before production moved to Malaysia between 1995-97. Malaysia is keen to establish itself as a leading builder of composite technology with the Eagle becoming the first stepping stone to larger more complex aircraft.

Variants and operators
X-TS 100: Australian built aircraft X-TS 200: Malaysian production version

Payload
Passengers: 2
Cargo: none
Range: 963 km (520 nm)

Length: 6.5 m (21 ft 5 in) Wingspan: 7.2 m (23 ft 6 in) Height: 2.3 m (7 ft 5 in)

Features: High/straight wing; low/straight foreplane; single piston engine

353

ENAER Namcu Chile

Light sports aircraft

The first ENAER aircraft to be designed entirely in Chile, the Namcu first flew in 1989. Under Euro-ENAER agreement the aircraft will also be assembled in the Netherlands. All-composite design to meet a requirement for inexpensive club aircraft.

Variants and operators
Namcu: initial production version **Namcu future version 1**: with 115 hp engine **Namcu future version 2**: with 119 hp engine

Payload
Passengers: 2
Cargo: 20 kg (44 lb)
Range: 927 km (501 nm)

Features: Low/straight wing; single piston engine; raised cab

Length: 7 m (23 ft 11 in) Wingspan: 8.3 m (27 ft 3 in)
Height: 2.4 m (7 ft 11 in)

EXTRA 300 Germany

Light aerobatic aircraft

Designed for unlimited aerobatics, around 70 aircraft have been sold since production began in 1988. The Extra 300 has transparent sections in the fuselage floor for additional visibility during close formation flying.

Variants and operators

Extra 200: earlier version with no floor windows **Extra 300:** standard production version **Extra 300S:** shortened version **Extra 300L:** low-wing version with two seats

Payload

Passengers: 1 or 2
Cargo: none
Range: 974 km (526 nm)

Length: 7.1 m (23 ft 4 in) Wingspan: 8 m (26 ft 3 in) Height: 2.6 m (8 ft 7 in)

Features: Mid/straight wing; single piston engine; bubble canopy

Fournier/Sportsavia RF6-180 Sportsman France/Germany

Light sports aircraft

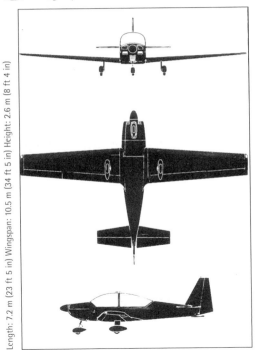

Features: Low/straight wing; single engine; bubble canopy

Length: 7.2 m (23 ft 5 in) Wingspan: 10.5 m (34 ft 5 in) Height: 2.6 m (8 ft 4 in)

First flown in 1973, the Sportsman is built in Germany to a French design. The RF-6B Club is broadly similar, but has a smaller canopy and seating for two pilots only. Early aircraft had the tailplane mounted on top of the fuselage (see silhouette); later aircraft had this moved halfway up the fin (picture).

Variants and operators

RF6-180: Standard production version RF-6B
Club: two seat aerobatic version

Payload

Passengers: 4
Cargo: n/a
Range: 1,510 km (815 nm)

Fuji FA-200 Aero Subaru Japan

Light sports aircraft

First flown in 1965, around 300 were built before production ceased in 1982. The designations FA-200-160 or FA-200-180 refer to the horsepower of the engine installed, 160 hp and 180 hp respectively.

Variants and operators

FA-200-160: initial production version FA-200-180: re-engined version

Payload

Passengers: 4
Cargo: 100 kg (220 lb)
Range: 1,215 km (655 nm)

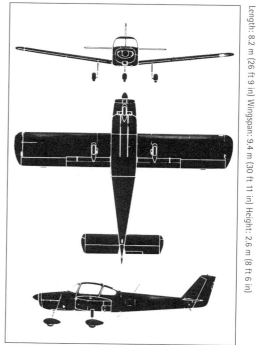

Length: 8.2 m (26 ft 9 in) Wingspan: 9.4 m (30 ft 11 in) Height: 2.6 m (8 ft 6 in)

Features: Low/straight wing; single piston engine; dihedral wing

357

FFA AS202 Bravo Switzerland

Light sports aircraft

Length: 7.2 m (23 ft 5 in) Wingspan: 9.7 m (31 ft 11 in) Height: 2.8 m (9 ft 2 in)

Features: Low/straight wing; single piston engine; bubble canopy

First flown in 1969, the Bravo was developed in conjunction with SIAI-Marchetti of Italy. The Wren is used by the BAe flying college for elementary training. The Turbine Bravo is fitted with an Allison 250-B17C turboprop.

Variants and operators

Bravo: standard production version **Wren:** elementary trainer **Turbine Bravo:** longer nose section for turboprop engine

Payload

Passengers: 2
Cargo: 100 kg (220 lb)
Range: 1,140 km (615 nm)

FLS Optica UK

Light observation aircraft

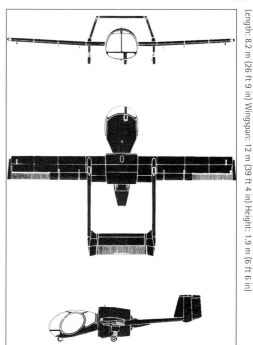

Brooklands Aviation designed the Optica for slow-flying surveillance duties. First flown in 1979 production started in 1983 but was suspended following acquisition by FLS. Production has yet to be re-started and the whole programme is up for sale.

Variants and operators
Optica: Standard production version

Payload
Passengers: 3
Cargo: 231 kg (510 lb)
Range: 1,056 km (570 nm)

Length: 8.2 m (26 ft 9 in) Wingspan: 12 m (39 ft 4 in) Height: 1.9 m (6 ft 6 in)

Features: Mid/straight wing; twin boom tail; bubble cabin

359

General Avia Pinguino Italy

Length: 7.4 m (24 ft 3 in) Wingspan: 7.4 m (27 ft 10 in) Height: 2.8 m (9 ft 3 in)

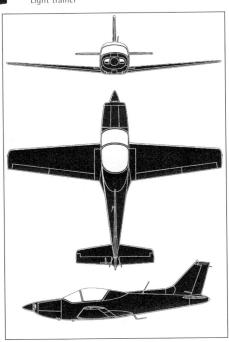

First flown in 1989, deliveries began in 1993. The Pinguino is mainly used at club level for basic training. Of the major variants the most significant are the A and B models with fixed landing gear and the C and R models with retractable landing gear.

Variants and operators

F.22–A/B: with 116 hp and 160 hp engines respectively **F.22–C/R:** 180 hp and 160 hp engine respectively with retractable landing gear

Payload

Passengers: 2
Cargo: none
Range: 1,352 km (730 nm)

Features: Low/straight wing; single piston engine; retractable landing gear

Grob G115 Germany

Light sports aircraft

First flown in 1985, production ceased during the early 1990s but has restarted at 10 per month. The Bavarian was developed for the US market, with fuel in the wings and revised instrument panel.

Variants and operators
G115: standard production version G115
Bavarian: for US market G115D1: strengthened for aerobatics

Payload
Passengers: 2
Cargo: none
Range: 1,204 km (650 nm)

Features: Low/straight wing; single piston engine; wheel spats

361

Grob G115T Acro Germany

Light trainer

Aimed at the USAF Enhanced Flight Screener competition, Grob is now offering it for the civil training market. Because its design fitted US military standards the type is well suited to other military programmes.

Variants and operators
G115TA: standard production variant

Payload
Passengers: 2
Cargo: 450 kg (992 lb)
Range: 1,612 km (870 nm)

Features: Low/straight wing; single piston engine; bubble canopy
Length: 8.8 m (28 ft) Wingspan: 10 m (32 ft 9 in) Height: 2.6 m (8 ft 5 in)

Grob GF 200 Germany

Light touring aircraft

First flown in 1991 with support from the German government, the aircraft was originally to have a Porsche engine. Various engine layouts are available for the single pusher propeller, including a turboshaft version and twin piston engines.

Variants and operators

GF 200: 4 seat with single piston engine **GF 250/6:** stretched 6 seat version **GF 300:** 6 seat turboshaft powered version **GF 350:** 6/8 seat twin piston engined version

Payload

Passengers: 4
Cargo: 580 kg (1,278 lb)
Range: 1,810 km (977 nm)

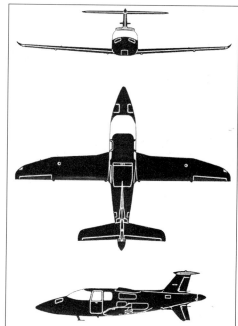

Features: Low/straight tapered wing; single pusher piston engine; T-tail

Length: 8.7 m (28 ft 6 in) Wingspan: 11 m (36 ft) Height: 3.3 m (10 ft 10 in)

Gulfstream AA-1C USA

Light sports aircraft

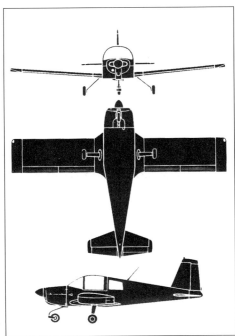

Length: 5.9 m (19 ft 3 in) Wingspan: 7.5 m (24 ft 5 in) Height: 2.3 m (7 ft 6 in)

Features: Low/straight wing; single piston engine; tricycle landing gear

First flown in 1970 as a development of the American Aviation AA-1 Yankee trainer. The AA-1C was introduced in 1977 incorporating a more powerful engine, and minor structural changes. The T-cat and Lynx versions have identical exteriors but include a number of equipment changes.

Variants and operators

AA-1C: standard production version T-cat: internal changes to equipment Lynx: trainer/aerobatic aircraft

Payload

Passengers: 2
Cargo: 45 kg (100 lb)
Range: 711 km (384 nm)

Gulfstream AA-5A Cheetah USA

Light sports aircraft

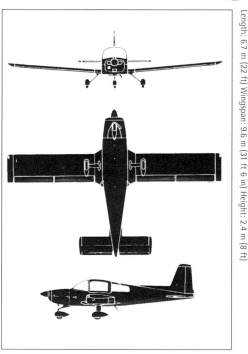

Length: 6.7 m (22 ft) Wingspan: 9.6 m (31 ft 6 in) Height: 2.4 m (8 ft)

First flown in 1970 the Cheetah was originally a Grumman design. Once known as the Traveller, the Cheetah is a larger version of the AA-1C. The Tiger has an improved interior, greater fuel load and more powerful engine.

Variants and operators
Cheetah: Standard production version **Tiger:** advanced version

Payload
Passengers: 4
Cargo: 54 kg (120 lb)
Range: 1,509 km (814 nm)

Features: Low/straight wing; single piston engine; low tail

Gulfstream GA-7 Cougar USA

Light transport

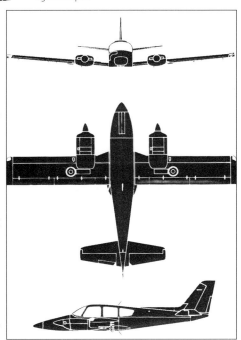

Features: Low/straight wing; twin engines; dihedral wing and tailplane

Like the other Gulfstream light aircraft the Cougar started life as a Grumman design in 1974. The aircraft was significantly improved before production commenced in 1977. The type is also used extensively as a two-engine trainer.

Variants and operators
Cougar: standard production version

Payload
Passengers: 4
Cargo: n/a
Range: 2,035 km (1,098 nm)

Istravision ST-50 Israel

Light business aircraft

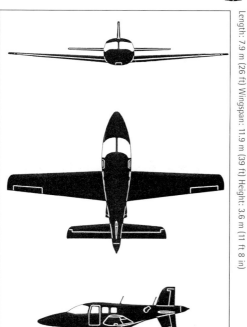

Length: 7.9 m (26 ft) Wingspan: 11.9 m (39 ft) Height: 3.6 m (11 ft 8 in)

Istravision bought the rights to the Cirrus ST-50 aircraft, which entered series production in 1997. The all-composite design allows for a light but strong aircraft. The wing gives good low-speed handling without drag penalties at normal operating speeds.

Variants and operators
ST-50: standard production version

Payload
Passengers: 5
Cargo: 136 kg (300 lb)
Range: 2,037 km (1,100 nm)

Features: Low/straight wing; single pusher piston engine; ventral tailfin

Lake La-250 Renegade USA

Light amphibian

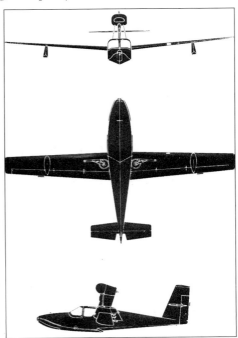

Length: 8.6 m (28 ft 4 in) Wingspan: 11.7 m (38 ft 4 in) Height: 3.1 m (10 ft)

Features: Mid/straight wing; single overwing piston engine; amphibian hull

Produced in two main variants, the Turbo 270 has a turbocharged piston engine for extra performance and has set a world altitude record for amphibians by reaching 7,465 m (24,500 ft). The Special Edition Seafury is equipped to operate from salt water sites and includes a custom interior and survival package.

Variants and operators

La-4 Buccaneer: early version **La-250:** standard production model **Turbo Renegade:** with turbocharged engine

Payload

Passengers: 6
Cargo: 90 kg (200 lb)
Range: 1,668 km (900 nm)

Laverda Falco F8 Italy

Light sports aircraft

Length: 6.5 m (21 ft 4 in) Wingspan: 8 m (26 ft 3 in) Height: 2.3 m (7 ft 6 in)

First flown in 1955. Four main versions of the Falcon have been produced (see variants) while other versions have been built for specific customers. The Falcon is fully aerobatic and was a very popular trainer and aerobatic aircraft, becoming a rarer sight today.

Variants and operators

F8 Series I: initial production version **F8 Series II:** re-engined with 135 hp engine **F8 America:** built in the USA for the US market **F8 Series IV:** re-engined America

Payload

Passengers: 2
Cargo: 40 kg (90 lb)
Range: 1,400 km (755 nm)

Features: Low/straight wing; single piston engine; bubble canopy

Let L-200 Morava Czech Republic

Light transport aircraft

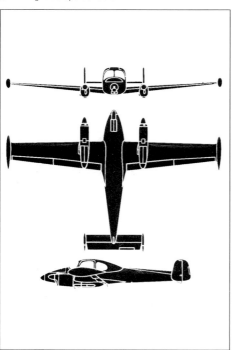

Length: 8.6 m (28 ft 3 in) Wingspan: 12.3 m (40 ft 4 in) Height: 2.3 m (7 ft 4 in)

Features: Low/straight wing; twin piston engines; twin tails

The Morava was first flown in 1957, as a light business aircraft. Over 400 were built and are still in regular service in Eastern Europe. Stretchers can be carried in the fuselage when the aircraft is fitted as an air ambulance.

Variants and operators
Let-200: standard production version

Payload
Passengers: 5
Cargo: 135 kg (297 lb)
Range: 1,710 km (921 nm)

Mooney Ranger USA

Light sports aircraft

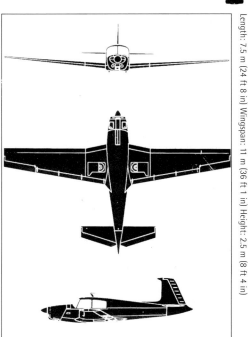

Mooney developed a number of aircraft based on the Ranger, all of them using the distinctive forward swept tail fin. The original Ranger first flew in 1961 with 1,860 being built so far and production continuing.

Variants and operators

Ranger: original production version **Encore:** high performance aircraft with more powerful engine **Ovation:** touring aircraft new interior layout

Payload

Passengers: 4
Cargo: 54 kg (120 lb)
Range: 1,961 km (1,059 nm)

Features: Low/straight wing; single engine; forward swept tailfin

371

Mudry CAP 10B France

Light aerobatic aircraft

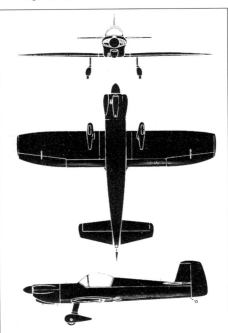

Length: 7.2 m (23 ft 6 in) Wingspan: 8.1 m (26 ft 5 in) Height: 2.6 m (8 ft 4 in)

First flown in 1968 the original CAP 10B has been superseded in production by the CAP 231 (silhouette) and the CAP 232 single seaters. Many ex-French Navy aircraft are finding their way in to civil hands, some being refitted as Glider tugs.

Variants and operators

CAP-10B: initial production version CAP-10R: Glider Tug CAP-231: single seat CAP-232: with carbonfibre wing

Payload

Passengers: 2
Cargo: 20 kg (44 lb)
Range: 1,000 km (539 nm)

Features: Low/straight wing; single piston engine; bubble canopy

Piper PA-18 Super Cub USA

Light utility aircraft

The Super Cub is the last in the Cub series of aircraft, the first of which flew in 1931. First flown in 1949 over 40,000 were built. Used extensively in agricultural spraying, Super cubs were also used as elementary trainers. Piper was bought out of bankruptcy in 1995 by Newco Pac Inc. and is now known as New Piper.

Variants and operators
E-2 Cub: original 1931 aircraft Super Cub: main production version

Payload
Passengers: 2
Cargo: 22 kg (50 lb)
Range: 741 km (400 nm)

Length: 6.8 m (22 ft 6 in) Wingspan: 10.8 m (35 ft 3 in) Height: 2.1 m (6 ft 8 in)

Features: High/braced straight wing; single piston engine; rounded wingtips

Piper PA-23 Aztec USA

Light transport aircraft

Length: 9.5 m (31 ft 2 in) Wingspan: 11.3 m (37 ft 2 in) Height: 3.2 m (10 ft 4 in)

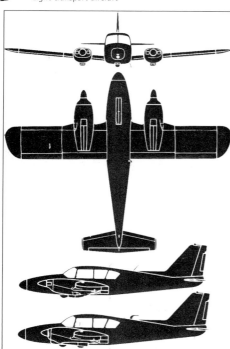

Features: Low/straight wing; twin piston engines; low tail

First flown in 1958. The Aztec has undergone a number of modifications since production began in 1959. The initial versions were 5 seaters; Aztec Bs introduced the longer nose baggage compartment and six seats. A number of different engines have been fitted including turbocharged units on the Aztec F.

Variants and operators

Aztec A: initial production version Aztec B: long nose version Aztec C/D (top side view): re-designed engine nacelles Aztec F: turbocharged version

Payload

Passengers: 6
Cargo: 725 kg (1,600 lb) max
Range: 2,445 km (1,320 nm)

Piper PA-28 Cherokee USA

Light sports aircraft

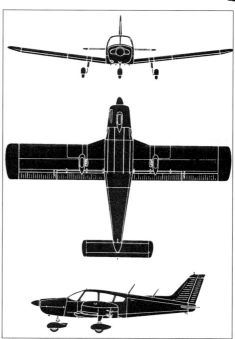

The first Cherokee flew in 1964, and has formed the basis of a number of Piper aircraft including the Saratoga, Lance and Arrow. The Warrior appeared in 1973 and has a longer wing, the SIX has a larger cabin with four windows on each side.

Variants and operators

Cherokee: standard production model **Warrior:** long wing version **Archer:** tourer version **Dakota:** with 235 hp engine **SIX:** with larger cabin

Payload

Passengers: 4
Cargo: 90 kg (200 lb)
Range: 1,168 km (630 nm)

Length: 7.2 m (23 ft 9 in) Wingspan: 10.7 m (35 ft) Height: 2.2 m (7 ft 3 in)

Features: Low/straight wing; single piston engine; fixed landing gear

375

Piper PA-30 Twin Commanche USA

Light transport aircraft

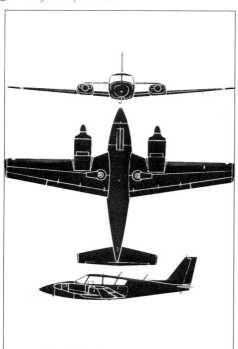

Features: Low/straight wing; twin piston engines; low tail

First flown in 1961, it was developed from the earlier single engined Commanche. The Turbo Commanche features turbocharged engines. The wing tip tanks can be removed. Very similar to the Aztec, the Commanche has a pointed nose were the single engine used to be.

Variants and operators
Twin Commanche: standard production model
Turbo Commanche; with turbocharged engines

Payload
Passengers: 8
Cargo: 113 kg (250 lb)
Range: 2,190 km (1,180 nm)

Length: 7.7 m (25 ft 2 in) Wingspan: 10.9 m (35 ft 11 in) Height: 2.5 m (8 ft 2 in)

Piper PA-31 Navajo USA

Light transport aircraft

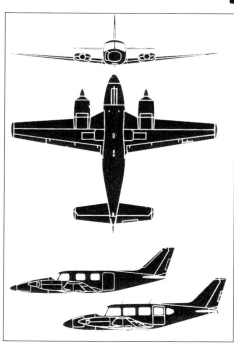

The Navajo has been progressively modified since it first flew in 1964. The main variants include the stretched PA-31P (top side view) and the standard PA-31 feederliner (bottom view). The Turbo Navajo is fitted with turbocharged engines.

Variants and operators
PA-31: standard feederliner **PA-31P**: stretched version **PA-31C**: long range version **Turbo-Navajo**: with turbocharged engines

Payload
Passengers: 6
Cargo: 159 kg (350 lb)
Range: 1,973 km (1,065 nm)

Features: Low/straight wing; twin piston engines; square windows

377

Piper PA-31 Cheyenne II USA

Light transport aircraft

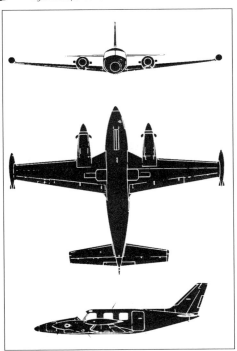

Length: 10.6 m (34 ft 8 in) Wingspan: 13 m (42 ft 8 in) Height: 3.9 m (12 ft 9 in)

Features: Low/straight wing; twin turboprops; wingtip pods

First flown in 1969, the Cheyenne was Piper's first turboprop design. Using the main fuselage and wing sections of the Navajo Piper added two turboprops to make the Cheyenne. The T-1040 Commuter has the forward fuselage of the Chieftain with the nose, tail and wings of the Cheyenne.

Variants and operators
Cheyenne II: standard production model T-1040
Commuter: enlarged commuter version

Payload
Passengers: 8
Cargo: 227 kg (500 lb)
Range: 2,796 km (1,510 nm)

Piper PA-32 Saratoga USA

Light sports aircraft

Largest of the Cherokee family of aircraft, over 800 Saratogas have been produced. The Saratoga can be found with fixed or retractable landing gear, turbocharged models have a pronounced intake under the engine.

Variants and operators

Saratoga: standard production version **Saratoga SP:** with retractable landing gear **Turbo Saratoga:** with turbocharged engine

Payload

Passengers: 6
Cargo: 90 kg (200 lb)
Range: 1,778 km (960 nm)

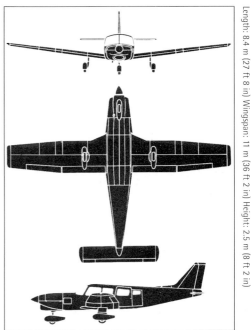

Length: 8.4 m (27 ft 8 in) Wingspan: 11 m (36 ft 2 in) Height: 2.5 m (8 ft 2 in)

Features: Low/straight wing; single piston engine; stretched fuselage

379

Piper PA-34 Seneca USA

Light transport aircraft

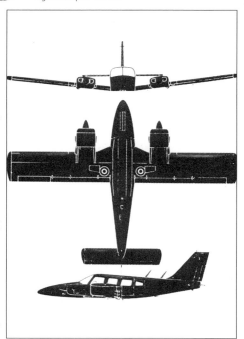

Length: 8.7 m (28 ft 7 in) Wingspan: 11.8 m (38 ft 10 in) Height: 3 m (9 ft 10 in)

Features: Low/straight wing; twin piston engines; large square windows

First flown in 1971, the Seneca is very similar to the earlier Twin Commanche. It can be recognised through the number of windows (four) along each side. The type was also built under licence in Poland.

Variants and operators

Seneca: standard production version PZL-112
M-20 Mewa: Polish-built version

Payload

Passengers: 6
Cargo: 90 kg (200 lb)
Range: 1,635 km (882 nm)

Piper PA-42 Cheyenne III USA

Light transport aircraft

Length: 13.2 m (43 ft 4 in) Wingspan: 14.5 m (47 ft 8 in) Height: 4.5 m (14 ft 9 in)

Developed from the original Cheyenne, the Cheyenne II features a T-tail and a longer fuselage. The Cheyenne 400 is fitted with two Garrett TPR331-14A turboprops. Used mainly in the feederliner and business taxi role.

Variants and operators

Cheyenne III: standard production version
Cheyenne III: turboprop powered version

Payload

Passengers: 11
Cargo: 1,140 kg (2513 lb)
Range: 4,204 km (2,270 nm)

Features: Low/straight wing; twin turboprops; long, thin fuselage

Piper PA-44 Seminole USA

Light transport aircraft

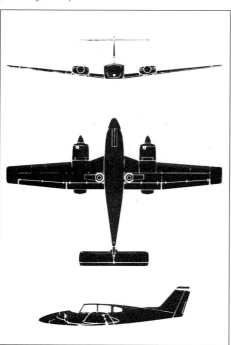

Length: 8.4 m (27 ft 7 in) Wingspan: 11.7 m (38 ft 7 in) Height: 2.6 m (8 ft 6 in)

Features: Low/straight wing; twin piston engines; T-tail

First flown in 1976, the Seminole is very similar to the Beechcraft Duchess. The Seminole can be recognised by its engine nacelles protruding over the trailing edge of the wing.

Variants and operators

Seminole: standard production version **Turbo Seminole:** with turbocharged engines

Payload

Passengers: 4
Cargo: 91 kg (200 lb)
Range: 1,695 km (915 nm)

Piper PA-46 Malibu Mirage USA

Light touring aircraft

Developed from the original Malibu which entered service in 1983. The Malibu Mirage was the first single-engined pressurised light aircraft on the civil market. The pressurised cabin and high lift wing enable the Malibu Mirage to reach 7,620 m (25,000 ft).

Variants and operators
Malibu: initial production version **Malibu**
Mirage: standard production version

Payload
Passengers: 6
Cargo: 45 kg (100 lb)
Range: 2,335 km (1,260 nm)

Length: 8.7 m (28 ft 7 in) Wingspan: 13.1 m (43 ft) Height: 3.5 m (11 ft 6 in)

Features: Low/straight wing; single piston engine; low tail

383

Piper PA-28 Arrow USA

Light sports aircraft

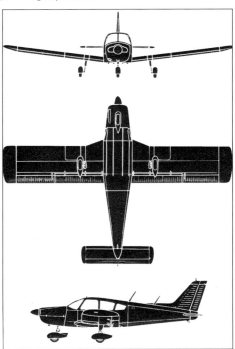

Length: 7.5 m (24 ft 8 in) Wingspan: 10.8 m (35 ft 5 in) Height: 2.4 m (7 ft 10 in)

Features: Low/straight wing; single piston engine; dihedral wing

Developed from the earlier Archer, the Arrow first flew in 1975. The Arrow IV was introduced in 1979 featuring a new T-tail, but main production switched back to a low-mounted design. The Archer can be recognised by its fixed landing gear.

Variants and operators

Archer: earlier model **Arrow:** standard production version **Arrow IV:** with T-tail

Payload

Passengers: 4
Cargo: 90 kg (200 lb)
Range: 1,621 km (875 nm)

PZL-Warszawa PZL-104 Wilga Poland

Light utility aircraft

Almost 1,000 Wilgas have been built since it first flew in 1962. The basic airframe has been adapted to many roles including glider tug, floatplane, agricultural sprayer, armed border patrol and utility aircraft. The Wilga 2000 dispensed with the rotary engine and had a refined fuselage and systems for the Western markets.

Variants and operators

Wilga 35: standard production version **Wilga 80:** westernised version **Wilga 2000:** improved version with flat six engine

Payload

Passengers: 4
Cargo: 35g (77 lb)
Range: 510 km (275 nm)

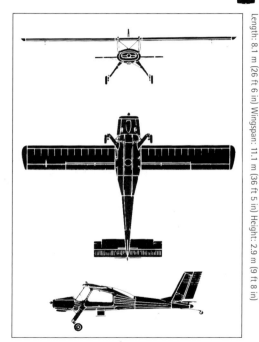

Length: 8.1 m (26 ft 6 in) Wingspan: 11.1 m (36 ft 5 in) Height: 2.9 m (9 ft 8 in)

Features: High/straight wing; single radial engine; forward swept landing gear

Raytheon (Beechcraft) B58 Baron USA

Light transport aircraft

Length: 9.1 m (29 ft 10 in) Wingspan: 11.5 m (37 ft 10 in) Height: 3 m (9 ft 9 in)

Features: Low/straight wing; twin piston engines; re-tractable landing gear

Developed from the Baron 55 the Baron 58 has a longer fuselage and a fourth window on each side. Some 2,500 Barons have been delivered many being used as training aircraft by the major airlines.

Variants and operators
Baron 55: initial production version **Baron 58:** Standard production version

Payload
Passengers: 6
Cargo: 317 kg (700 lb)
Range: 2,917 km (1,575 nm)

Raytheon (Beechcraft) B60 Duke USA

Light touring aircraft

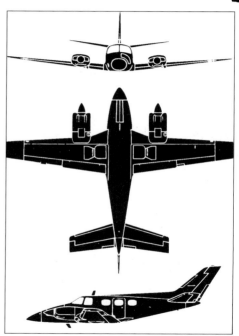

First flown in 1966, almost 600 Dukes were built. The Duke features a pressurised cabin and turbocharged engine enabling it to operate up to 9,145 m (30,000 ft). Two major versions were built: the standard A60 and B60 with TIO-541 engines.

Variants and operators

A60: standard production version **B60:** re-engined version

Payload

Passengers: 6
Cargo: n/a
Range: 2,079 km (1,112 nm)

Length: 10.3 m (33 ft 10 in) Wingspan: 11.9 m (39 ft 3 in) Height: 3.8 m (12 ft 4 in)

Features: Low/straight wing; twin piston engines; long tailfin strake

Raytheon (Beechcraft) B76 Duchess USA

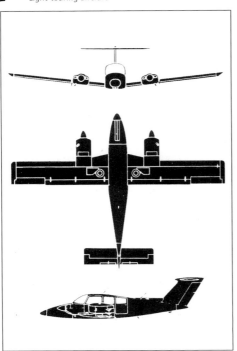

Light touring aircraft

Length: 8.9 m (29 ft) Wingspan: 11.6 m (38 ft) Height: 2.9 m (9 ft 6 in)

By using fuselage sections from the Sierra single engined aircraft to build the Duchess, Beech were able to keep costs down and production simple. First flown in 1977. Designed as a personal light transport and trainer aircraft over 400 were built.

Variants and operators
Duchess: standard production version

Payload
Passengers: 4
Cargo: 90 kg (200 lb)
Range: 1,583 km (843 nm)

Features: Low/straight wing; twin piston engines; T-tail

Raytheon (Beechcraft) F33A Bonanza USA

Light sports aircraft

First flown in 1959, the F33A was developed from the original F35 Bonanza. Main differences between the two include the change from a butterfly tail to a conventional unit on the F33A. The last version the A36 was introduced in 1968 with a longer fuselage.

Variants and operators

F33A: standard production version **A36:** improved version now in production

Payload

Passengers: 5
Cargo: 123 kg (270 lb)
Range: 1,648 km (889 nm)

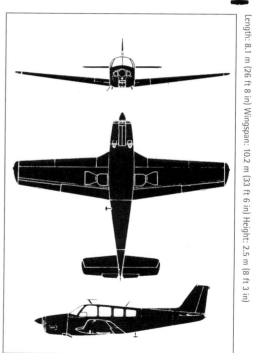

Length: 8.1 m (26 ft 8 in) Wingspan: 10.2 m (33 ft 6 in) Height: 2.5 m (8 ft 3 in)

Features: Low/straight wing; single piston engine; low tail

Raytheon (Beechcraft) **V35B Bonanza** USA

Light sports aircraft

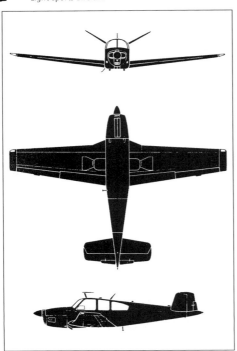

Length: 8.1 m (26 ft 5 in) Wingspan: 10.2 m (33 ft 6 in) Height: 2.3 m (7 ft 7 in)

Features: Low/straight wing; single piston engine; butterfly tail

The original Bonanza, the V35 first flew in 1945. When production ceased in 1985 15,000 aircraft had been built with the butterfly tail (see photo) before production switched to the A36. Few changes were made to the structure in its forty year history.

Variants and operators
V35B: standard production version

Payload
Passengers: 5
Cargo: 123 kg (270 lb)
Range: 1,648 km (889 nm)

Raytheon (Beechcraft) Sierra 200 USA

Light sports aircraft

First flown as the Musketeer Super R in 1969, the Sierra was renamed when deliveries began in 1974. The Sundowner has a lower powered engine and non retractable landing gear.

Variants and operators
Sierra: standard production version
Sundowner: simplified version

Payload
Passengers: 4
Cargo: 123 kg (270 lb)
Range: 1,271 km (686 nm)

Features: Low/straight wing; single piston engine; retractable landing gear

Length: 7.8 m (25 ft 9 in) Wingspan: 9.9 m (32 ft 9 in) Height: 2.5 m (8 ft 1 in)

391

Raytheon (Beechcraft) Skipper USA

Light training aircraft

Length: 7.3 m (23 ft 10 in) Wingspan: 9.1 m (30 ft) Height: 2.3 m (7 ft 6 in)

Features: Low/straight wing; single piston engine; T-tail

First flown in 1975, the Skipper was designed for the light training market. The first aircraft had a low mounted tail, before it was replaced in the production versions with a T-tail. Over 300 were built.

Variants and operators
Skipper: standard production version

Payload
Passengers: 3
Cargo: none
Range: 764 km (413 nm)

Robin ATL Club France

Light sports aircraft

Length: 6.7 m (22 ft) Wingspan: 10.2 m (33 ft 7 in) Height: 2 m (6 ft 6 in)

An easily identified design with forward swept wings and a butterfly tail. The Club first flew in 1983 and is powered by a conventional Volkswagen car engine. Used for basic training at club level over 140 have been produced. Known as the Bijou in the UK.

Variants and operators
Club: standard production model **Voyage:** tourer version with larger engine and four seats

Payload
Passengers: 2
Cargo: none
Range: 1,000 km (539 nm)

Features: Low/forward swept wing; boom fuselage; butterfly tail

393

Robin HR100 France

Light sports aircraft

Length: 7.6 m (24 ft 10 in) Wingspan: 9.1 m (29 ft 9 in) Height: 2.7 m (8 ft 10 in)

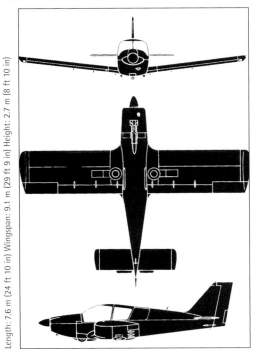

Features: Low/straight wing; single piston engine; low tail

The first Robin HR100 flew in 1971. The 100/200TR is fitted with a fuel injection engine of 250 hp for better performance. The Tiara has retractable landing gear, while the 100 4+2 has extra seating for 6 people.

Variants and operators

HR100: standard production version
HR100/250TR: re-engined version **HR100 Tiara:** with retractable landing gear **HR100 4+2:** with extra seats

Payload

Passengers: 5
Cargo: none
Range: 2,130 km (1,149 nm)

Robin HR200 France

Light training aircraft

First flown in 1971, the Robin HR200 was taken out of production in 1976. Production was re-started in 1992, with 150 aircraft being built.

Variants and operators
HR200: standard production version **HR200**
Club: with landing gear spats

Payload
Passengers: 2
Cargo: none
Range: 1.050 km (566 nm)

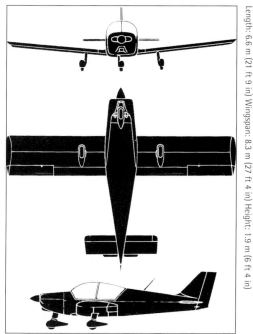

Length: 6.6 m (21 ft 9 in) Wingspan: 8.3 m (27 ft 4 in) Height: 1.9 m (6 ft 4 in)

Features: Low/straight wing; single piston engine; bubble canopy

Robin DR400 France

Light sports aircraft

Length: 6.9 m (22 ft 10 in) Wingspan: 8.7 m (29 ft 7 in) Height: 2.2 m (7 ft 3 in)

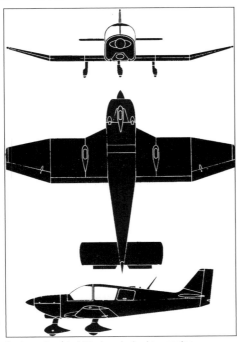

First flown in 1972, the DR400 has been through a constant process of development. The first versions seated two adults and two children, later versions seating up to five adults. Remo Glider tugs can be recognised by their double silencers under the fuselage

Variants and operators
DR400: standard production version **DR400 Cadet:** light trainer **DR400 Remo:** glider tug

Payload
Passengers: 5
Cargo: 55 kg (121 lb)
Range: 860 km (464 nm)

Features: Low/straight wing; single piston engine; dihedral wingtips

Robin R3000 France

Light sports aircraft

First flown in 1980 the R3000 was designed to accept a number of different engines and interior fittings. Of the seven models proposed only two have entered production, as described in variants.

Variants and operators
DR3000/160: production model with 160 hp engine **DR3000/180:** production model with 180 hp engine

Payload
Passengers: 4
Cargo: 40 kg (88 lb)
Range: 1,480 km (799 nm)

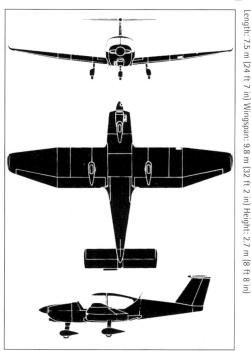

Features: Low/straight wing; single piston engine; T-tail

Length: 7.5 m (24 ft 7 in) Wingspan: 9.8 m (32 ft 2 in) Height: 2.7 m (8 ft 8 in)

Rockwell Commander USA

Light sports aircraft

Length: 7.6 m (25 ft) Wingspan: 10.8 m (35 ft 7 in) Height: 2.6 m (8 ft 5 in)

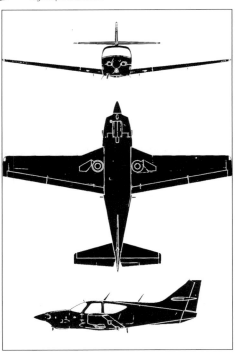

First flown in 1970, both versions have an identical external appearance. Main changes lie in the powerplant and auxiliary systems. Both have a characteristic mid-set tail.

Variants and operators
Commander 112: with 210 hp engine
Commander 114: 260 hp engine

Payload
Passengers: 4
Cargo: n/a
Range: 1,569 km (846 nm)

Features: Low/straight wing; single piston engine; mid tail

Socata TB9 Tampico France

Light sports aircraft

The Tampico first flew in 1977, and has formed the basis of several other aircraft. Original Tampicos had 119 hp engine and fixed landing gear. The Tobago had the same fuselage and landing gear but was fitted with a 180 hp engine. The Trinidad having retractable landing gear.

Variants and operators

Tampico: initial production version **Tobago:** re-engined version **Tobago XL:** with 200 hp engine and extra seat **Trinidad:** with retractable landing gear **Trinidad TC:** with turbocharged engine

Payload

Passengers: 5
Cargo: 45 kg (100 lb)
Range: 1,210 km (653 nm)

Features: Low/straight wing; single piston engine; fixed or retractable landing gear

Length: 7.6 m (25 ft) Wingspan: 9.8 m (32 ft) Height: 3.2 m (10 ft 6 in)

399

Socata Rallye France

Light sports aircraft

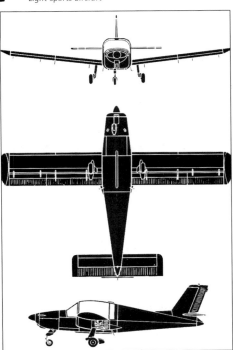

Length: 7.3 m (23 ft 10 in) Wingspan: 9.7 m (31 ft 11 in) Height: 2.8 m (9 ft 2 in)

Features: Low/straight wing; single piston engine; low tailplane

Since it first flew in 1959 the Rallye has undergone a number of changes to its powerplant. The designation numbers following its name refer to the horsepower of the engine fitted (see variants). Armed versions of the Rallye are called Guerrier and are operated by Rwanda and Senegal.

Variants and operators

Rallye 125, 150, 180, 220, 235: standard production versions and corresponding engine size **Guerrier:** armed version with two wing hardpoints **Koliber:** Polish version

Payload

Passengers: 4
Cargo: 110 kg (242 lb)
Range: 1,250 km (675 nm)

Sukhoi Su-26 Russia

Light aerobatic aircraft

The other Sukhoi aerobatic aircraft the Su-29 is broadly similar but has a greater wingspan and length for increased maneouverability. There is a two-seat version of the Su-29 for training, see three-view (right). The pilot's seat in the Su-26 is inclined at 45 deg to counter the effects of g forces.

Variants and operators

Su-26: standard production version **Su-29:** larger version

Payload

Passengers: 1 or 2
Cargo: none
Range: 800 km (432 nm)

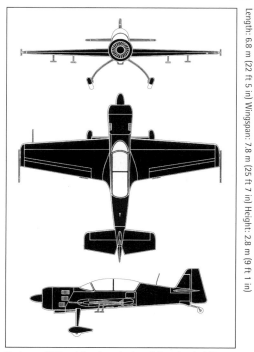

Length: 6.8 m (22 ft 5 in) Wingspan: 7.8 m (25 ft 7 in) Height: 2.8 m (9 ft 1 in)

Features: Mid/straight wing; single radial engine; bubble canopy

TAAL Hansa 3 India

Light training aircraft

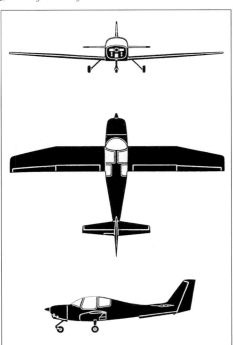

Length: 7.2 m (23 ft 7 in) Wingspan: 10.4 m (34 ft 4 in) Height: 2.6 m (8 ft 6 in)

Features: Low/straight wing; single piston engine; swept wingtips

First flown in 1993 the Hansa was designed as an elementary training aircraft. Docile handling qualities were built in along with robust construction and low cost. Several prototypes were built each with different engines and equipment packages before the standard production version was chosen.

Variants and operators

Hansa 2: second prototype **Hansa 3**: standard production version

Payload

Passengers: 2
Cargo: none
Range: 842 km (455 nm)

Zlin **Z50L/Z** Czech Republic

Light aerobatic aircraft

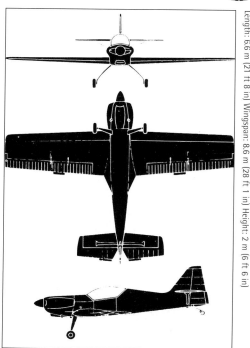

First flown in 1975, the L50 family are all stressed to G limits of +9g to -6g. The 50LS is powered by a 300 hp engine. The standard production version can be fitted with auxiliary wingtip tanks or smoke canisters.

Variants and operators

Z50L: initial production version **Z50LE:** short wingspan version **Z50LS:** standard production version with more powerful engine **Z50LX:** with integral fuel tanks in the wing roots **Z50M:** with a longer slimmer nose

Payload

Passengers: 1
Cargo: none
Range: 640 km (345 nm)

Length: 6.6 m (21 ft 8 in) Wingspan: 8.6 m (28 ft 1 in) Height: 2 m (6 ft 6 in)

Features: Low/straight wing; single piston engine; bubble canopy

403

Zlin **Z142** Czech Republic

Light sports aircraft

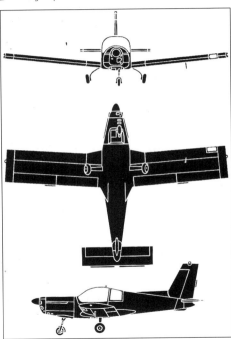

Length: 7.1 m (23 ft 1 in) Wingspan: 9.1 m (29 ft 10 in) Height: 2.7 m (8 ft 10 in)

Features: Low/straight wing; single piston engine; forward swept wing

First flown in 1978, the Z142 was designed as an aerobatic trainer, but found uses as a light tourer and general trainer. The Z242 has a straight leading edge and improved engine for the Western markets. The Z143 is a standard Z142 with a Lycoming engine for the Western markets. Over 770 aircraft have been built.

Variants and operators

Z142: initial production version **Z143:** standard production version **Z242:** westernised version with straight wing

Payload

Passengers: 2
Cargo: 45 kg (100 lb)
Range: 530 km (286 nm)

HELICOPTERS

Agusta A 109 Italy

Light helicopter

Length: 11.4 m (37 ft 6 in) Rotorspan: 11 m (36 ft 1 in) Height: 3.5 m (11 ft 5 in)

Features: Four rotor; twin turbine; retractable landing gear

First flown in 1971, the A 109 was the first helicopter to be designed entirely by Agusta Military and civil versions of the A 109 have been built, military versions having numerous modifications including armoured seats and external stores hardpoints. Some military aircraft have fixed landing gear, as have all naval versions. UK aircraft are operated by 22 SAS regiment.

Variants and operators

A109: Argentina; Belgium; Greece; Italy; Libya; Malaysia; Morocco; Paraguay; Saudi Arabia; Singapore; Slovenia; South Africa; UAE; UK; Venezuela

Payload

Accommodation: 2 pilots; 6 passengers
Cargo: 907 kg (2,000 lb)
Hardpoints: 2 fuselage
Weapons: TOW; Stinger; gun pods; rockets

Agusta A 129 Mangusta Italy

Attack helicopter

Length: 12.3 m (40 ft 3 in) Rotorspan: 11.9 m (39 ft) Height: 3.3 m (11 ft)

Europe's first dedicated attack helicopter design, the A 129 first flew in 1983. In service with the Italian Army, initial aircraft were dedicated to the anti-tank role. Later developments include the multi-role A 129 with higher all-up weight and more powerful transmission; this version will also be fitted with a nose cannon. An export model the A 129 International has uprated engines and avionics and also has a chin turret.

Variants and operators

A129: Italy

Payload

Accommodation: 2 pilots
Warload: 1,200 kg (2,645 lb)
Hardpoints: 4 wing
Weapons: TOW; Hellfire; AIM-9 Sidewinder; Mistral; gun pods; rockets

Features: Four rotor/twin turbine; tandem seats: TOW sight on nose

Agusta-Bell AB 212 Italy

Shipborne anti-submarine

Length: 12.9 m (42 ft 4 in) **Rotorspan:** 14.7 m (48 ft 2 in) **Height:** 4.5 m (14 ft 10 in)

Features: Twin rotor/single turbine; skids; radar over cockpit

The standard AB 212 was a licence built Bell UH-1. Agusta modified it, as the AB 212ASW to perform a range of shipborne roles including anti-submarine warfare, anti-ship strike, SAR and over the horizon targeting. The latest version, the AB 412, has a four blade rotor assembly, and can also be fitted with radar and FLIR.

Variants and operators

AB 212: Austria; Greece; Iran; Israel; Italy; Lebanon; Libya; Morocco; Oman; Saudi Arabia; Spain; Sudan; Turkey; UAE; Yemen; Zambia **AB 212ASW:** Greece, Iran, Italy; Peru; Spain; Turkey; Venezuela **AB 412:** Finland; Italy; Lesotho; Netherlands; Sweden; UAE; Uganda; Venezuela; Zimbabwe

Payload

Accommodation: 2 pilots; 2 crew or 7 passengers
Cargo: 2270 kg (5000 lb)
Hardpoints: 2 fuselage
Weapons: Marte Mk 2; Sea Skua; ASW torpedoes; depth charges

Agusta A 119 Koala Italy

Light helicopter

First flown in 1995, the Koala was designed to achieve the greatest internal space from a single turbine helicopter. Agusta claims it has 30 percent more space than any other single engine helicopter. The Koala has only just finished its testing phase and is expected to go into full production soon. Orders have been received for 20 aircraft.

Variants and operators
A 119: orders from Italy; USA

Payload
Accommodation: 2 pilots; 6 passengers
Cargo: 1,320 kg (2,910 lb)

Length: 11.1 m (36 ft 3 in) Rotorspan: 11 m (36 ft 1 in) Height: 3.3 m (10 ft 10 in)

Features: Four rotor/single turbine; skids; large tail skid

Agusta/Sikorsky AS-61 Italy

Shipborne anti-submarine helicopter

Length: 16.7 m (54 ft 9 in) Rotorspan: 18.9 m (62 ft) Height: 4.7 m (15 ft 6 in)

Features: Five rotor/twin turbine; twin stabilizing floats; ventral radar

Agusta began licence building the Sikorsky S-61 in 1967. Several versions have been developed including the ASH-3D Anti-submarine helicopter with ventral radar, the Pelican search and rescue helicopter with rear loading ramp and the AS-61N offshore transport.

Variants and operators
AS-61: Egypt; Iran; Iraq; Italy; Libya; Malaysia; Peru; Saudi Arabia; Venezuela **ASH-3D:** Argentina; Brazil; Iran; Italy; Peru

Payload
Accommodation: 2 pilots; 2 sonar operators or 31 troops
Cargo: 3,630 kg (8,000 lb)
Hardpoints: 4 fuselage
Weapons: Marte Mk2; Exocet; AS.12; ASW torpedoes; depth charges

Bell Model 47 USA

Ultra light helicopter

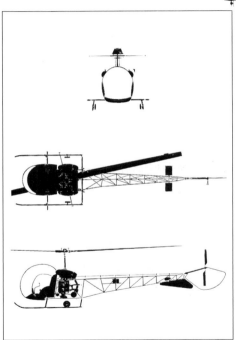

Made famous by the opening scene in MASH, the Bell 47 first flew in 1947. Produced in Italy by Agusta and the UK by Westland as well as the USA. In the MASH air ambulance role two stretchers could be carried on the skids, in the agricultural role tanks and spray bars are fixed to the skids.

Variants and operators

Bell 47: Croatia; Greece; Malaysia; Malta; New Zealand; Tanzania; Uruguay; Zambia **OH-13 Sioux**: Colombia; Greece; Paraguay

Payload

Accommodation: 2 pilots; 1 passengers; 2 stretchers
Cargo: 455 kg (1,000 lb)

Features: Twin rotor/piston engined; bubble canopy; lattice tail boom

Length: 9.6 m (31 ft 7 in) Rotorspan: 11.3 m (37 ft 1 in) Height: 2.8 m (9 ft 3 in)

411

Bell Model 206 JetRanger USA

Light helicopter

Length: 9.5 m (31 ft 2 in) Rotorspan: 10.2 m (33 ft 4 in) Height: 2.9 m (9 ft 6 in)

Features: Twin rotor/single turbine; skids; pointed nose

Over 7,000 JetRangers have been built since deliveries began in 1971. The stretched LongRanger (next entry) has an extra window and small fins on the tail boom. A JetRanger was the first helicopter to fly around the world. The armed Kiowa version is described separately (p. 147).

Variants and operators

JetRanger: Australia; Brazil; Brunei; Canada; Croatia; Chile; Ecuador; Guatemala; Guyana; Indonesia; Jamaica; South Korea; Oman; Pakistan; Poland; Slovenia; Sri Lanka; Thailand; Uganda; UAE; Venezuela **TH-67 Creek:** Taiwan; US Army

Payload

Accommodation: 2 pilots; 3 passengers
Cargo: 635 kg (1,500 lb)

Bell Model 206L-4 LongRanger USA

Utility helicopter

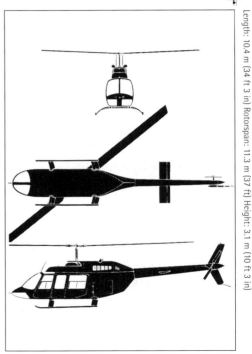

The LongRanger followed the JetRanger in 1974. The Cabin was increased in size to allow the carriage of two stretchers. In this guise the LongRanger is often used as an air ambulance and Police helicopter. Over 1,100 aircraft have been delivered. Some LongRangers have been fitted with a second engine, and are known as TwinRangers.

Variants and operators

LongRanger: Algeria; Bangladesh; Cameroon; Colombia; Cyprus; Guatemala; Israel; Mexico; Nepal; Thailand; UAE; Venezuela

Payload

Accommodation: 2 pilots; 5 passengers
Cargo: 1,024 kg (2,258 lb)

Length: 10.4 m (34 ft 3 in) Rotorspan: 11.3 m (37 ft) Height: 3.1 m (10 ft 3 in)

Features: Twin rotor/single turbine; skids; three side windows

413

Bell Model 430 USA

Executive transport helicopter

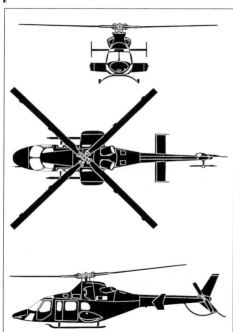

Length: 12.8 m (42 ft 2 in) Rotorspan: 12.8 m (42 ft) Height: 3.5 m (11 ft 6 in)

Features: Four rotor/twin turbine; retractable landing gear; side pods

The latest development of the Bell 222 and 230, the 430 features a four blade rotor assembly, producing a 10 percent increase in power. Utility versions are fitted with skid landing gear and can be seen fitted with FLIR and TV pods for police work. A Bell 430 holds the round-the-world speed record for helicopters. Heli-Dyne of the USA have modified the 230 for a number of specialist roles including reconnaissance, border patrol and search and rescue.

Variants and operators

Bell 430: Utility versions are in service with a number of Police and Law Enforcement agencies in Canada and the USA. Albania and UAE also operate Utility versions, Chile has the sole shipborne maritime surveillance version.

Payload

Accommodation: 2 pilots; 7 passengers
Cargo: n/a

Bell UH-1 Iroquois (Huey) USA

Utility helicopter

Built in huge numbers between 1959 and 1987 in the USA. In its operational configuration, two troops are replaced by a pair of door gunners and pintle- mounted machine guns. The earlier model 204 UH-1 had a smaller cabin with one window each side.

Variants and operators

UH-1: Argentina; Australia; Bolivia; Bosnia; Brazil; Canada; Chile; Colombia; Dominican republic; Ethiopia; Germany; Greece; Guatemala; Honduras; Japan; Jordan; South Korea; Lebanon; Mexico; Myanmar; New Zealand; Pakistan; Panama; Papua New Guinea; Peru; Philippines; El Salvador; Singapore; Spain; Taiwan; Thailand; Tunisia; Turkey; Uruguay; USA; Venezuela

Payload

Accommodation: 2 pilots; 2 crew; 12 troops
Cargo: 1,759 kg (3,880 lb)
Hardpoints: 2 fuselage
Weapons: door guns; gun pods; rockets

Length: 17.6 m (41 ft 9 in) Rotorspan: 14.6 m (48 ft) Height: 4.4 m (14 ft 5 in)

Features: Twin rotor/single turbine; skids; large side doors

Bell UN-1N Iroquois (Twin Huey) USA

Utility helicopter

Originally designed for the Canadian government as the CH-135, the Twin Huey was also adopted by the USMC and US Navy. Also produced in Italy, the latest version is the 412 with a four rotor assemble to reduce noise and vibration and increase cargo capacity.

Variants and operators

UH-1N: Canada, USMC, US Navy **412:** Botswana; Bahrain; Canada; Honduras; Mexico; Nigeria; Slovenia; South Korea; Sri Lanka; Thailand; UK; Venezuela; Zimbabwe

Payload

Accommodation: 2 pilots; 2 crew; 14 passengers
Cargo: 2,268 kg (5,000 lb)

Features: Twin rotor/twin turbine; skids; longer nose section

Bell OH-58D Kiowa USA

Reconnaissance helicopter

Developed from the standard JetRanger, the first Kiowa entered service in 1969. All US Army OH-58s will be upgraded to Kiowa Warrior standard with mast mounted sight and two weapons stations. The mast mounted sight can acquire, track and illuminate targets for other helicopters to fire Hellfire missiles at. A stealth kit can be fitted to reduce IR and radar cross section.

Variants and operators
OH-58D: Taiwan; Turkey; US Army

Payload
Accommodation: 2 pilots; 2 passengers
Warload: 907 kg (2,000 lb)
Hardpoints: 2 fuselage
Weapons: Hellfire; Stinger; gun pods; rockets

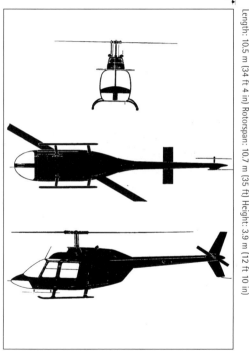

Length: 10.5 m (34 ft 4 in) Rotorspan: 10.7 m (35 ft) Height: 3.9 m (12 ft 10 in)

Features: Twin rotor/single turbine; skids; mast mounted sight

417

Bell AH-1 Cobra/SuperCobra USA

Attack helicopter

Length: 13.9 m (45 ft 6 in) Rotorspan: 14.6 m (48 ft) Height: 4.1 m (13 ft 6 in)

Developed in 1965 for a US Army requirement for a faster gunship than the UH-1 Huey, the AH-1 uses the same powerplant and transmission as the Huey with a slimmer, faster fuselage and more efficient weapons and crew stations. The SeaCobra and SuperCobra (bottom silhouette) both use the twin engine layout from the Twin Huey and is used by the USMC.

Variants and operators

AH-1: Bahrain; Greece; Iran; Israel; Japan; Jordan; South Korea; Pakistan; Thailand; Turkey; US Army **AH-1W SeaCobra:** South Korea; USMC **AH-1W SuperCobra:** Taiwan; Turkey

Payload

Accommodation: 2 pilots
Warload: 1,118 kg (2,466 lb)
Hardpoints: 4 wing
Weapons: M197 20 mm cannon; TOW; Hellfire; gun pods; rockets

Features: Twin rotor/single or twin turbine; skids; tandem cockpit

Bell/Boeing V-22 Osprey USA

Tilt-rotor transport

The only tilt-rotor aircraft in production, the V-22 is expected to enter service with the USMC in 1999 and with other branches of the US Armed Forces after 2000. The US Army has withdrawn its requirement for 231 V-22s but may order some for medevac and special operations. US Navy aircraft will be used for Combat Search and Rescue (CSAR) US Air Force aircraft for long-range special operations.

Variants and operators
V-22: US Air Force; USMC; US Navy

Payload
Accommodation: 2 pilots; 2 crew; 24 troops
Cargo: 9,072 kg (20,000 lb)
Weapons: door guns; (Naval version) ASW torpedoes; depth charges

Length: 17.5 m (57 ft 4 in) Rotospan: 11.6 m (38 ft) each Height: 5.4 m (17 ft 8 in)

Features: Twin tilt rotors; twin tails; high/straight wing

419

Boeing (McDonnell Douglas) AH-64 Apache USA

Attack helicopter

Length: 15.5 m (51 ft) Rotorspan: 14.6 m (48 ft) Height: 3.8 m (12 ft 7 in)

Features: Four rotor/twin turbine; ventral cannon; tandem cockpit

Over 1,000 Apaches have been delivered since the type first flew in 1975. AH-64Ds have the mast-mounted Longbow radar, and advanced avionics enabling them to communice securely with JSTARS and JTIDS equipped aircraft. The Netherlands AH-64Ds will lack the Longbow radar. WAH-64Ds are externally identical, but are powered by Rolls Royce engines.

Variants and operators

AH-64: Egypt; Greece; Israel; Saudi Arabia; UAE; USA **AH-64D:** Netherlands; USA **WAH-64D:** UK

Payload

Accommodation: 2 pilots
Warload: 1,500 kg (5000 lb)
Hardpoints: 6 wing
Weapons: M230 30 mm Cannon; Hellfire; Stinger; Starstreak; Sidearm; AIM-9 Sidewinder; rockets

Boeing CH-46 Sea Knight USA

Medium–lift helicopter

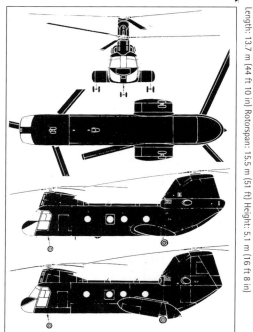

First flown in 1958 the CH-46 was due to be replaced by the V–22 in the early 1980s; overruns on the V–22 programme mean they will have to soldier on until 2000+. Known to the Marine Corps as the Frog, the CH-46 is often mistaken for the Chinook, but the Frog has tricycle landing gear while the Chinook has four wheels.

Variants and operators
CH-47: Canada; Japan; Sweden; USMC; USN

Payload
Accommodation: 2 pilots; 2 crew; 25 troops
Cargo: 4,082 kg (9,000 lb)
Weapons: door guns

Features: Tandem rotor/twin internal turboshafts; tricycle landing gear; side pods

Length: 13.7 m (44 ft 10 in) Rotorspan: 15.5 m (51 ft) Height: 5.1 m (16 ft 8 in)

Boeing CH-47 Chinook USA

Heavy lift helicopter

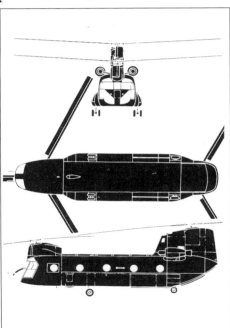

Length: 15.5 m (51 ft) Rotorspan: 18.3 m (60 ft) each Height: 5.8 m (18 ft 11 in)

Features: Tandem rotor/twin turbine; quad landing gear; long side pods

The big CH-47 Chinook first flew in 1961, and remains the primary heavy transport of a number of armies. The UK Royal Air Force operate a number of special operations Chinooks, fitted with extra armour, weapons and defensive aids. The US Army's MH-47E is a more extensive refit with terrain following radar, FLIR, ECM and in-flight refueling probes (picture).

Variants and operators

CH-47: Argentina; Australia; Canada; Greece; Japan; Iran; Italy; Libya; Morocco; South Korea; Netherlands; Singapore; Spain; Taiwan; Thailand; Turkey; UK; USA

Payload

Accommodation: 2 pilots; 2 crew; 55 troops; 24 stretchers
Cargo: 12,210 kg (26,918 lb)
Weapons: door guns

Boeing (McDonnell Douglas) MD-500 Defender USA

Light helicopter

Developed from the US Army's OH-6A Cayuse observation helicopter, the civil version entered service in 1968. Civil production has been shifted to the Model 500E (see next entry). Military versions included an anti-submarine version for the Taiwanese Navy, the 500MD with a mast-mounted sight and the 500MD/TOW with a nose-mounted sight (bottom silhouette).

Variants and operators

Defender: Argentina; Bahrain; Brazil; Colombia; Costa Rica; Croatia; Cyprus; Denmark; El Salvador; Finland; Honduras; Indonesia; Iraq; Israel; Japan; Jordan; Peru; Philippines; Kenya; Mexico; South Korea; North Korea; Spain; Taiwan; USA

Payload

Accommodation: 2 pilots; 2 passengers
Hardpoints: 2 stub wing
Weapons: TOW; Stinger; gun pods; rockets

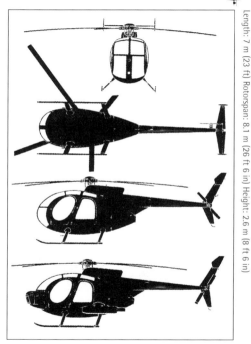

Length: 7 m (23 ft) Rotorspan: 8.1 m (26 ft 6 in) Height: 2.6 m (8 ft 6 in)

Features: Four rotor/single turbine; boom tail; round canopy

423

Boeing (McDonnell Douglas) Model 500E USA

Light helicopter

Length: 7.5 m (24 ft 7 in) Rotorspan: 8.1 m (26 ft 5 in) Height: 2.7 m (8 ft 9 in)

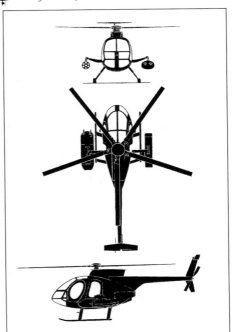

Features: Five rotor/single turbine; boom tail; pointed nose

The Model 500E replaced the standard 500 in production in 1982. The Cabin was enlarged with more space for pilots and passengers. A new engine was also fitted, some aircraft have been fitted with the No Tail Rotor system (NOTAR) using a ducted fan to replace the standard tail rotor. Armed versions have been produced as the MD 530.

Variants and operators
MD 530: Argentina; Chile; Colombia; Mexico; Philippines;

Payload
Accommodation: 2 pilots; 4 passengers
Cargo: 907 kg (2,000 lb)
Hardpoints: 2 stub wing
Weapons: TOW; Stinger; gun pods; rockets

Boeing (McDonnell Douglas) Model 520 USA

Utility helicopter

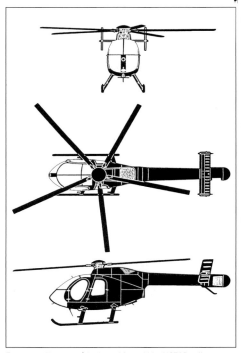

Length: 9.3 m (30 ft 6 in) Rotorspan: 8.4 m (27 ft 6 in) Height: 2.6 m (8 ft 8 in)

A NOTAR (No Tail Rotor) development of the standard Model 500, deliveries began in 1991. The NOTAR assembly reduces noise and increases safety. A stretched version the MD 600 is also in production, which has three side windows. Armed versions have been developed but have yet to secure order.

Variants and operators

MD520: standard production version in service with a number of police and law enforcement agencies. **MD600:** stretched version

Payload

Accommodation: 2 pilots; 6 passengers
Cargo: 1,247 kg (2,750 lb)

Features: Five rotor/single turbine; skids; NOTAR tail

Boeing (McDonnell Douglas) Explorer USA

Utility helicopter

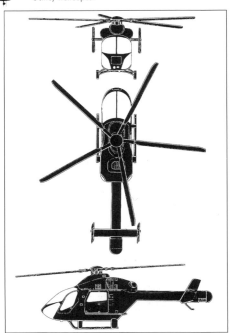

Length: 9.7 m (31 ft 10 in) Rotorspan: 10.3 m (33 ft 10 in) Height: 3.6 m (12 ft)

Features: Five rotor/twin turbine; skids; NOTAR tail

The first helicopter to be designed specifically for the NOTAR system, the Explorer first flew in 1992. Firm orders for 70 have been secured, future markets are expected to call for 1,000 aircraft. The NOTAR design and relocated engine exhausts make the Explorer particularly suited to air ambulance roles, where it may have to work in confined spaces.

Variants and operators

Explorer: civil versions in service in Belgium; Germany; Japan; Luxembourg; South Korea; Sweden; Switzerland; USA

Payload

Accommodation: 2 pilots; 6 passengers
Cargo: 1,458 kg (3,215 lb)

Boeing/Sikorsky RAH-66 Commanche USA

Reconnaissance/attack helicopter

The first helicopter to be designed with stealth features, the fuselage is made from radar absorbent material and angled to reflect radar. The weapons bay can be retracted into the hull to further reduce the radar cross section. Designed for nap-of the earth flying in all weathers, the pilots have glass cockpits and advanced night sights. Some may also be fitted with the Longbow radar.

Variants and operators
RAH-66: US Army

Payload
Accommodation: 2 pilots
Warload: 1,185 kg (2,612 lb)
Hardpoints: internal weapons bays; 2 optional stub wing
Weapons: three barrel 20 mm cannon; Hellfire; Stinger; fuel tanks; rockets

Features: Five rotor/twin turbine; fenestron tail rotor; tandem cockpit

Length: 13.2 m (43 ft 4 in) Rotorspan: 11.9 m (39 ft) Height: 3.4 m (11 ft 1 in)

Brantly B-2 USA

Ultra light helicopter

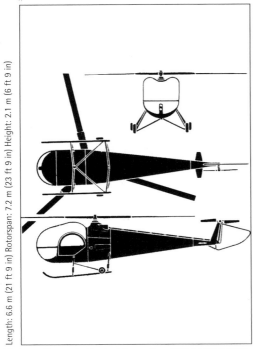

First flown in 1953, the B-2 was put back in to production in 1990 as a cheap helicopter trainer. Production has again ceased, but many remain in service, especially in Japan.

Variants and operators
B-2: main production version

Payload
Accommodation: 2 pilots
Cargo: 22.7 kg (50 lb)

Length: 6.6 m (21 ft 9 in) Rotorspan: 7.2 m (23 ft 9 in) Height: 2.1 m (6 ft 9 in)

Features: Three rotor/single piston engine; skids; bubble canopy

Denel (Atlas) **Rooivalk** South Africa

Attack helicopter

First flown in 1990, the Rooivalk was South Africa's first indigenous helicopter design. Developed using technology from the licence built AS 330 Puma transport helicopter, the Rooivalk uses the same engine and rotor system. Several prototypes are flying, each with minor differences in avionics and nose mounted equipment.

Variants and operators
Rooivalk: South Africa

Payload
Accommodation: 1 pilot; 1 gunner
Warload: 1,371 kg (3,022 lb)
Hardpoints: 2 wingtip; four wing
Weapons: nose-mounted 20 mm cannon; ZT-3 Swift or ZT-35 AT missiles; V3C Darter; rockets

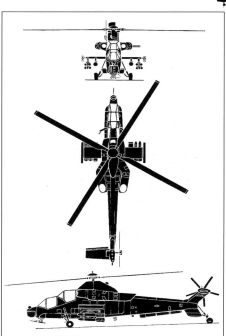

Length: 16.4 m (53 ft 9 in) Rotorspan: 15.6 m (51 ft 1 in) Height: 4.6 m (15 ft)

Features: Four rotor/twin turboshaft; twin cockpits in tandem; ventral tailfin

EHI EH-101 Merlin Italy/UK

Shipborne anti-submarine helicopter

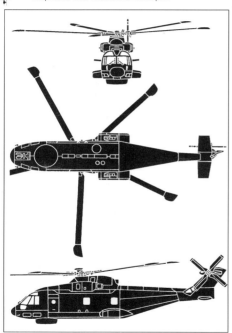

Length: 22.8 m (74 ft 10 in) Rotorspan: 18.6 m (61 ft) Height: 6.6 m (21 ft 10 in)

Features: Five rotor/three turbine; tricycle landing gear; ventral radar

First flown in 1987 the EH 101 was designed primarily for anti-submarine warfare. It is now being studied as an AEW, ECM and SAR platform as well. A civil version the Heliliner has been developed, seating 30 passengers. The utility version has a rear loading ramp and no radar.

Variants and operators

EH-101: Italy; UK

Payload

Accommodation: 2 pilots; 2 crew
Cargo: 3,900 kg (8,598 lb)
Hardpoints: 4 fuselage
Weapons: Sea Eagle; Marte Mk2; Sea Skua; ASW torpedoes; depth charges

EHI EH-101 Merlin Utility Italy/UK

Shipborne transport helicopter

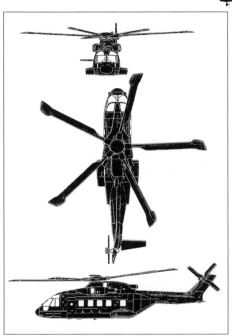

First flown in 1989 the utility version of the EH 101 was developed at the request of the Italian government who needed a replacement for the AS-61 Pelican transport helicopter. The Royal Navy and Royal Air Force will also receive them as a Commando and Wessex replacement. Can be fitted with stub wings or a nose-mounted cannon.

Variants and operators

EH-101 Utility : Canada; Italy; Japan; UK

Payload

Accommodation: 2 pilots; 1 crew; 45 troops
Cargo: 5,443 kg (12,000 lb)
Weapons: door guns

Features: Five rotor/three turbine; tricycle landing gear; rear loading ramp

431

Enstrom F28 USA

Light helicopter

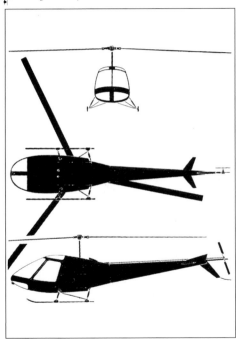

Length: 8.9 m (29 ft 3 in) Rotorspan: 9.7 m (32 ft) Height: 2.8 m (9 ft 2 in)

Features: Three rotor/single piston engine; skids; straight tail boom

Used by Chile, Colombia and Peru for basic helicopter training, over 170 are in service with civilian and police operators. The 480 is powered by an Allison 250-C20W turboshaft for greater speed and range. The rotor gearbox is larger on the 480, requiring a larger fuselage mounting.

Variants and operators

F28/280: standard piston engined production version **Sentinel:** Police surveillance version **480:** turboshaft powered version

Payload

Accommodation: 1 pilot; 2 passengers
Cargo: 49 kg (108 lb)

Eurocopter (Aerospatiale) SA 330 Puma France

Medium lift helicopter

The Puma was designed to meet the French Army requirement for a helicoptère de manoeuvre. Capable of operating in all weathers, day or night, it was the first western helicopter to be certified for such operations. The first prototype flew in 1965, 695 were built before production switched to the Super Puma. South Africa has developed an armed version, the Oryx, with nose-mounted sight and two weapons stations.

Variants and operators

SA 330: Argentina; Algeria; Belgium; Brazil; Cameroon; Chile; Congo; Ecuador; Ethiopia; France; Gabon; Iraq; Ivory Coast; Kenya; Kuwait; Lebanon; Malawi; Mexico; Morocco; Nepal; Nigeria; Pakistan; Philippines; Portugal; Romania; Senegal; Senegambia; South Africa; Spain; Sudan; Togo; UAE; UK; Zaire

Payload

Accommodation: 2 pilots; 1 crew; 20 troops
Cargo: 3,200 kg (7,055 lb)
Hardpoints: 2 stub wings
Weapons: door guns; gun pods; rockets

Features: Four rotor/twin turbine; retractable landing gear; side pods

Length: 14.1 m (46 ft 1 in) Rotorspan: 15 m (49 ft 2 in) Height: 5.1 m (16 ft 10 in)

433

Eurocopter AS 332 Super Puma France/Germany

Medium lift helicopter

Length: 15.5 m (50ft 11 in) Rotorspan: 15.6 m (51 ft 2 in) Height: 4.9 m (16 ft 1 in)

Derived from the original Puma, the Super Puma first flew in 1978. The main changes were confined to the fuselage which was stretched and the main rotor bearings. The standard Super Puma has been developed into a VIP transport, airborne radar platform and anti-ship aircraft. Military versions are called AS 532 Cougar.

Variants and operators

AS 332: Argentina; Brazil; Chile; Congo; Finland; France; Gabon; Germany; Japan; Jordan; South Korea; Mexico; Nepal; Oman; Spain; Sweden; Switzerland; Thailand; Togo; UAE; Venezuela;
AS 532 Cougar: Chile; France; Kuwait; Netherlands; Saudi Arabia; Singapore; Spain; Sweden; Turkey; UAE; Zimbabwe

Payload

Accommodation: 2 pilots; 1 crew; 25 troops
Cargo: 4,500 kg (9,920 lb)
Hardpoints: 2 fuselage
Weapons: door guns; gun pods; rockets (naval version) Exocet; ASW torpedoes; depth charges;

Features: Four rotor/twin turbine; retractable landing gear; side pods

434

Eurocopter AS 550/555 Ecureuil France/Germany

Light helicopter

First flown in 1974, over 2,000 have been built. Also built under licence in Brazil as the Helibras Esquillo. The AS 550 Fennec is a purpose built military version with attachments for TOW missiles, gun pods and rockets. Some Ecureuils have been retrofitted with roof mounted sights and weapons stations.

Variants and operators

AS 350P: A Ibania; Algeria; Argentina; Australia; Benin; Botswana; Brazil; Cambodia; Central African Republic; Comores; Ecuador; France; Guinea Republic; Iceland; Mali; Malawi; Paraguay; Peru; Tunisia; UK **AS 550:** Argentina; Brazil; Denmark; France; Mexico; Singapore

Payload

Accommodation: 2 pilots; 4 passengers
Cargo: 1,400 kg (3,086 lb)
Hardpoints: 2 stub wings
Weapons: TOW; gun pods; rockets

Length: 10.9 m (35 ft 10 in) Rotorspan: 10.7 m (35 ft) Height: 3.3 m (10 ft 11 in)

Features: Three rotor/single turbine; skids; long tail boom

435

Eurocopter AS 365 Dauphin 2 France/Germany

Light helicopter

Length: 10.9 m (36 ft) Rotorspan: 11.5 m (37 ft 8 in) Height: 3.5 m (11 ft 6 in)

Features: Four rotor/single turbine; fenestron tail; tricycle landing gear

Developed as the successor for the AS 361 Dauphin which first flew in 1972. The Dauphin 2 can be recognised by its longer nose section and retracting tricycle landing gear. The US Coast Guard operate over 100 as search and rescue aircraft, where they are known as HH-65 Dolphins. The AS 565 Panther was designed specifically for the military market. The three-view shows AS 565 MA.

Variants and operators

AS 365: Cambodia; China; Congo; Dominican Republic; France; Iceland; Israel; Ivory Coast; Malawi; Morocco; Saudi Arabia; South Africa; UAE; US Coast Guard

AS 565: Angola; Argentina; Brazil; China; France; Saudi Arabia; UAE

Payload

Accommodation: 2 pilots; 8 passengers
Cargo: 4,250 kg (9,369 lb)
Weapons: AS 15TT; gun pods; rockets

Eurocopter EC 135 France/Germany

Light helicopter

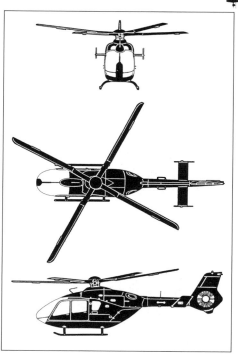

Length: 10.2 m (33 ft 4 in) Rotorspan: 10.2 m (33 ft 5 in) Height: 3.6 m (11 ft 10 in)

First flown in 1988, as the BO108 technology demonstrator, the EC135 was a stretched, more powerful development of the BO105. The use of advanced materials and a fenestron tail rotor have reduced drag by 30 percent. 42 aircraft have been ordered and production began in 1996.

Variants and operators

EC135: standard production version EC635: military version

Payload

Accommodation: 2 pilots; 6 passengers
Cargo: 900 kg (1,984 lb)

Features: Four rotor/twin turbine; fenestron tail rotor; skids

Eurocopter (Aerospatiale) SA 315B Lama II France

Light helicopter

Length: 10.3 m (33 ft 8 in) Rotorspan: 11 m (36 ft 1 in) Height: 3.1 m (10 ft 1 in)

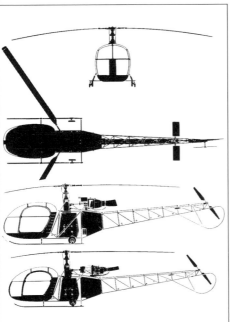

Features: Three rotor/single turbine; bubble canopy; lattice tail boom

The SA315B was developed from the earlier series of Alouettes specifically for the Indian Army. It used the airframe of the Alouette II with the power plant and rotor system of the Alouette III. Production continues in India, where it has set a number of helicopter altitude records.

Variants and operators

SA 313 (bottom silhouette): Indonesia; Belgium; Cameroon; France; Senegal SA 315 Lama: Angola; Argentina; Bolivia; Chile; Ecuador; Ethiopia; India; Morocco; Namibia; Nepal; Pakistan; Seychelle Islands; Togo

Payload

Accommodation: 1 pilot; 4 passengers
Cargo: 1,135 kg (2,500 lb)

Eurocopter (Aerospatiale)
SA 316/319 Alouette III France

Light helicopter

The last development of the Alouette family the SA316 had a larger cabin and a more powerful engine. First flown in 1959. Licence built production was undertaken in India and Romania. In 1977 an Alouette III in Canada rescued a climber from 4,235 m (13,900 ft) up Mount Logan, the highest hoist rescue ever.

Variants and operators

SA 316: Argentina; Austria; Burundi; Chad; Congo; Congo (Democratic Republic); Ecuador; Ethiopia; France; Ghana; Guinea-Bissau; Indonesia; Iraq; Ireland; Jordan; Lebanon; Libya; Malaysia; Malta; Pakistan; Rwanda; South Africa; Surinam; Switzerland; Tunisia; Venezuela; Zimbabwe **SA 319:** A lbania; Austria; Belgium; Cameroon; France; Greece; India; Mexico; Pakistan; Peru; Romania

Payload

Accommodation: 2 pilots; 5 passengers
Cargo: 750 kg (1,650 lb)
Hardpoints: 2 stub wings
Weapons: AS.12; ASW torpedoes; gun pods; rockets

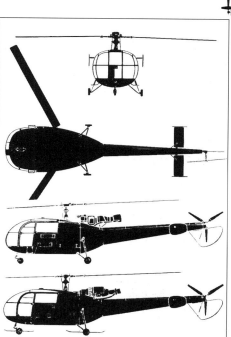

Length: 10.2 m (33 ft 4 in) Rotorspan: 11 m (36 ft 1 in) Height: 2.9 m (9 ft 9 in)

Features: Three rotor/single turbine; tricycle landing gear; exposed engine

Eurocopter (Aerospatiale) SA 341 Gazelle France

Light observation helicopter

Length: 11.9 m (39 ft 3 in) Rotorspan: 10.5 m (34 ft 5 in) Height: 3.2 m (10 ft 2 in)

Features: Three rotor/single turbine; Fenestron tail rotor; bubble canopy

The first helicopter to feature a fenestron tail rotor, the Gazelle first flew in 1967. Production was also undertaken in the UK by Westland and the Former Yugoslavia by Soko. Yugoslav versions carried the SA-7 Grail air-to-air missile and the AT-3 Sagger anti-tank missile.

Variants and operators

SA 341: Angola; Burundi; Cameroon; China; Croatia; Cyprus; Ecuador; Egypt; France; Gabon; Guinea Republic; Iraq; Ireland; Kuwait; Lebanon; Libya; Morocco; Qatar; Republika Srpska; Rwanda; Syria; UAE; UK; Federal Yugoslavia

Payload

Accommodation: 1 pilot; 4 passengers
Cargo: 700 kg (1,540 lb)
Hardpoints: 2 stub pylons
Weapons: AS.11; AS.12; HOT; AT-3; gun pods; rockets

Eurocopter (MBB) BO-105 Germany

Light helicopter

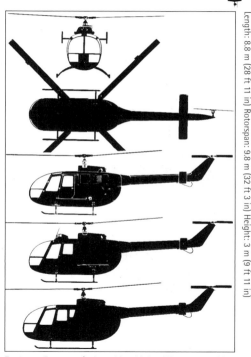

Length: 8.8 m (28 ft 11 in) Rotorspan: 9.8 m (32 ft 3 in) Height: 3 m (9 ft 11 in)

First flown in 1967, the BO-105 has been developed into a number of civil and military versions. The top silhouette shows the standard BO105CB, the middle view the armed BO105SP or PAH-1, which carries HOT anti-tank missiles, the bottom silhouette shows the stretched BO105CBS. Over 1,300 aircraft have been built.

Variants and operators
BO105: Brunei; Bahrain; Chile; Colombia; Czech Republic; Germany; Indonesia; Iraq; Kenya; Lesotho; Mexico; Netherlands; Nigeria; Peru; Philippines; Spain; Sudan; Sweden; Trinidad and Tobago; UAE

Payload
Accommodation: 2 pilots; 3 passengers
Cargo: 800 kg (1,764 lb)
Hardpoints: 2 stub pylons
Weapons: TOW; HOT; gun pods; rockets

Features: Four rotor/twin turbine; high tail boom; round fuselage

441

Eurocopter Tiger France/Germany

Attack helicopter

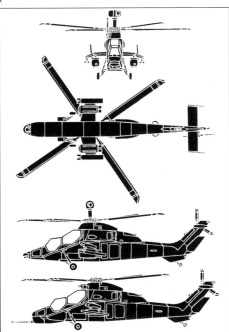

Length: 14 m (45 ft 11 in) Rotorspan: 13 m (42 ft 7 in) Height: 4.3 m (14 ft 2 in)

Features: Four rotor/twin turbine; tandem cockpits; mast or nose-mounted sight

First flown in 1991, the Tiger is expected to enter service in 2003. Trials have been carried out on several versions including the HAP escort helicopter (bottom silhouette) and HAC anti-tank helicopter for France and UHT anti-tank and support helicopter for Germany (top silhouette). Unlike most other attack helicopters the pilot is seated at the front, the gunner behind.

Variants and operators

Tiger: France; Germany

Payload

Accommodation: 2 pilots
Hardpoints: 4 wing
Weapons: Trigat; HOT; Mistral; Stinger; gun pods; rockets

GKN Westland Lynx UK

Multi-role helicopter

Length: 15.2 m (49 ft 9 in) Rotorspan: 12.8 m (42 ft) Height: 3.5 m (11 ft 6 in)

Developed in conjunction with France, the Lynx first flew in 1971. The bottom silhouette shows the Naval Lynx fitted with tricycle landing gear and nose mounted radar. The latest naval versions have a 360 deg radar mounted under the nose. UK Army Lynxes (top silhouette) can carry TOW missiles, but will be re-rolled as utility aircraft when the WAH-64D Apache comes into service.

Variants and operators

Naval Lynx: Brazil; Denmark; France; Germany; Netherlands; Norway; Pakistan; Portugal; South Korea; UK **Army Lynx:** UK

Payload

Accommodation: 1 pilot; 1 observer or 2 pilots; 9 troops
Cargo: 907 kg (2,000 lb)
Hardpoints: 2 fuselage
Weapons: (naval) Sea Skua; ASW torpedoes; depth charges; gun pods; (military) door guns; TOW

Features: Four rotor/twin turbine; long nose section; tricycle or skid landing gear

GKN Westland Sea King UK

Shipborne anti submarine helicopter

Length: 17.2 m (57 ft 2 in) Rotorspan: 18.9 m (62 ft) Height: 4.7 m (15 ft 6 in)

Features: Five rotor/twin turbine; dorsal radar; amphibious hull

Westland obtained a licence to produce the Sikorsky SH-61 in 1959. They developed the aircraft for the Royal Navy by installing Rolls-Royce Gnome engines and a new five-blade tail rotor. The radar is mounted above the tail boom unlike US aircraft. Some 245 Sea Kings have been built in several different models, including an AEW version with a large ventral radar radome. The transport Commando version lacks the dorsal radar and sponsons. Two different debris guards can be fitted above the cockpit, a flat plate or a sand filter box.

Variants and operators

Sea King: Australia; Belgium; Egypt; Germany; India; Norway; Pakistan; UK **AEW Mk2:** Spain; UK **Commando:** Egypt; Qatar; UK

Payload

Accommodation: 2 pilots; 2 systems operators; 45 troops (Commando)
Cargo: 3,628 kg (8,000 lb)
Hardpoints: 4 fuselage
Weapons: Sea Eagle; ASW torpedoes; depth charges

GKN Westland Wasp UK

Shipborne anti-submarine helicopter

First flown in 1958, the Wasp entered Royal Navy service in 1963. Designed to operate from frigate sized warships its familiar four poster landing gear is fitted with casters to enable easy movement in a limited space. The land-based version, the Scout, is no longer in service.

Variants and operators

Wasp: Indonesia; Malaysia

Payload

Accommodation: 1 pilot 4 passengers
Warload: 680 kg (1,500 lb)
Hardpoints: 2 fuselage
Weapons: AS.12; ASW torpedoes; depth charges

Features: Four rotor/single turbine; quad landing gear; exposed engine

Length: 9.2 m (30 ft 4 in) Rotorspan: 9.8 m (32 ft 3 in) Height: 3.6 m (11 ft 8 in)

GKN Westland Wessex UK

Utility helicopter

Length: 14.7 m (48 ft 4 in) Rotorspan: 18.9 m (62 ft) Height: 5.1 m (16 ft 10 in)

Westland began building the Sikorsky S-58 under licence in 1957. The powerplant on the Wessex differed significantly from the S-58 by using two Rolls-Royce Gnome turboshafts in place of the original piston engines. The twin exhausts beneath the cockpit are a major feature. Most of the 377 built have been withdrawn from service, only the Royal Air force and Uruguayan Navy still operate them.

Variants and operators
Wessex: UK; Uruguay

Payload
Accommodation: 2 pilots; 16 troops
Cargo: 3,628 kg (8,000 lb)
Weapons: door guns

Features: Four rotor/twin turbine; high set cockpit; nose-mounted engine

HAL Advanced Light Helicopter India

Multi-role light helicopter

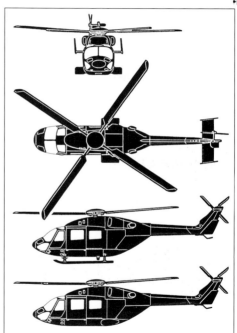

Length: 13.4 m (44 ft) Rotorspan: 13.2 m (43 ft 3 in) Height: 3.9 m (12 ft 10 in)

Based on the MBB family of helicopters the first Indian aircraft flew in 1992. HAL intends to produce several versions including an attack/SAR version for the army and airforce, a naval version with retractable landing gear, a gunship version with a tandem two seat cockpit and a civil version with skid landing gear.

Variants and operators
ALH: deliveries expected to begin in 1998 to Indian Army, Air Force, Navy and Coast Guard

Payload
Accommodation: 2 pilots; 10 passengers
Cargo: 1,500 kg (3,307 lb)
Hardpoints: 4 stub pylons
Weapons: anti-ship/anti-tank missiles; gun pods; rockets

Features: Four rotor/twin turbine; (civil) skids; (military) tricycle landing gear

447

Hiller UH-12E USA

Light utility helicopter

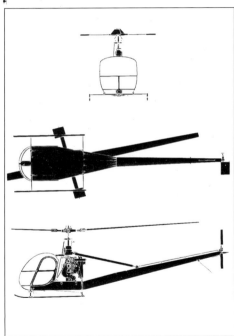

Length: 8.7 m (28 ft 6 in) Rotorspan: 10.8 m (35 ft 5 in) Height: 3.1 m (10 ft 1 in)

Features: Twin rotor/single piston engine; bubble canopy; thin sloped tail boom

The original UH-12 first flew in 1948 and had been developed for the US Army. Used during the 1950s by the US armed forces the aircraft was taken out of production as bigger helicopters came along. Put back into production for the civil market in 1991 it was intended to fill the trainer market but ended up being used for agricultural work.

Variants and operators
UH-12E: standard production version

Payload
Accommodation: 2 pilots; 1 passenger
Cargo: Limited. No official figures available.

Kaman K-max USA

External lift helicopter

The Kaman K-Max first flew in 1991, and was designed for maximum lift for carrying underslung loads. The unique intermeshing rotor system enables all power to be directed to produce lift; the single cockpit and lack of a cabin reduce the weight of the aircraft. With these features the K-max can lift more than its own weight.

Variants and operators
K-Max: standard production version

Payload
Accommodation: 1 pilot
Cargo: 2,721 kg (6,000 lb)

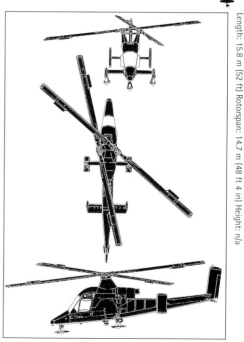

Length: 15.8 m (52 ft) Rotorspan: 14.7 m (48 ft 4 in) Height: n/a

Features: Twin intermeshing rotors/single turbine; single cockpit; tricycle landing gear

449

Kaman SH-2 SeaSprite USA

Shipborne anti-submarine helicopter

Length: 12.2 m (40 ft) Rotorspan: 13.5 m (44 ft 4 in) Height: 4.6 m (15 ft)

Features: Four rotor/twin turbine; retractable landing gear; ventral radar

First flown in 1959 as a single-engined ASW helicopter the SeaSprite was known as the LAMPS I in naval service. From 1967 all single engined aircraft were refitted with a second engine. Put back into production in 1981, with new engines and upgraded avionics.

Variants and operators

SH-2G: Australia; Egypt; Taiwan; US Navy **SH-2F:** New Zealand

Payload

Accommodation: 2 pilots; 1 sonar operator; 4 passengers
Cargo: 1,814 kg (4,000 lb)
Hardpoints: 2 stub wings
Weapons: door guns; Penguin; Maverick; Sea Skua; ASW torpedoes; depth charges

Kamov Ka-25 Hormone Russia

Shipborne anti-submarine helicopter

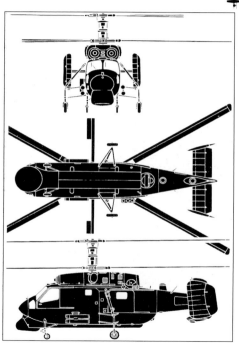

The Kamov bureau was created in 1947 to take advantage of the German research data gathered at the end of the second world war. The unique co-axial rotor system is a feature of all Kamov helicopters, the first of which was the Hormone in 1961. Used by the Russian Navy for ASW and over the horizon targeting it is being replaced by the larger Ka-27 Helix in Russian service.

Variants and operators

Ka-25: Bulgaria; India; Russia; Syria; Ukraine; Vietnam

Payload

Accommodation: 2 pilots; 12 passengers
Cargo: 1,300 kg (2,866 lb)
Hardpoints: internal bomb bay; 2 fuselage
Weapons: ASW torpedoes; depth charges

Features: Twin coaxial rotors/twin turbine; quad landing gear; twin tails

Kamov Ka-27 Helix A Russia

Shipborne anti-submarine helicopter

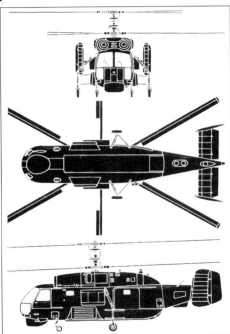

Length: 11.3 m (37 ft 1 in) Rotorspan: 15.9 m (52 ft 2 in) Height: 5.4 m (17 ft 8 in)

Kamov began developing the basic Hormone design to overcome its inability to hover and operate a dipping sonar at night or in foul weather. The Helix first flew in 1973, and is operated from Sovremenny and Udaloy class destroyers and later cruisers. Earlier warships were unable to operate the Helix because their hangers were already a tight fit for the much smaller Hormone.

Variants and operators

Ka-27: Russia; Ukraine **Ka-28 Helix D (export version)**: India; Vietnam

Payload

Accommodation: 2 pilots; 1 sonar operator
Cargo: 5,000 kg (11,023 lb)
Hardpoints: 2 fuselage
Weapons: ASW torpedoes; depth charges

Features: Twin coaxial rotors/twin turbine; twin tails; smaller radar than Ka-25

Kamov Ka-29 Helix-B Russia

Shipborne multi-purpose helicopter

Developed from the standard Ka-27 anti-submarine helicopter, the Ka-29 and Ka-31 were designed to perform a range of missions from the projected aircraft carriers and amphibious landing ships. Ka-29s have weapons pylons and a gatling-type gun housed in an articulated door in the nose. Ka-31s have a large flat array radar under the fuselage for radar picket duties.

Variants and operators
Ka-29: Russia; Ukraine **Ka-31:** Russia; India

Payload
Accommodation: 2 pilots; 16 troops
Cargo: 4,000 lb (8,818 lb)
Hardpoints: 4 pylons
Weapons: Spiral; gun pods; rockets

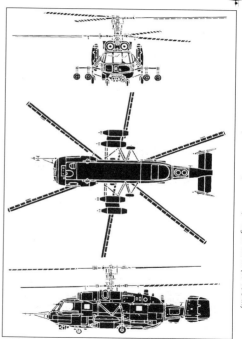

Length: 11.3 m (37 ft 1 in) Rotorspan: 15.9 m (52 ft 2 in) Height: 5.4 m (17 ft 8 in)

Features: Twin coaxial rotors/twin turbine; square nose section; no ventral radar

Kamov Ka-50 Hokum Russia

Attack helicopter

First flown in 1982 the Hokum was the world's first single seat attack helicopter. Only 8 are in service with the Russian Army with full-scale production only just beginning. The Hokum's long development is a result of its many unique features: the single pilot, an ejector seat and an advanced avionic systems to allow single pilot operation. A two seat version the Ka-52 (bottom silhouette) is also being developed to overcome some of these problems.

Variants and operators
Ka-50: Russia **Ka-52:** Russia

Payload
Accommodation: 1 or 2 pilots
Warload: 3,000 kg (6,610 lb)
Hardpoints: 4 wing
Weapons: single 2A42 30 mm cannon; Kh-25MP; Igla; AT-12 Vikhr; gun pods; rockets

Features: Twin coaxial rotors/twin turbine; side-by-side or single seat cockpit; retractable tricycle landing gear

Length: 16 m (52 ft 6 in) Rotorspan: 14.5 m (47 ft 7 in) Height: 4.9 m (16 ft 2 in)

Kamov Ka-126 Hoodlum Russia

Utility helicopter

Developed from the earlier Ka-26, which first flew in 1965, the first Ka-126 flew in 1986. The new model boasted a turboshaft engine to increase performance and has a revised rotor layout. Used in a variety of agricultural roles, it can be safely operated by a single pilot.

Variants and operators

Ka-26: early piston engined version **Ka-126:** standard production version with turboshaft engine **Ka-226:** advanced development version

Payload

Accommodation: 2 pilots; 6 passengers
Cargo: 1,000 kg (2,205 lb)

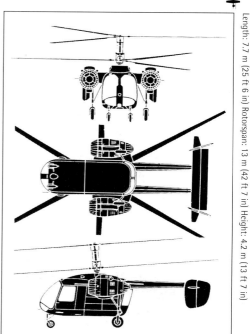

Length: 7.7 m (25 ft 6 in) Rotorspan: 13 m (42 ft 7 in) Height: 4.2 m (13 ft 7 in)

Features: Twin coaxial rotors/single turbine; bubble canopy; twin boom tail

Kawasaki XOH-1 Japan

Attack and observation helicopter

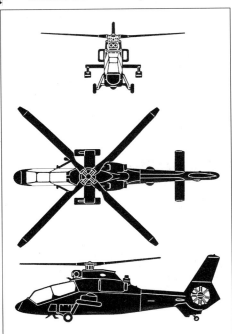

Length: 12 m (39 ft 4 in) Rotorspan: 11.5 m (37 ft 8 in) Height: 3.8 m (12 ft 5 in)

Features: Four rotor/twin turbine; tandem cockpit; fenestron tail rotor

Japan's first home-designed helicopter, design work began in 1992 and the first flight took place in 1996. Designed to replace the OH-6 observation helicopter the programme is also known as the Kogata Kansoku (new small observation helicopter) in Japan. The Japanese Self-Defence Agency has a requirement for 150 aircraft with deliveries beginning in 2000.

Variants and operators
XOH-1: Japan

Payload
Accommodation: 2 pilots
Warload: n/a
Hardpoints: 2 wing
Weapons: Type 91 AAMs

Mil Mi-2 Hoplite Russia/Poland

Light helicopter

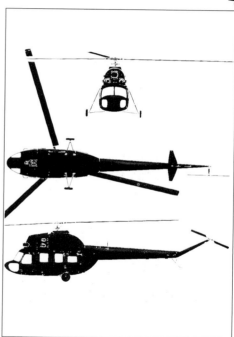

Although designed and first flown in Russia in 1961, the Mi-2 has been built in Poland since 1965 and is sometimes called the PZL (Mil) Mi-2. The aircraft has gone though a number of modifications and formed the basis of the PZL W-3 helicopter. Several versions are still in production including a gunship, light observation helicopter and civil agricultural versions.

Variants and operators

Mi-2: Bulgaria; Cuba; Czech Republic; Djibouti; Estonia; Georgia; Hungary; Kazakhstan; North Korea; Latvia; Lithuania; Myanmar; Poland; Russia; Slovak Republic; Syria; Ukraine

Payload

Accommodation: 2 pilots; 8 passengers
Cargo: 800 kg (1,763 lb)
Hardpoints: 2 pylons
Weapons: Sagger; Strela; cannon or gun pods; rockets

Features: Three rotor/twin turbine; tricycle landing gear; high tail boom

Length: 11.4 m (37 ft 4 in) Rotorspan: 14.5 m (47 ft 6 in) Height: 3.7 m (12 ft 3 in)

Mil Mi-6 Hook Russia

Heavy lift helicopter

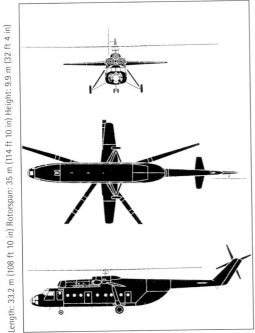

Length: 33.2 m (108 ft 10 in) Rotorspan: 35 m (114 ft 10 in) Height: 9.9 m (32 ft 4 in)

When first flown in 1957 the Mi-6 was the largest helicopter in the world. More than 860 have been built since for civil and military operators. Elements of the Mi-6 were used to build the single Mi-12 which remains the largest helicopter ever. The Mi-22 is a command version which can be recognized by its large antenna on the tail boom. The wings can be removed.

Variants and operators

Mi-6: Algeria; Belarus; Egypt; Iraq; Kazakhstan; Laos; Peru; Russia; Syria; Ukraine; Uzbekistan; Vietnam **Mi-22:** Belarus; Russia; Ukraine

Payload

Accommodation: 2 pilots; 3 crew; 70 troops
Cargo: 12,000 kg (26,450 lb)

Features: Five rotor/twin turbine; glazed nose; high mounted straight wing

Mil Mi-8 Hip Russia

Medium lift helicopter

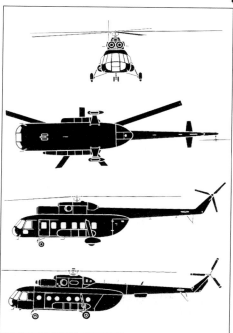

Designed to replace the piston engined Mi-4, the Mi-8 first flew in 1961. More than 12,000 Hips have been built of both Mi-8 and Mi-17 configuration. The Mi-17 is a later development of the Mi-8 and can usually be recognised by the position of its tail rotor, starboard on the Mi-8 and port on the Mi-17.

Variants and operators

Mi-8: Afghanistan; Algeria; Angola; Armenia; Azerbaijan; Bangladesh; Belarus; Bhutan; Bosnia; Bulgaria; Burkina Faso; Republika Srpska; Cambodia; Central African Republic; China; Congo; Croatia; Cuba; Czech Republic; Djibouti; Egypt; Estonia; Ethiopia; Finland; Georgia; Germany; Guyana; Hungary; India; Iraq; Kazakhstan; North Korea; Laos; Libya; Lithuania; Madagascar; Maldives; Mali; Mexico; Moldova; Mongolia; Mozambique; Pakistan; Palestine; Peru; Poland; Romania; Russia; Slovak Republic; Sudan; Syria; Tajikistan; Turkey; Ukraine; Uzbekistan; Vietnam; Yemen; Yugoslavia; Zambia

Payload

Accommodation: 2 pilots; 24 troops; 12 stretchers
Cargo: 4,000 kg (8,820 lb)
Hardpoints: 4 pylon
Weapons: Swatter; gun pods; rockets

Features: Five rotor/twin turbine; starboard tail rotor; rear clamshell doors

459

Mil Mi-14 Haze Russia

Land-based anti-submarine helicopter

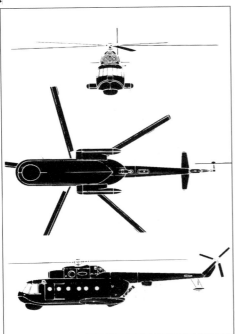

Length: 18.4 m (60 ft 3 in) Rotorspan: 21.3 m (69 ft 10 in) Height: 6.9 m (22 ft 9 in)

Features: Five rotor/twin turbine; amphibious hull;
ventral nose radar

Using many parts developed for the Mi–8/Mi-17 series, the Mi-14 was equipped with an amphibious hull and internal weapons bay to carry out anti-submarine warfare from shore bases. Also used for search and rescue and firefighting.

Variants and operators
Mi-14: Bulgaria; Germany; North Korea; Libya; Poland; Romania; Syria; Vietnam; Yugoslavia

Payload
Accommodation: 2 pilots; 2 systems operators
Cargo: n/a
Hardpoints: Internal bomb bay
Weapons: ASW torpedoes; depth charges; nuclear depth charge

Mil Mi-17 Hip Russia

Medium lift helicopter

Using the same engines and rotor system as the Mi-14 the Mi-17 replaced the Mi-8 in production as Russia's standard tactical helicopter. Early versions still carried the Mi-8 designation and some retain the starboard tail rotor. Mi-17s are fitted with a thimble radar or single 12.7 mm gun in the nose and most military versions also carry 3 weapons pylons.

Variants and operators

Mi-17: Afghanistan; Angola; Armenia; Azerbaijan; Bangladesh; Bulgaria; Burkina Faso; Cambodia; China; Colombia; Croatia; Costa Rica; Cuba; Czech Republic; Ethiopia; Hungary; India; Kazakhstan; Macedonia ; Malaysia; Nicaragua; Pakistan; Palestine; Peru; Poland; Romania; Russia; Sierra Leone; Slovak Republic; Syria; Turkey; Uganda; Ukraine; Uzbekistan; Venezuela; Vietnam

Payload

Accommodation: 2 pilots; 24 troops; 12 stretchers
Cargo: 4,000 kg (8,820 lb)
Hardpoints: 6 pylon
Weapons: Swatter; Spiral; gun pods; rockets

Length: 18.4 m (60 ft 5 in) Rotorspan: 21.3 m (69 ft 10 in) Height: 4.7 m (15 ft 7 in)

Features: Five rotor/twin turbine; port tail rotor; high tail boom

Mil Mi-24 Hind Russia

Assault helicopter

Length: 17.5 m (57 ft 5 in) Rotorspan: 17.3 m (56 ft 9 in) Height: 3.9 m (13 ft)

Features: Five rotor/twin turbine; tandem cockpits; central troop compartment

When it first appeared in 1974 the Hind had a large glasshouse cockpit in place of the familiar tandem arrangement. The ability to carry troops in the central compartment is unique among gunships. Of the major versions, the Mi-24P has a side mounted 23 mm cannon and the latest Mi-35 has a twin 23 mm gun turret. NBC recce, artillery recce and internal security versions have also been built.

Variants and operators

Mi-24: Afghanistan; Algeria; Angola; Armenia; Azerbaijan; Belarus; Bulgaria; Croatia; Cuba; Czech Republic; Ethiopia; Georgia; Germany; Hungary; India; Iraq; Kazakhstan; North Korea; Kyrgizia; Libya; Mongolia; Mozambique; Peru; Poland; Russia; Sierra Leone; Slovak Republic; Sri Lanka; Sudan; Syria; Ukraine; Uzbekistan; Vietnam; Yugoslavia; Zimbabwe

Payload

Accommodation: 1 pilot; 1 gunner; 8 troops
Warload: 2,400 kg (5,290 lb)
Hardpoints: 6 wing
Weapons: single YakB-12.7 mm gun or fixed twin 23 mm cannon; Swatter; Spiral; chemical weapons dispensers; gun pods; rockets

Mil Mi-26 Halo Russia

Heavy lift helicopter

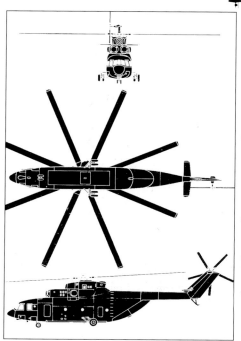

Design work began on a helicopter which could carry twice the payload of the Mi-6 in the early 1970s. The Mi-26 first flew in 1977 and over 200 have been built so far, making it the largest helicopter in production. The cargo compartment is similar in size to the C-130 Hercules, and has been used as a tanker, flying hospital, flying crane and geological survey aircraft.

Variants and operators
Mi-26: Belarus; India; Kazakhstan; Peru; Russia; Ukraine

Payload
Accommodation: 2 pilots; 2 crew; 80 troops; 60 stretchers
Cargo: 20,000 kg (44,090 lb)

Features: Eight rotor/twin turbine; rear loading ramp; tricycle landing gear

Length: 33.7 m (110 ft 8 in) Rotorspan: 32 m (105 ft) Height: 8.2 m (26 ft 8 in)

Mil Mi-28 Havoc Russia

Attack helicopter

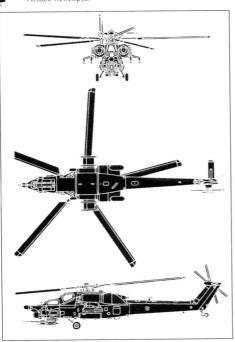

Length: 17 m (55 ft 9 in) Rotorspan: 17.2 m (56 ft 5 in) Height: 4.7 m (15 ft 5 in)

Features: Five rotor/twin turbine; tandem cockpits; thimble nose radar

Design work started in 1980 as a successor to the Mi-24 Hind. The first aircraft flew in 1982, but no large scale orders have been received. The end of the Cold War slowed development and only a few have been built for testing and evaluation.

Variants and operators

Mi-28: Russia

Payload

Accommodation: 1 pilot; 1 gunner
Warload: 1,814 kg (4,000 lb)
Hardpoints: 4 wing
Weapons: single 2A42 30 mm cannon; Gimlet; Spiral; gun pods; rockets

Mil Mi-34 Hermit Russia

Light helicopter

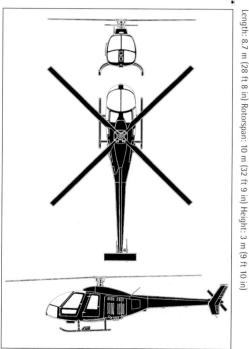

Length: 8.7 m (28 ft 8 in) Rotorspan: 10 m (32 ft 9 in) Height: 3 m (9 ft 10 in)

Intended for training and aerobatic flying the Mi-34 was the first Russian helicopter able to carry out full loops and rolls. First flown in 1986, versions are being sold for police duties and light transport. The standard production model is powered by a radial piston engine but a westernised version is also available with a Textron Lycoming engine.

Variants and operators
Mi-34: Russia

Payload
Accommodation: 2 pilots; 2 passengers
Cargo: 550 kg (1,212 lb)

Features: Four rotor/single piston engine; skids; bubble canopy

NHi NH-90 France/Germany/Italy/Netherlands

Multi-role helicopter

Length: 16.1 m (52 ft 10 in) Rotorspan: 16.3 m (53 ft 5 in) Height: 5.4 m (17 ft 10 in)

Features: Four rotor/twin turbine; side pods; high flat tail boom

The NH 90 was designed as a naval/army multipurpose helicopter along the lines of the Westland Lynx. Capable of carrying out tactical transport and ASW. The programme was suspended in 1994 and subjected to rigorous cost examination. The partner nations have reduced costs and now intend to bring it into service in 2003-2005, 10 years after its initial in-service dates.

Variants and operators

NH 90: requirement for over 700 from France, Germany, Italy and the Netherlands

Payload

Accommodation: 2 pilots; 3 systems operators or 20 troops
Cargo: 4,600 kg (10,141 lb)
Hardpoints: 2 fuselage
Weapons: anti-ship missiles; ASW torpedoes; depth charges

PZL Swidnik W-3 Sokol Poland

Light helicopter

Length: 14.2 m (46 ft 7 in) Rotorspan: 15.7 m (51 ft 6 in) Height: 3.8 m (12 ft 5 in)

Having produced the Mi-2 Hoplite under licence for many years PZL Swidnik began work on a larger utility helicopter in the late 1970s. The Sokol (Falcon) first flew in 1979. Production began in 1985 and over 100 have been built so far. Several armed versions have been designed to fill light gunship roles but none put into production.

Variants and operators

W-3: Czech Republic; Germany; South Korea; Myanmar; Nigeria; Poland

Payload

Accommodation: 2 pilots; 12 passengers
Cargo: 2,100 kg (4,630 lb)
Hardpoints: four pylons
Weapons: twin GSh-23L 23 mm cannon; gun pods; rockets

Features: Four rotor/twin turbine; tricycle landing gear; troop door at rear

PZL SW-4 Poland

Light helicopter

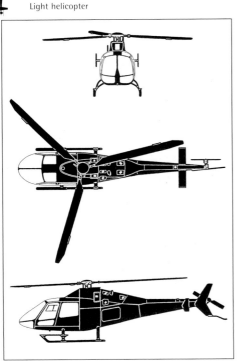

Length: 8.2 m (27 ft) Rotorspan: 9 m (29 ft 6 in) Height: 2.9 m (9 ft 7 in)

Features: Three rotor/single turbine; skids; long tail skid

Design work began in 1985 as a light civil helicopter and trainer. A major re-design took place in 1989 when it was fitted with an Allison turboshaft, and more streamlined fuselage. Full production has yet to begin but several versions are on offer including a more powerful Pratt&Whitney powered aircraft.

Variants and operators
SW-4: several prototypes flying awaiting full certification and production

Payload
Accommodation: 2 pilots; 3 passenger
Cargo: 750 kg (1,653 lb)

Robinson R22 Beta USA

Ultra light helicopter

Design work began in 1973 as an affordable light helicopter for police forces and training schools. Prices start from around $139,000 a copy, with running costs no more than an average family car. Other versions include an aerial crane trainer and agricultural sprayer. Over 2,200 have been delivered.

Variants and operators

R22: standard production model **R22 Police:** with stabilized TV cameras **R22IFR:** trainer **R22 mariner:** with floats for amphibious work.

Payload

Accommodation: 2 pilots
Cargo: 181 kg (400 lb)

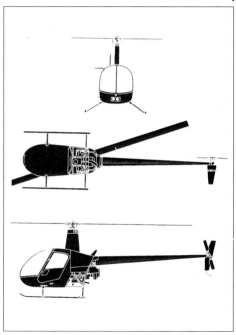

Length: 6.3 m (20 ft 8 in) Rotorspan: 7.7 m (25 ft 2 in) Height: 2.7 m (8 ft 9 in)

Features: Twin rotor/single piston engine; high-mounted rotorhead; long thin tail boom

Robinson R44 Astro USA

Light helicopter

Length: 11.6 m (38 ft 2 in) Rotorspan: 10.1 m (33 ft) Height: 3.3 m (10 ft 9 in)

Based on the earlier R22, the R44 has a larger four seat cabin and conforms to higher standards of comfort and safety. The success of the R22 Police with its single pilot and stabilized TV camera pod, led several US News companies to buy R44s fitted with similar equipment for real-time news gathering.

Variants and operators

R44: standard production model **R44 Clipper:** float equipped version

Payload

Accommodation: 2 pilots; 2 passengers
Cargo: n/a

Features: Twin rotor/single piston engine; two side windows; high-mounted rotorhead

Schweizer Model 300 USA

Light helicopter

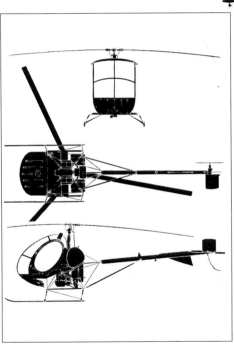

The Model 300 was originally a Hughes design from the 1960s. Schweizer bought the production rights in 1983, and then bought the entire programme in 1986. Hughes built 2,800 aircraft in military and civil versions, Schweizer has since sold around 500. A later model the 330 (shown above) has a larger pointed cabin and a fully enclosed tail boom and engine cove (picture).

Variants and operators
Model 300: Colombia; El Salvador; Greece; Japan; Nigeria; Sweden; Thailand; Turkey
Model 330: improved model

Payload
Accommodation: 2 pilots; 1 passenger
Cargo: 45 kg (100 lb)

Features: Three rotor/single piston engine; bubble canopy; thin tail boom

Sikorsky S-58 USA

Utility helicopter

Length: 14.4 m (47 ft 3 in) Rotorspan: 17.1 m (56 ft) Height: 4.8 m (15 ft.11 in)

First flown in 1954, the S-58 was a development of the earlier S-55 which had a similar high-mounted cockpit, but had four wheels. The first versions were powered by a Wright R-1820 piston engine, from 1970s onwards many were refitted with a Pratt&Whitney turboshaft. Very similar to the Wessex, the main difference is the twin exhausts under the Wessex cockpit.

Variants and operators
S-58: Indonesia; Thailand

Payload
Accommodation: 2 pilots; 16 passengers
Cargo: 3,628 kg (8,000 lb)

Features: Four rotor/twin turbine; high-mounted cockpit; twin nose inlets

Sikorsky S-61 Sea King USA

Shipborne multi-purpose helicopter

Length: 16.7 m (54 ft 9 in) Rotorspan: 18.9 m (62 ft) Height: 4.7 m (15 ft 6 in)

First flown in 1959, the S-61 was designed as an anti-submarine helicopter to replace the S-58. The S-61 has embodied 15 military and civil variants and was built under licence in Italy, Japan and the UK. Now being replaced in US Navy service by the Seahawk. The 900 military and 130 civil S-61s flew just under 4 million hours in their first 20 years.

Variants and operators

S-61: Argentina; Canada; Brazil; Denmark; Japan; Malaysia; Spain; USA

Payload

Accommodation: 2 pilots; 2 systems operators; 26 troops
Warload: 3,630 kg (8,000 lb)
Hardpoints: 4 fuselage
Weapons: ASW torpedoes; depth charges

Features: Five rotor/twin turbine; amphibious hull; ventral or thimble nose radar

473

Sikorsky S-61N USA

Offshore transport helicopter

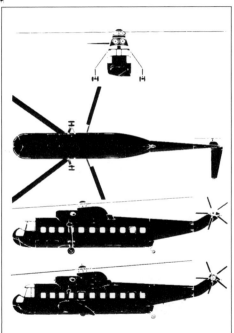

Length: 22.2 m (72 ft 10 in) Rotorspan: 18.9 m (62 ft) Height: 5.2 m (17 ft)

Developed from the military S-61 the S-61N was designed to support the offshore oil industry as a personnel transport. The type also found use as a Coastguard helicopter and was built under licence in Italy. The S-61L (top silhouette) was the initial production version and lacked the twin sponsons and amphibious capability.

Variants and operators

S-61L: initial production version S-61N: standard production version S-61 Payloader: dedicated cargo version

Payload

Accommodation: 2 pilots; 30 passengers
Cargo: 3,560 kg (7,850 lb)

Features: Five rotor/twin turbine; amphibious hull; square windows

Sikorsky S-61R CH-3 USA

Medium lift helicopter

Another development of the standard S-61 the CH-3 differs by having a rear loading ramp to ease the loading of troops and cargo. The USAF converted 50 into the original Jolly Green Giants and used them for combat search and rescue. Jolly Greens were fitted with inflight refueling probes, heavy armour and drop tanks. Also known as the Pelican in Coastguard service.

Variants and operators
CH-3: Italy

Payload
Accommodation: 2 pilots; 30 troops; 15 stretchers
Cargo: 2,270 kg (5,000 lb)
Weapons: door guns

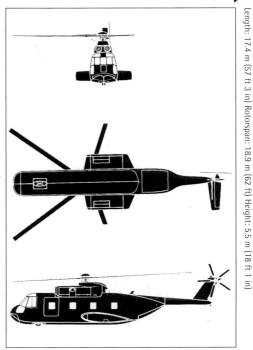

Length: 17.4 m (57 ft 3 in) Rotorspan: 18.9 m (62 ft) Height: 5.5 m (18 ft 1 in)

Features: Five rotor/twin turbine; side pods; rear loading ramp

Sikorsky S-62 USA

Utility helicopter

Length: 13.6 m (44 ft 6 in) Rotorspan: 16.2 m (53 ft) Height: 4.3 m (14 ft 2 in)

First flown in 1958, the S-62 was influenced by the S-61 in design being the smallest of that family. Built only in small numbers it was used mainly by the US Coast Guard. It was also built in Japan. HH-52As have a small FLIR turret in the nose.

Variants and operators

S-62: initial production version **HH-52A:** US Coast Guard search and rescue version

Payload

Accommodation: 2 pilots; 12 passengers
Cargo: 1,335 kg (2,943 lb)

Features: Three rotor/single turbine; twin floats; amphibious hull

Sikorsky S-64 Skycrane USA

Heavy lift helicopter

Length: 21.4 m (70 ft 3 in) Rotorspan: 21.9 m (72 ft) Height: 7.7 m (25 ft 5 in)

Designed to carry a variety of cargo pods or underslung loads, the Skycrane has set a number of world records including time-to-height, payload-height and altitude. Cargo pods could carry 45 troops, a fully fitted command post or a complete surgical hospital segment, they were also used to retrieve aircraft that had been shot down.

Variants and operators

S-64: Standard production version
CH-54 Tarhe: US Army

Payload

Accommodation: 2 pilots; 1 crew
Cargo: 9,072 kg (20,000 lb)

Features: Six rotor/twin turbine; cockpit pod; boom fuselage

477

Sikorsky S-65A/CH-53 Sea Stallion USA

Heavy lift helicopter

Length: 20.5 m (67 ft 2 in) Rotorspan: 22 m (72 ft 3 in) Height: 7.6 m (24 ft 11 in)

Features: Six rotor/twin turbine; long side pods; rear loading ramp

First flown in 1964, the S-65 was based on many of the proven parts of the S-64 Skycrane. The aircraft took over the combat search and rescue role from the S-61 and as a result is often mistakenly called Jolly Green Giant. Other roles included special forces insertion and minesweeping.

Variants and operators
CH-53: Germany; Israel; Iran; US Navy; US Air Force; USMC

Payload
Accommodation: 2 pilots; 2 crew; 37 troops; 24 stretchers
Cargo: 9,070 kg (20,000 lb)
Weapons: door guns

Sikorsky S-70 UH-60 Black Hawk USA

Utility helicopter

First flown in 1974, over 2,000 have been built. The standard airframe has been modified to carry out a variety of missions and can be seen sporting auxiliary fuel tanks or hellfire missiles on stub wings. Electronic warfare versions have been fitted with SLAR and ECM equipment, command and control aircraft have a large ventral antenna spike.

Variants and operators

UH-60: Argentina; Australia; Bahrain; Brunei; Chile; China; Colombia; Egypt; Greece; Hong Kong; Israel; Japan; Jordan; Mexico; Morocco; Philippines; Saudi Arabia; South Korea; Taiwan; Turkey; USA

Payload

Accommodation: 2 pilots; 2 crew; 14 troops
Cargo: 3,629 kg (8,000 lb)
Hardpoints: 2 stub wings
Weapons: door guns; Hellfire; Stinger; rockets

Features: Four rotor/twin turbine; tall tail fin; low/wide fuselage

479

Sikorsky MH-60 Pave Hawk USA

Special operations helicopter

Length: 15.3 m (50 ft) Rotorspan: 16.4 m (53 ft 8 in) Height: 5.1 m (16 ft 10 in)

The US Army operate a number of specialized Black Hawks under the designation MH-60. The 160th Special Operations Regiment operate several versions of the Pave Hawk including the AH-60L assault gunship. Standard features include defensive aids, stub wings, FLIR turrets and terrain following radar. Various in-flight refueling probes, auxiliary fuel tanks and weapons can be fitted according to a particular mission.

Variants and operators

MH-60G: US Army; US Air Force **MH-60K:** US Army Special Operations **AH-60L:** US Army gunship

Payload

Accommodation: 2 pilots; 2 crew; 14 troops
Cargo: 3,629 kg (8,000 lb)
Hardpoints: 2 stub wings
Weapons: door guns; Hellfire; Stinger; rockets

Features: Four rotor/twin turbine; inflight refueling probe; thimble nose radar/FLIR

480

Sikorsky S-70A SH-60B Seahawk USA

Shipborne anti-submarine helicopter

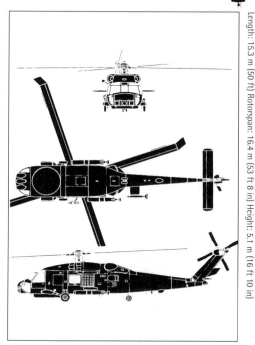

Developed from the Black Hawk the Seahawk has folding rotors and tail unit to facilitate storage aboard frigates and cruisers. The rear tailwheel is further forward than the land based Black Hawk and it has a ventral radar. The HH-60H is used to support Naval special forces while the Jayhawk has advanced avionics and search equipment to hunt drug smugglers.

Variants and operators

SH-60B: Australia; Greece; Japan; Spain; Taiwan; Thailand; Turkey; US Navy **HH-60H/J Jayhawk:** US Navy/US Coast Guard

Payload

Accommodation: 2 pilots; 1 systems operator
Warload: 3,551 kg (7,829 lb)
Hardpoints: 2 fuselage
Weapons: Penguin; Hellfire; ASW torpedoes; depth charges

Features: Four rotor/twin turbine; smaller side doors; straight tail wheel

481

Sikorsky S-76 USA

Utility helicopter

Length: 13.4 m (44 ft) Rotorspan: 13.4 m (44 ft) Height: 4.4 m (14 ft 5 in)

Features: Four rotor/single turbine; retractable landing gear; twin side doors

First flown in 1977, the S-76 was designed using the aerodynamics and technology of the Black Hawk. Tailored for the civil market it was aimed at the offshore oil industry, business transport and medical evacuation markets. Over 400 have been produced some fitted with weapons stations for the Philippine Air Force.

Variants and operators

S-76: standard civil transport version **S-76 Eagle:** military version **S-76 Utility:** with stronger floor for lifting cargo

Payload

Accommodation: 2 pilots; 14 passengers
Cargo: 1,497 kg (3,300 lb)

Sikorsky S-80 CH-53E Super Sea Stallion USA

Heavy lift helicopter

Developed from the standard S-65 Sea Stallion, the Super Sea Stallion was fitted with a third engine and a fully articulated seven-blade main rotor. The MH-53E Sea Dragon is a dedicated minesweeper and can be recognised by its larger side sponsons. An in-flight refueling probe can be fitted but is not carried as standard.

Variants and operators
CH-53E: USMC transport helicopter **MH-53E:** Japan; US Navy **MH-535:** US Air Force

Payload
Accommodation: 2 pilots; 2 crew; 55 troops
Cargo: 13,607 kg (30,000 lb)
Hardpoints: 2 fuselage
Weapons: door guns

Length: 22.3 m (73 ft 4 in) Rotorspan: 24.1 m (79 ft) Height: 8.9 m (29 ft 5 in)

Features: Six rotor/ triple turbine; inflight refueling probe; rear loading ramp

483

A Guide to Recognition

The briefest study of aircraft recognition shows how aircraft designed for similar purposes tend to display similar characteristics. Combat aircraft designed for strength, speed and fighting have internal turbojets, large area swept wings, bubble canopies and underwing weapon stations. Civil Airliners built for high altitude cruising with high passenger capacity have slender swept wings, wide bodies and external turbofans.

This simple fact is dictated by the laws of aerodynamics, and serves to make recognition a difficult task. As designers search for the most efficient way of meeting their requirements, they eventually end up in the same ball-park. However no two designers come to identical conclusions, and every aircraft has its own set of recognition features to trace.

Tracing these features is a process of deduction. To ease the burden of identifying the 464 aircraft in this book, they are broken down into nine groupings, each covering a specific area of aviation:

Combat Aircraft
Combat Support
Combat Trainers

Civil Jet Airliners
Civil Turboprop Airliners
Civil Utility Aircraft

Private Executive Aircraft
Private Light Aircraft

Helicopters

484

Opposite page:
Top left: F-14 Tomcat of the US Navy.
Bottom left: MiG-23 of the Libyan Air Force.
Far right: F-15 of the US Air Force refuelling from a KC-10

A Guide to Recognition

This basic deduction process can get you familiar with the main features: wing, engines and tail section. However with many aircraft all three are the same, the Mirage family and their offspring the Kfir and Cheetah are all tailless deltas with a single turbojet and single swept tail. To tell them apart you have to go one stage further and look at radomes, canards, notches and cranks.

The layout of this book enables you to compare any two silhouettes side-by-side by folding the pages. By flicking your eyes from one to the other you immediately notice individual features - a crank in the wing, and extra notch in the tailfin. The more obvious details are listed in each entry, but it helps to pick out your own - for years I told the difference between the Boeing 757 and the Tupolev Tu-204 by the way the 757's canopy made it look stern.

Three view silhouettes can tell you a lot about the features of an aircraft, but features can change or be obscured when viewed from different angles. The photographs in this book have been chosen to show the aircraft at a different angle to the silhouettes, so you can identify these changes.

A serious student of recognition should try and view an aircraft from as many angles as possible. Airshows are a superb way of getting familiar with aircraft. Good multi-national shows display scores of different aircraft, with an opportunity to get close up views on the ground and realistic views when their airborne. The aircraft are also clearly marked for easy recognition.

Right: A very stern looking 757 returns home.

Modelling also provides an interactive hands-on recognition aid. The process of building model aircraft and then having a 3D image to view, can permanently lodge shape, size and characteristics in your memory. Military recognition instructors place high value in models - briefing room models provided hours of entertainment with mock dogfights over tea while carrying out the major military pastime - waiting.

Students of recognition should be prepared for the ways in which aircraft can change shape in flight and on the ground. Swing wing aircraft change dramatically in-flight, at high speeds they resemble delta wing aircraft, at low speeds the resemble straight wing aircraft. When aircraft land or are on the ground they drop flaps, landing gear and in the case of Concorde the nose. All these can change the profile of the aircraft.

Above: A Concorde on final approach, its nose, landing gear and flaps down.

A Guide to Recognition

Those military aircraft without internal bomb bays, carry their offensive armament on wing and fuselage pylons. These pylons are called hardpoints and can be fitted with an array of waepons, drop tanks, or electronic countermeasure pods. Knowing where the hardpoints are located, and what they can carry, prepares the student for the change in profile.

Away from recognition features, the information contained in the text and specifications can also gives clues to identify. Getting familiar with what countries or airlines operate what aircraft, can act as an aid to recognition. If you see a delta winged aircraft in Israeli colours you know it is not a Mirage 2000. If you spot a turboprop airliner in the livery of Cityflyer you can tell its an ATR and not ATP.

When you have mastered the basics of features, functions and markings, one can choose to delve deeper into configurations. The McDonnell Douglas DC-8 has been stretched and stretched by designers retaining many of the same features but increasing passenger load. The C-130 Hercules can be found mounting howitzers, signals intelligence equipment, terrain following radar or airborne data gathering probes. At this level the recognition enthusiast should keep abreast of the major aviation magazines as configurations and equipment can change regularly.

The importance of recognition goes beyond spotting. In the military field, recognition is important as an aid to intelligence. If you spot three hostile helicopters, and identify them correctly you can get a good idea of how many men they are carrying, and from that likely enemy intentions. Knowing what capabilities hostile combat aircraft have you can deduced the enemy's hitting power and react accordingly.

Some of the many guises of the C–130 Hercules

1

2

3

5

4

6

1. *AC-130 Spectre gunship*
2. *C-130 BL on skis*
3. *C-130 Firefighter*
4. *DC-130H Drone launcher*
5. *NC-130B Data gatherer*
6. *EC-130E Commando Solo*

Index

Index

Index

Index

Index

Index

Index

Index

Index

Index

Index

OTHER TITLES IN THE JANE'S RECOGNITION GUIDE SERIES

Jane's Warship Recognition Guide

THE ESSENTIAL GUIDE TO WARSHIPS OF THE WORLD

Jane's Warship Recognition Guide is the most comprehensive handbook on modern warships. First published in 1994 it is now revised to take account of the sweeping changes affecting the world's navies. Over 200 classes of warship are covered with

- CLASSES AND SHIP NAMES
- WEAPON SYSTEMS AND RADARS
- DETAILED LINE DRAWINGS
- FULL PAGE PHOTOGRAPHS OF EVERY WARSHIP
- KEY RECOGNITION FEATURES

Jane's
WARSHIP
RECOGNITION
GUIDE

Jane's Guns Recognition Guide

THE ESSENTIAL GUIDE TO WEAPONS AVAILABLE TODAY

Jane's Guns Recognition Guide features all the military rifles, pistols, revolvers, machine-guns and sub-machine guns
in action today. From the US Army's newest infantry rifle to former Soviet weapons now in terrorist hands, as well as ex-World War II
guns still soldiering on, this essential book enables you to identify them all, with information on

- BARREL MARKINGS
- TECHNICAL DATA
- SERVICE HISTORIES
- SAFETY INSTRUCTIONS

PISTOLS,
RIFLES AND
MACHINE GUNS

Jane's
GUNS
RECOGNITION
GUIDE

Jane's Tank Recognition Guide

THE ESSENTIAL GUIDE TO TANKS AND COMBAT VEHICLES

Jane's Tank Recognition Guide is the most comprehensive handbook on military combat vehicles ever published, covering

- TECHNICAL DATA
- KEY RECOGNITION FEATURES
- DETAILED LINE DRAWINGS
- OVER 400 COMBAT VEHICLES

Jane's
TANK
RECOGNITION GUIDE
BY CHRISTOPHER F. FOSS
HOW TO IDENTIFY MODERN TANKS AND COMBAT VEHICLES

Jane's Historic Military Aircraft Recognition Guide

ALL THE WORLD'S HISTORIC MILITARY AIRCRAFT

From jet interceptors recently retired from military service to World War I bi-planes, *Jane's Historic Military Aircraft Recognition Guide* is a complete directory of military aircraft preserved today

- RECENT PHOTOGRAPHS
- HISTORIC DETAILS
- TECHNICAL DATA
- LOCATION GUIDE